DISCOVERIES AND REVIEWS

# DISCOVERIES
# AND
# REVIEWS

*from Renaissance to Restoration*

A. L. ROWSE

BARNES & NOBLE

**BOOKS**

10 East 53d St., New York 10022

(a division of Harper & Row Publishers, Inc.)

*First published 1975 by*
THE MACMILLAN PRESS LTD
*London and Basingstoke*

*Published in the U.S.A. 1975 by*
HARPER & ROW PUBLISHERS, INC.
BARNES & NOBLE IMPORT DIVISION

ISBN 0-06-496009-9

*Printed in Great Britain*

To Fredson Bowers,
great scholar,
and good companion

# Contents

# Preface

In this book I have brought together a number of essays, addresses and reviews on topics in my main field of interest, the history and literature of the sixteenth and seventeenth centuries. I trust they have a certain unity of interest, revolving as they do round the Tudor period, the Elizabethan Age, Shakespeare as its foremost expression in literature, and then moving forward to the Civil War and its consequences.

I hope, too, that the treatment of different subjects at different times, as they arise in books under review, may also be not without unity in the point of view expressed. I attach most importance to common-sense judgement, sense of the past, the understanding of human beings in their real environment as against theorising and theses, reducing history to an inferior kind of sociology.

Thus some sociological points of contemporary interest emerge, some reflections on the society of today. One phenomenon is a kind of academic sub-culture, in which academics write for each other, not for the general intelligent public – unlike G. M. Trevelyan, R. H. Tawney, Samuel Eliot Morison in history; Keynes or Bertrand Russell, Gilbert Murray or T. S. Eliot in other disciplines. To some extent this is a result of the over-specialisation of our time; it cuts them off from vital currents of thought and loses them the advantage, and the inspirations, of cross-fertilisation. Nowhere are these advantages greater than in the allied subjects of history and literature. It is indeed necessary to study them together: historians without literary sense, and writers on literature without a sense of history, are indeed deprived, without a limb.

Throughout this book I have done my best to bring them together; and I do not regret the repetitions necessary to bring home the lesson. The study of our greatest Elizabethan writer, Shakespeare, has been the chief sufferer from this unimaginative divorce of literature from history – utterly un-Elizabethan, I may add.

Most of the books noticed are good of their kind and deal with subjects of permanent importance, historical or literary. Only very occasionally have I included a bad book as a salutary example, how *not* to do it; equally, there may be one or two instances where the estimate is possibly too generous, e.g. over McFarlane's work on Memling.

I am grateful to the many editors who have been ready and willing to let me have my say on these topics. It was Voltaire who said that the great advantage of being a writer is that one can say exactly what one thinks.

*New Year, 1975*                                    A. L. ROWSE

# Acknowledgements

Acknowledgements are made to the following, in which some of these pieces have appeared: *The Times, Times Educational Supplement, Books and Bookmen, Spectator, Listener, English Historical Review, History Today, New York Times Book Review, Wall Street Journal;* and also to the Royal Society of Literature and the bodies to which I owe the invitations to give various addresses.

A.L.R.

# Discoveries

I have been asked to write about my attitude to historical writing and research. This is a tall order – too much so for here and now. I can only say at this point that, with me, literature – in particular, the writing of poetry – came long before history. It may be that that is the right order – Macaulay thought poetry belongs to the childhood of a civilisation, and 'as civilisation advances, poetry almost necessarily declines'.

Whether this is true or not, my youth was much more given to literature, and poetry in particular; the thought of writing history positively frightened me. It is true that in the Oxford of my younger days a great song-and-dance was made of historical research: the technicians made a cult of their expertise, rather frightening one off the premises than encouraging one to enter – and I developed an acute inferiority-complex about the Public Record Office, the British Museum Research Room, the inner recesses of the Bodleian, Duke Humphrey and Selden End; the demands of palaeography, diplomatic, state papers; patent rolls, close rolls, and the rest of it. In those days there were no seminars or classes for beginners – one was just thrown into the pool to sink or swim. I hesitated for long, shivering on the brink.

Later on, G. M. Trevelyan – always encouraging – said to me, 'When you were young, we thought that you were never going to begin; but, my goodness, once you got started! ...' All the same, it was a long time before I did begin; it was not like Churchill's brief hesitation before starting to paint: 'I saw that the canvas could not hit back – so, wallop into the paint-pot, splash on to the canvas', and the picture was started.

It took me years in the Public Record Office – I thought I

should never get out; I still have masses of material in my
bottom-drawer which I accumulated then and still haven't
used. They were so frightening, those whiskered academic
ladies: I used to recite a litany of them as I occasionally
surfaced to draw a breath of fresh air within the prison-
railings of the P.R.O. Miss Rose Graham, Miss Helen Cam,
Miss Helen Chew, Miss Isobel Thornley, the lady whose name
I have forgotten, who was the world's greatest expert on the
Pipe Roll of 1272, Surrey membrane. She once reproved me,
brushing my pencil aside as I pointed to some thorny entry in
the Recusants' Roll, submitting a tentative explanation;
putting her own pencil to her learned forehead, she paused
and said, 'Well, correct: but not scholarly.'

That made me laugh: I didn't mind about the form of the
thing, so long as I had got the kernel of the matter right. I
have often thought of that comic exchange – it might well
serve as epigraph for much of my work forty years after. The
good lady bent on scholarly 'form' – like so many others –
never emerged with anything to show for it, never produced
anything. That was the real lesson to learn: never to make an
end of the means, never to be so immersed in the medium,
the formulae, the techniques, as to forget the end to which
they were but subsidiary.

As it happened, a book – or more than one book – was
forming in my mind. I had gone to the P.R.O., as we
affectionately called it, to collect material on the Reformation in Cornwall: I wanted to know what the process was,
what happened in concrete detail and thus what the
Reformation *meant*, when you examined it under the
microscope for a given area. I have always remained attached
to that method as the right one – as this book bears out – as
against generalising theses about the Rise of the Gentry, the
Crisis of the Aristocracy, of the Seventeenth Century, with
the profitless discussions these have given rise to. True
historical method means the patient accumulation of concrete detail: that yields better and more certain results. As an
eminent classical scholar recently said to me, 'when you work

hard at a subject for a long time, you see connections which other people haven't thought of and can't see'. This book offers some examples.

It never occurred to me in the days of my immersion that I should make any historical discoveries – I wasn't looking for them. And that again is correct historical method – not to start out with a thesis, a preconception, and then look round for the facts to 'prove' it. As it might be, to start out looking for a 'Mr. W. H.' or a Dark Lady who might be Shakespeare's mistress – nothing is discovered that way: a completely wrong way of going about things. If you go about it the right way, something unexpected – and richly rewarding – may turn up.

After two or three years working away at Tudor Cornwall in general, I found myself concentrating on everything I could find about Sir Richard Grenville of the *Revenge*. Here was an obvious gap to fill among biographies of the Elizabethan seamen, and I at length began to understand why. All the private and personal correspondence of his family had been destroyed, when the great house of Stowe on the cliffs of North Cornwall had been rebuilt and then pulled down. When I went to Bideford, which Grenville had largely controlled in his time, the town archives had been destroyed – the only two documents to survive had Grenville signatures.

If only letters to and from the family had survived one could make a more rounded portrait, in depth, of the man. Frustrated on this front, I decided to go and see all the places where he had lived and been active, describe the house which he formed out of Buckland Abbey where he lived, the old Barbican and back-streets of Plymouth, the Devon and Cornish scenes he looked on, the Elizabethan houses where he visited which still remained – Trerice of the Arundells, Godolphin, Penheale built by his cousin George Grenville and inherited by the Specotts. And so on. I took a leaf out of Macaulay's notebook, who used to write down what the places looked like while they were under his eye.

There were, besides, technical reasons which made the
biography of Grenville difficult to write – though the
ground here had been cleared for me by the indispensable
work of the admirable old Devon antiquary, R. Pearse Chope,
whom I went to consult in his then inaccessible lair out on
the cliffs of Hartland.

Then, one day in the Record Office, I made my first
find; it wasn't very important, but I remember the cold thrill
of excitement as I realised what I had come upon. There,
staring at me from those dreary Patent Rolls – unpublished
then – was an account of an affray in which young Grenville,
not yet of age, was involved, had killed his man, fled and was
pardoned on account of his minority. One November day in
1562 in the parish of St Clement Danes – in the Strand, I
suppose, or one of those narrow lanes running down to the
Thames – two groups of young men were fighting. On one
side, Sir Edward Unton of Faringdon – brother of the
ambassador, of whom we have the famous picture depicting
his whole life[1] – Fulke Greville, father of the poet, and
Robert Bannester a Londoner; on the other side, Richard
Grenville and his cousin, Nicholas Specott. Each side with
their respective attendants. Suddenly Grenville ran through
Bannester with his sword, giving him a mortal wound six
inches in depth of which he died within the hour. Grenville
and Specott fled, and were outlawed.

It was not important; but what excited me was that no one
had known about it since Grenville died, or within a
generation or so, nothing had ever appeared about it in any
book – and yet it was so characteristic of the man he
became, the fighting tough. I suppose that, from the
beginning, though unaware of it, what thrilled me was to be
in touch with, to come as close as possible to, the *life* of
these long-dead men, to renew their lives as an historian. I
have remained faithful to that idea all along: it has been a

---

[1] Years later I used this for the jacket of *The Elizabethan Renaissance: the Life of
the Society.*

chief inspiration of my work — not, at any rate, to write dead history.

Much more important was the last episode in Grenville's life, the famous battle of Flores in the Azores where the *Revenge* — Drake's favourite ship — was lost. Hitherto there had been no full or satisfactory account, for all its fame: there was only Ralegh's narrative from the English side, and that at second-hand for he had not been present. It occurred to me that there must somewhere be a Spanish account. That summer on the beach at home — for I was now ill and struggling with a duodenal ulcer — I learned enough Spanish to be able to read Fernandez Duro's history of the Spanish Navy at the time. There, sure enough, were indispensable references to the Spanish manuscript account, unpublished, lying in the Museo Geographico in Madrid.

I was just in time, before the Civil War broke out, to get transcripts of that and other documents — I don't know today whether the documents, or the Museo, survived the destruction, but I still have the transcripts. Here the help of my old friend J. A. Williamson — admirable historian and a good sailing man himself — was indispensable: he was able to read the winds and currents. The result was, for the first time, a complete account of the battle of Flores and the loss of the *Revenge* — quite different in some important particulars from what had been previously thought, but not to be impugned for it rested upon both Spanish and English accounts checking each other. Anyone who wants to know what happened can read the book — no room for it here.

It was my first work of historical research: it had a good reception from the public, for all my disappointment that there could be little of Grenville's personal life in it. There was, however, little enthusiasm among my closest friends at Oxford: at that time, with Namierism all the rage and Namier's way of writing history regarded as the last word, there was a snooty writing down of historical biography among my friends, the academic elect. That didn't deflect, though it irritated, me; I was bent on writing living books — and, in the end, their mentor Namier wasted the last years of his life writing scores of short biographies of insignificant eighteenth-century Members of Parliament.

Academics have a wonderful way of discouraging each other; but my friends were doubly wrong, for, if I had not had the experience of writing a biography first — for, with a biography, the form is already given — I should never have been able to manage a portrait of a whole society, if on a small scale, as with *Tudor Cornwall* which followed. My advice to young historians is never to listen to such discouragements — academics have an instinct for stinging each other into frustration. Both McFarlane and Richard Pares — excellent technical historians as they were — had a curious effect in discouraging their pupils from writing (they weren't so very good at it themselves: perhaps this was why), with the result that some of their chosen pupils have hardly written anything. These experts had no such effect on me: I listened respectfully to what they said, learned all the time from both of them — and went on writing my book.

One little discovery in the Record Office I have not even yet done my duty by. In the course of those years — though ill, yet young and ardent then, I look back upon it nostalgically now that I am old and coming to the end of my work — I lighted upon a fascinating little Diary of an Elizabethan Cornishman, William Carnsew of Bokelly[2] in St Kew. Though I drew upon it in those first two research books, and wrote a *Spectator* article about it, I have still not edited it, along with its dependent material, letters, etc. For one thing, it is in so very minute and crabbed a hand — far worse than Simon Forman, who is not difficult but tricky, so that it is possible to make mistakes with him, as Halliwell-Phillips did. For another, Carnsew is so laconic and brief in his entries — hard to make it interesting for the general reader: one would have to expand.

The very opposite was the case with my next find, the Throckmorton Diary. This consisted of three folio volumes,

[2] This means the dwelling by the grove.

perhaps nearly a thousand pages, the fullest and most detailed of all extant Elizabethan diaries, usually so brief and bitty. This was unpublishable as it stands, unless as a long-term venture by some archaeological society — and then it would be unreadable. The problem was how to deal with this bonanza.

It was not really my find: I had been told of its existence, in the Chapter Library at Canterbury, by an old scholar-friend. I salted away the information until I was free, some years later, to go into it. The Chapter, through the intervention of Canon John Shirley, allowed me to have the volumes at All Souls for a couple of years where I could study them at leisure.

They proved absolutely fascinating as a whole, for they were the diaries of Sir Walter Ralegh's brother-in-law, Sir Arthur Throckmorton, from which one could re-create the life of a typical Elizabethan gentleman: service in the wars, France and the Netherlands; the Continental tour through Germany and Austria to Italy, Renaissance life there, book-buying, music; the companionship of other well-known Elizabethans in Venice, Padua, Florence; country occupations, rides across England, calling on familiar figures; the intellectual and artistic life of the time; the crowded activities of London and the Court, play-going, friendships and disputes; building and equipping an Elizabethan house, farming, indispensable (if immensely detailed) information about commodities, wages and prices. In short, a tapestry against which moved well-known figures — various members of the Throckmorton family; Carews, Darcys, Howards, Wottons; Walsingham and Leicester; a few new touches for the poet Donne and the scientist Hariot.

But the real excitement, which made news, was the discovery of the circumstances of Ralegh's disgrace with the Queen, the birth of a child unknown to history, baptised by the name of Damerei — D'Amory, a West Country name of royal descent — for whom Essex, of all people, though Throckmorton's leader, stood sponsor! What a find! — but the name gave me trouble, and was elucidated later (by a member of the Ralegh clan). Of course there were people knowing nothing whatever about the subject who wouldn't believe it; I remember one ageing journalist for the *Daily Telegraph*, who wanted to see the Diary. Fortunately, it was still in my possession and I politely invited the old buffer down to All Souls to inspect it. That settled his hash: no more trouble from that quarter.

It did not settle the hash of a more academic acquaintance in America, an alumna of a women's college with the acidulated traits of the type. Her own work is of a still and marmoreal perfection, totally dead. When she heard of my find, and the use I had made of the Diary to create *Ralegh and the Throckmortons*, she said crisply, 'I could have killed you'. I thought, in my innocence, that this was an expression of amicable envy. Not a bit of it; it was the disapproval of a pedant: she thought that I should have edited the Diary *in extenso, verbatim, apparatus criticus*, and the rest of it. Mind you, she had never *seen* the Diary: she did not know that that was not a practicable proposition, virtually impossible — it could not have seen the light of day to this moment. She had not troubled to read my book. So much for the justice of mind of these people.

The real problem was a literary and artistic one — how to handle this vast mass of rebarbative material. The new information about Ralegh was what was exciting and significant; one could hardly write a whole book about the Diary as such. The solution was to portray Ralegh, with the new facts about him, against the background of the Throckmortons, the family into which he married, a more important one than the Raleghs were. Hitherto I had never been able to get upsides with Ralegh, had never felt that I fully understood him (G. N. Clark later told me that he had had the same feeling); now at last I felt that I had *got* him. One result of this was a significant contribution to general history: I was able to explain, for the first time, the mystery of Ralegh's conduct after James I's accession in 1603, for which Ralegh was condemned to death, what precisely he had been up to. This had never been accounted for hitherto — no room for it here: one should consult the book.

Such a book, with its dual structure, was not easy to write. It was a matter of regret to me that it was not a West Country diary: if only it had been, I sighed, I should already have known most of the people to occur in it, a good deal about them, where precisely they lived, and so on. The Diary was mostly about Northamptonshire and its Elizabethan denizens: I didn't know who they were, in unfamiliar territory. However, it was conveniently on the threshold of Oxford, and for a couple of years I had an enjoyable time of it making historical expeditions, looking up houses and churches, looking down on my characters upon their tombs, exploring their fields and following their tracks and traces.

Joan Wake — the wonderful old Northants antiquarian to whom we owe so much, for the preservation of archives, what not — was fascinated: she said that the portrait of Elizabethan life there was so much like the country life she had known, essentially unchanged, in Victorian days. Everybody displayed good Midlands kindness and hospitality, peers and parsons alike. When the book came out, I thanked them by name for the courtesy and help I had received. A less polite professor of lower middle-class manners and Leftist leanings (whom I had sponsored for his doctorate), in reviewing the book wrote that my expression of thanks was more becoming an eighteenth-century clergyman than a modern Fellow of All Souls! This is the kind of thing one has had to put up with from these inferior people — a generation ago, they would have known their place. Modestly as ever, I asked Joan Wake what she thought: she said that these old persons in Northants were delighted to be mentioned — their only chance of appearing in a book anyway!

However, the best — and rudest — was yet to come: over Shakespeare.

No need to go into the facts and findings here — I have done that in subsequent essays in this book; merely a brief

word on the personal side. When I went to the Huntington
Library in 1962 to write *William Shakespeare: A Biography*,
I naturally assumed — what we had all been told — that the
'problems' of Shakespeare's biography, the identity of
'Mr. W. H.', of the young man, the rival poet and the dark
lady, were insoluble. I was not out to solve them: that was
not my idea. What, I put it to myself, was the particular
point and justification of my tackling the biography of the
greatest writer of the Elizabethan Age?

Well, I was by this time, after a lifetime of research on it,
very familiar with the life of the age — more so than anybody
else writing about Shakespeare. I felt assured, modestly again,
that I should be able (a) to illuminate the background, the
social life of Warwickshire, Stratford and London, and bring
it to life; and (b) to elicit the underlying political and social
implications of the plays, which are so important a part of
their message, little appreciated up to our time. (One needs,
indeed, a good knowledge of the age in order to be able to
understand and appreciate it.) Actually, on the intellectual
side, this is the part of my book on which I set most store.
Embarking on my task — a bit ruefully, five thousand miles
away from the Cotswolds and Stratford, the scenes of his
life — I consoled myself with the thought that, after all,
Shakespeare was the most historically-minded of dramatists:
what more appropriate than that an Elizabethan historian —
someone deeply in sympathy with that age, rather than
ours — should write his biography and interpret him in terms
of his time, the appropriate ones?

It never occurred to me that the so-called 'problems' would
work out and fall into place, naturally, consistently, convincingly. I was astonished, and electrified. Wouldn't you be,
dear reader, if you found that the supposedly greatest
'problem' in literature had resolved itself — and the crucial
period in the life of our greatest writer, described in his
own autobiography, the Sonnets — lay open at last? I have
gone into the process elsewhere, in the relevant books; so I
will say no more about it here, except that at no point did

the explanations come up against any obstacle — this was obviously the true account of the matter unfolding itself before my astonished eyes.

The one exception was the Dark Lady — there was no clue to her, and I never wasted a moment looking for one. There were only the *internal* indications in Shakespeare's work, in the Sonnets and *Love's Labour's Lost* — one would need corroboration from the *external* world, and that was very unlikely to be forthcoming. Conservatively minded, quite unexperimental, detesting anything radical or eccentric, I dismissed the possibility from my mind. What is more important, it is a radically wrong method to put up some clay-pigeon of a 'candidate' for the Dark Lady, and then to look round for evidence to support what is only a thesis. In my later research into Simon Forman's papers I was not looking for her — though it is true that his Case-Books offered the likeliest place where she might turn up; the evidence itself overwhelmed me. I have no 'candidate' for Shakespeare's Dark Lady: this is the woman.

Let me say *tout court*: in the complex web of my findings about Shakespeare, in which structure everything is subtly interdependent — the solutions now of all the 'problems' — if these were not the answers it should be possible to fault it at half-a-dozen points. But it is not possible to do so, for the simple reason that it is the true story of the matter — it would be beyond anyone's powers to invent it, without slipping up somewhere.

Looking back over the long years of work, now that it is coming to an end, I sometimes feel that there has been a benevolent providence watching over it — something like what my friend W. S. Lewis, Horace Walpole's Mr Lewis, has named 'serendipity'. If I hadn't tackled the biography of Sir Richard Grenville first, I could never have coped with a portrait of a society, even a small one, such as Tudor Cornwall; then, too, if I had not had the experience gained in writing that — with the cross-rhythms, the curves, the consciously contrived ascents and descents in its structure — I

certainly could not have managed a portrait of the whole
society, in my quartet of volumes on *The Elizabethan Age*.
As my friend the classical scholar said, it is only after you
have worked long and deeply at a subject that you see the
connections that others do not. This is its own reward.

# Simon Forman and the
# Dark Lady

Who was Simon Forman? He was someone whom
Shakespeare would certainly have known of, for several
people in Shakespeare's immediate circle came to consult
Forman, medically and astrologically. Shakespeare's colleague, Ben Jonson, mentions Dr Forman two or three
times, and his play *The Alchemist* owes something to
Forman's career. Then, too, Forman is well known to
Shakespeare scholars, for he is the one person to give us an
account of seeing some of Shakespeare's plays at the Globe in
the spring of 1611. Again, Forman's name was cited in a
famous trial, that of the wicked young Countess of Somerset
and her husband for the poisoning of Sir Thomas Overbury in
the Tower of London. Overbury was murdered in 1613.
Forman had nothing to do with that; he had died two years
before. But the young Countess had been a client of his – she
had come to him for love-potions and erotic figurines to
compel the love of Robert Carr, who was King James I's
boyfriend. Whether owing to Forman's arts or no, she
succeeded in marrying Carr. It all made a great scandal, in
which the poor King and the Archbishop of Canterbury were
both involved. Ben Jonson wrote the masque for the

notorious marriage. And Forman's name was unfairly be-smirched by these proceedings in high society.

There is a fairly full account of Forman in the *Dictionary of National Biography*; but again, he is treated there as a quack and a charlatan – quite wrongly. As an astrologer he was not a charlatan. In Shakespeare's time everybody believed, more or less, in astrology; certainly Forman did, and he was a very successful practitioner. He was also a successful medical practitioner, though an unqualified one. Most were, in those days, and they were liable to be persecuted as such by the Royal College of Physicians or the local authorities. If you know much about the treatments Elizabethan doctors gave their patients, the violent purgings, the bleedings, their appalling concoctions, you might well have preferred to be treated by Forman. He didn't believe in all that bleeding and purging, nor much in going by people's urine. He seems to have preferred herbal treatments, and he had a long and very wide experience of disease, especially women's complaints. With this he had acute psychological perception, and undoubted psychic gifts.

Forman was a bit of a psychotic type himself. He longed to get an education and come to the university; but his father died young and he couldn't continue his schooling. Born just outside Wilton Park near Salisbury, he had some broken schooling there and at the Free School in the Close. He learnt enough Latin to be able to write it more fluently than most university men, but he could get to Oxford only as the personal servant of two frolicsome clerics, whom he rather despised. No wonder he developed an acute inferiority complex. When he set up to practise medicine in Salisbury, he was sent to prison by the local authorities. So he developed signs of paranoia too – but that gave him an insight into other queer types, and a sharper understanding of human beings in general.

When Forman got to London – about the time Shakespeare came to London, in all the excitement of the Spanish Armada, just before or after – life opened out for

him. Persecuted, in and out of prison for practising in the
City, Forman went to live at Lambeth out of the range of the
Doctors and under the more tolerant shadow of the
Archbishop. Finally, Forman got a licence from Cambridge
University to practise: he ended up, if not in the odour of
sanctity, at any rate a successful citizen. He married a young
lady of good birth and connections, and left a tidy
fortune – and all his fabulous papers, from which we learn
more, more intimately, about the Elizabethan Age than from
any other source.

It is strange that they have never been properly explored
before, but a great stroke of luck that they were left for me.
Forman left them to his friend, Richard Napier, rector of
Great Linford, Bucks; *he* left them to his nephew, Sir
Richard Napier, a Fellow of All Souls, through whom they
came to Ashmole, and so are among the Ashmolean MSS in
the Bodleian Library. The papers have every kind of interest.
To the psychologist, for instance. The psychologist Jung said
that Ashmole's record of his dreams was of great interest and
value as the earliest we have got. They are from the late
seventeenth century. But Forman's record of his dreams is
nearly a century earlier, from the Elizabethan Age. You
know how the poets and artists regarded Queen Elizabeth I,
as the semi-divine figure at the apex of the society, isolated in
her glory. People couldn't bear the idea of anyone coming
too near the Virgin Queen – Leicester, for instance, or the
Duke of Anjou. All very anthropological, in a society which
had only recently ceased to worship the Blessed Virgin Mary.
Well, what do you think was the response of the ordinary
normal male to the Virgin Queen on the throne? There is
never any evidence in history as to the most intimate
concerns of men's minds of that sort. But Forman's papers
afford the most searching glimpse that we have; in him we
discover an Elizabethan Pepys or a Boswell.

In 1597 – when Shakespeare was producing *Henry IV*,
with his creation of Falstaff – Forman dreamed that he was
walking with the Queen, a little elderly woman in a white

petticoat, 'all unready'. They came to a place where there was a tall man with a reddish beard, rather distracted, who spoke too familiarly to her and 'at last did take her and kiss her'. Forman protected her and led her away. The way was dirty and her coat trailed in front in the dirt. He held it up for her, and asked if he might wait upon her. Receiving permission, he said: 'I mean to wait *upon* you, and not under you, that I might make this belly a little bigger to carry up this coat out of the dirt.' 'Then she began to lean upon me ... and to be very familiar with me, and methought she would have kissed me.' A month later Forman dreamed of her again, coming to him all in black with a French hood. One hardly needs to be a Freud to spot the symbolism: the Virgin Queen at first all in white, then trailing in the dirt, finally appearing in black with a French hood. He would remember the primitive apprehension there was in the country at the thought of a French marriage, people's hatred of her marrying Catherine de Medici's son, Anjou. As for the tall man with the reddish beard, there is Essex, and that is just what he was doing at the time, bandying words with her, after Cadiz, and pressing her for the Azores Expedition later that year, 1597.

There is a great deal of confused talk today about pornography. The term has come now to have a more precise meaning, namely writing about sexual matters for the subsidiary purpose of stimulating sexual excitement. This is absolutely not Forman's line: his purpose is purely factual, to record the exact moment of intercourse, timing it, so that the horoscope might be as accurate as possible – otherwise, the calculations would go wrong and the forecast be no good. Remember that everybody believed that the stars influenced our fate, just as the sun and moon do. But the calculations had to be pinpointed. So Forman's recording of these experiences are not pornography, but anthropology – and may be of interest not only to psychologists but to medical men. His word for intercourse is *halek* – I don't know where it comes from, it may be cabbalistic; but he gives us a complete record of his sex-life with his wife, which I won't go into detail about here, as well as other people's.

The sub-culture of people's emotional and erotic life, their subconscious, the penumbra of the irrational, their most intimate yearnings and hopes and insatisfactions — all this is the most difficult area for the historian to penetrate into. Forman's papers are a marvellous source, practically unique for penetrating into the life of a society.

Here I have an important historical point to make. The Reformation dealt a blow to society's unconscious cult life, the semi-magical penumbra of experience which Catholicism had provided for — leaving people unsatisfied in this area. It was this gap that people like the famous Dr Dee, Queen Elizabeth's astrologer, and Forman helped to fill. The people who consult him offer a fascinating spectrum of society from the very top to (not quite) the bottom. Lord Chamberlain Hunsdon, the patron of Shakespeare's company, was a first cousin of the Queen. His daughter, Lady Hoby, consulted Forman about the health of her brother, the second Lord Hunsdon, whom Forman had met years before. This second Lord Hunsdon was also patron of Shakespeare's company; it looks pretty clear that the illness from which he died was v.d. The Elizabethans were much more diseased than we are, and also much more unrespectable. They were medievals, like Chaucer's people, for the most part free and easy in their sex-life.

One of the grandest and most regular clients of Forman is another Frances Howard, cousin of the beautiful poisoner, and a respectable character. Granddaughter of the Duke of Norfolk, she was left an orphan. Nevertheless, Forman prognosticated, she was born under a fortunate conjunction: she would change her state three times. She changed her state the first time when she married a rich vintner; when he soon died she was left well off. Only twenty, she is now after — whom do you think? Shakespeare's young patron and friend, the Earl of Southampton. The lady wants to know from Forman whether the Earl means anything to her; shall

she follow him down into the country, etc? When Southampton marries Elizabeth Vernon, Frances at length has to
give up — and settles for the elderly Earl of Hertford. When
he dies, he leaves her very rich. She changes her state for the
third time — as Forman had foretold — and enters the royal
family. She marries King James I's first cousin, the Duke of
Lennox, becomes a royal duchess, Duchess of Richmond and
Lennox. And is buried in Westminster Abbey, in a grand
marble four-poster just across from Henry VII, where you
may go and see her.

A leading sea-commander in the last years of the war with
Spain was Vice-Admiral Sir William Monson, of the *Naval
Tracts*. He never put to sea without having Forman cast the
horoscope how he should fare; on one occasion taking him
down to Plymouth where the fleet was assembling. Similarly
Nicholas Leate, Master of the Ironmongers Company, a
leading Turkey merchant. He is concerned for his cargoes of
goods on the merchantmen penetrating the Mediterranean:
have they left Algiers for Tripoli, have they arrived at
Alexandretta or are they returning from Zante, the centre of
the trade in currants? It is just like the beginning of *The
Merchant of Venice*, with Antonio and his friends discussing
the whereabouts of their argosies:

Plucking the grass to know where sits the wind,
Peering in maps for ports, and piers, and roads.

The more you delve in depth into Forman's papers the more
it brings home to you how real and expressive of Elizabethan
life Shakespeare's plays are, for all their Italian colouring. It
is not so much Venice as Shakespeare's and Forman's London,
of the Levant Company and Turkey merchants. So it is not at
all surprising that Shakespeare's known landlady turns up,
Marie Montjoie. We know independently that Shakespeare
was lodging with that French couple in Silver Street about
the time he wrote the French scenes in *Henry V* — for their
lodger, William Shakespeare, performed the betrothal of their
daughter to an apprentice. Mrs Mountjoy loses money out of

her purse going along Silver Street and comes to consult Forman.

The next person to turn up is Richard Field, the Stratford-born printer who printed Shakespeare's poems, *Venus and Adonis* and *The Rape of Lucrece*. Then William Jaggard turns up to consult Forman medically: this is the publisher who published several of Shakespeare's sonnets without his permission. Thomas Heywood, the playwright, tells us that 'the author, as I know, was much offended thereat.' And Shakespeare's close colleague in the Lord Chamberlain's Company, Augustine Phillips, next appears, along with several Burbages and Henslowes, names of theatre-folk, whom I cannot precisely identify. But I think we can identify the lady who next turns up. We are given so many clues, the closest possible parallel in circumstances, character, dating. And she comes not only out of the circle of the Lord Chamberlain's Company, Shakespeare's company, but was the Lord Chamberlain's own mistress, up to late in the year 1592, when she was discarded, being pregnant, and married off, for colour, to a musician with whom she was unhappy. Emilia was the daughter of another of the Queen's musicians, an Italian, Baptista Bassano. Her husband, Alfonso Lanier, also a musician to the Queen, was away on the expedition to the Azores, on which Southampton was in command of a ship. We learn independently that Southampton knew the Italian lady's husband, and also that Lanier served later, with Essex and Southampton, in Ireland.

You remember Shakespeare devoting a sonnet to his Dark Lady playing on the virginals—

How oft, my music, when thou music play'st

— with her fingers wandering over the keys, while the jacks leap up to kiss the tender inward of her hand, etc. And you will remember that it was at just this time, when the Lord Chamberlain discarded his young Italian mistress, that Shakespeare fell for his Dark Lady out of pity:

If thy unworthiness raised love in me,
More worthy I to be beloved of thee.

She *was* unworthy. She was a bad lot — nothing romantic about Shakespeare's affair with her. She was promiscuous, it was an adulterous relationship; she looked down on him, and demeaned him in talk with others. But he couldn't help himself, he couldn't but be infatuated.

O from what power hast thou this powerful might . . .
To make me give the lie to my true sight?

In the end she drove Shakespeare 'frantic-mad', he says; and the affair breaks off with him going off to Bath for treatment, 'a sad distempered guest.'

Simon Forman himself had a precisely similar experience at the hands of the Italian Lady. She was high-minded and ambitious, anxious to be a lady of title. Forman says she was 'not worthy thereof'. She had been maintained in pomp and luxury by the old Lord Chamberlain and had been made much of by other lords. Notice that, for Shakespeare's Dark Lady had entangled his young lord and patron, Southampton, in her snares. Emilia treated Forman just as the poet had been treated; she sent her manservant to bid him to her house, where he stayed all night, and was allowed every liberty, except the last. She drove him frantic, after encouraging him; later, she bade him up again. In the end, she alarmed Forman, the only woman to do so, with her tales about the invocation of spirits. After this he finished with her, and wrote her down roundly as 'a whore'.

Shakespeare had more compassion, and a greater capacity for suffering: he was the one who was tortured at her hands. But the immense advantage of Forman is that he gives you these people's ages, so that the whole situation becomes more real to us, and completely convincing. At the time when the affair was at its height, Shakespeare was twenty-nine — no longer young, for an Elizabethan, his life more than half over, a married man with three children. It *was* humiliating for him to be under the spell of a much younger woman — she was twenty-three or four, Southampton just twenty.

Next year the Lord Chamberlain's Company was founded, the old Lord Chamberlain, who had discarded Emilia Bassano the year or so before, being patron of the company, of which Shakespeare and Augustine Phillips were founder-members.

You see what a small circle this is, of people all known to each other, and connected by ties we know about independently. If these facts did not completely hold together to make an absolutely consistent factual account of the matter, it should be possible to challenge it at some point. But there is no point at which it can be challenged: it is perfectly clear that this is the true story and that here we have, at last — and quite unexpected by me — Shakespeare's Dark Lady. And that is only one of the many people whose most intimate affairs and activities we learn about from Simon Forman.

# I

# The Reception of My
## *William Shakespeare*[1]

The reception of my work on Shakespeare is an interesting story in itself, and one that is symptomatic of our time, not only of its literary life, but of academic and intellectual life in general, in the decline of standards, the lack of concern for what is true, the inability to recognise it when put forward by a leading authority on the age of Shakespeare, the preference for nonsense rather than commonsense, the obtuseness on the part of those who should know better. It is all characteristic of this age and its lowering of standards.

It may well be wondered how one can bear up against it all – and I have received some compliments on the score of courage, even a conditional tribute to my 'intuition and tenacity', in a snide review of my book in the *Times Literary Supplement* by a recognisable professor of the Shakespeare Establishment.

Well, it doesn't take much courage to stand up for commonsense – and besides I have been through it all before. In the 1930s practically the whole country went whoring after Neville Chamberlain and appeasing Hitler. It was absolute nonsense, yet they couldn't see it. I was a very lone voice, on the Left, constantly returning to the charge in letters to *The Times*, speeches as a young Labour candidate, frequent articles.

I have often felt as if I were going through it again in my campaign for commonsense about Shakespeare. For I have

[1] (Macmillan, 1963.)

been doing nothing other than that, reducing the so-called 'problems' to commonsense – nothing novel or radical (I should hate that), quite conservative and traditional, only firm and definite. Shakespeare did not write his Sonnets in order to create a puzzle: they should be susceptible of interpretation, their background worked out – if only one knows enough about the Elizabethan background to be able to do so. But very few people do – so that hardly anybody's opinion on these matters is of any account. The joke is that they don't realise that – journalist-clowns, witty enough in their vulgar way, haven't the sense of humour to realise that when it comes to the Elizabethan Age they don't know what they are talking about.

I have spent my whole life working on the Age of Shakespeare, particularly its social life, and I can tell you that most of the comments are simply rubbish and need not detain us. We have far more interesting things, and people, in view.

When I went to the Huntington Library to write my biography of Shakespeare ten years ago, I took it for granted, as we had been told, that the problems of Shakespeare's Sonnets were insoluble, that there was no knowing who Mr W. H. was, assuming that he was Shakespeare's young man, etc.

The first thing I noticed – and this was the stone that blocked the way to common sense about it all – was that Mr W. H. was not Shakespeare's young man, but the publisher Thorp's dedicatee. There is no disputing this: everybody knows that it was Thomas Thorp who dedicated the Sonnets to Mr W. H., not Shakespeare. But people had missed the significance of this: it meant that Mr W. H. was not Shakespeare's young man in the Sonnets at all, who was anyway a Lord. The majority of literary scholars, from Malone onwards, had always supposed this; I was merely one with the dominant literary tradition, but I had made it firm, removed the stone in the way.

It was always clear that the young Lord of the Sonnets

was the obvious person — Shakespeare's personal patron, the Earl of Southampton, recognisable in every detail of character and circumstance, a peer of state, rather feminine and ambivalent, who refused to marry in just these years, and so on.

All the books written under the mistaken idea that Thorp's Mr W. H. was Shakespeare's young Lord were just barking up the wrong tree: they had *created* the confusion and mixed people up. But they were mixed up themselves: both Chambers and Dover Wilson had got it wrong, just plumping for the Earl of Pembroke — years out. In any case he had never been a Mr W. H. — when young, he was Lord Herbert, i.e. Lord H., and when he grew up was anything but ambivalent, a roaring heterosexual. When the Sonnets began he was aged twelve — really, one does not write sonnets to a boy of twelve telling him to get married right quick and carry on the family.

The most absurd of these suggestions was put forward by Professor Hotson — also under the mare's-nest notion that Thorp's Mr W. H. was Shakespeare's young Lord. Looking out for anybody and everybody with the initials W. H., Hotson lighted upon an obscure William Hatcliffe, who had once been Prince of Purpoole at some Inn of Court revels. A crazy suggestion, of course. (But it took in Dame Veronica Wedgwood, the only scholar who fell for this nonsense.)

What the historian has to contribute is above all certainty with regard to dating: in fact here the Elizabethan historian is indispensable. I am not a textual scholar, a critic or historian of the drama, or a bibliographer: for those matters, one goes to the leading authorities, Fredson Bowers, Nevill Coghill, G. E. Bentley. I am delighted to take telling from them, not from journalist-clowns, or journalist-professors who should be getting on with their research, writing solid books and setting a better example in their faculty.

In working out the topical references in the Sonnets I found that they gave a perfectly intelligible reading in chronological order as they are — beginning in 1592, going on through 1593 and 1594, to end in the winter 1594—5. This also was in keeping with the dominant literary tradition, which had always thought they belonged to the early 1590s. Once more, nothing novel or radical, quite conservative and plain common sense; but the Elizabethan historian, familiar with events from year to year and month to month, was able to make the time-scheme firm and definite.

The consequences were important. The Southampton sequence, Sonnets 1 to 126, run from 1592 to 1594/5; the Dark Lady Sonnets, 127 to 152, fall within that period, mainly 1592—3. The Sonnets are in sensible order as they are. There is no point in re-arranging them, disarranging or de-ranging them, as people have done, only creating confusion. Further, it became obvious that the Rival Poet was the obvious person, Marlowe (and not some other nonsensical person out of the rag-bag, such as Gervase Markham, the poet of farriery. As ludicrous a suggestion as William Hatcliffe!). And what was the Rival Poet rivalling Shakespeare for? For the patronage of the patron, i.e. the Sonnets were written to the patron. Q.E.D.

The textual scholar, Hyder Rollins, had stated that *dating* was the clue to solving the 'unanswerable' problems of the Sonnets. And so it turned out: all the so-called 'problems' of the Sonnets turned out to be no problems at all. The answers stood revealed — all, except for the identity of the Dark Lady, for whom there was no clue from the external world to corroborate what Shakespeare himself told us.

I wrote home to tell the person whom I most respected in this field, and consult his opinion: my friend F. P. Wilson, Professor of English Literature at Oxford, our leading authority on the Elizabethan drama, a scholar of the soundest judgement. He wrote back: 'If Hotson had told me that he had solved the problems of the Sonnets, I should have known that it was another mare's nest. But since it is you who are telling me, I must take it seriously; I have always greatly respected your knowledge of Elizabethan society, particularly of family and personal relations.'

When I came home to Oxford, F. P. Wilson, though ill, came to my rooms on two afternoons to hear my two chapters on the period of the Sonnets and the related plays, *Love's Labour's Lost* and *A Midsummer Night's Dream.* At the end of the reading he said in his grave, pondered way: 'All I can say is, that I am deeply impressed, and have nothing whatever to urge against it.' (The only exception he made was to my reading of Don Armado too much in terms of Gabriel Harvey, and here F. P. Wilson was probably right.)

But he recognised E. K. Chambers at once from my allusion to a 'massive but imperceptive' scholar. The description is perfectly correct. We are all deeply indebted to Chambers for the enormous amount of material he assembled in the intervals of his full-time career as a civil servant. But by the same token he was imperceptive: quite wrong about Sir Thomas Malory; in his biography of Sir Henry Lee he failed to notice Lee's chief claim to fame as the creator of the Accession Day Tilts; and quite wrong about the Sonnets, in which he expressed not much interest – in a biography of Shakespeare, think of it, when they contain Shakespeare's autobiography! It is hardly surprising that he thought the heterosexual Pembroke to be the ambivalent young Lord of the Sonnets. The rather autocratic civil servant had not much human perception.

But Dover Wilson, who had perception, was very erratic, as all scholars know; especially, as F. P. Wilson pointed out, with regard to this early period, that of the Sonnets and *Love's Labour's Lost.* By the time my *William Shakespeare* came out F. P. Wilson was dead, and I was left alone to face the racket. I greatly missed him, his moderation, advice and help.

At the Quatercentenary celebrations at Stratford – where there was a marvellous evocation of the Age in the Exhibition created by Richard Buckle, and as little appreciated by the third-rate as my own work (but this is the Age of the Third-Rate) – Dover Wilson kindly came to my lecture. I was rather fond of old Dover, and afterwards I told him that I had found the answers to the problems of the Sonnets, except for the Dark Lady. I promised that I would send him a copy of my book. He said, 'I'm afraid I can't read it, I'm blind.' Taken aback, I said, 'But you could have it read to you.' He asked whom I thought to be the young man of the Sonnets. I told him, of course it was Southampton. Dover was still engaged in editing the Sonnets as the concluding volume of the *Cambridge Shakespeare*. He said, 'I'm afraid I am so far along on the other tack that I can't change course now.'

I was shocked at this. Dover was well into his eighties at the time, and partly blind. But he was not too old to indite a pamphlet, on the problems of the Sonnets 'for the benefit of historians', traversing this historian's work and repeating all the old confusions. When his edition of the Sonnets came out it was practically valueless, with all the old muddle about Pembroke. This time the *Times Literary Supplement* reviewer was careful not to notice it.

This was a sad episode, and rather a sad end for Dover. Though his pamphlet for the historian's benefit, written at eighty-three or so, is utterly muddled it is still referred to as if it had authority. But by people who do not know what they are talking about, have never gone into the subject and wouldn't know how to judge of it if they had. The last word on poor old Dover Wilson was said to me recently by one of the leading authorities at Stratford: 'Dover didn't really want to know the truth.'

This is what is so shocking in the whole story: they really do not want to know the truth, they do not want to have their old easy prejudices disturbed, they do not want the bother of thinking out anything new, they do not want to consider it — even when they are being told by a leading authority on the Age.

One of my colleagues, an authority on Italian history, said that he couldn't care less who the Dark Lady was. If he had discovered something fascinating and unknown about Michelangelo, I should be the first to be interested. It is our *raison d'être* as intellectuals to want to know — and how few of us qualify!

As for the *Times Literary Supplement*, that organ was badly let down by its reviewer in this field. Some years before, the reviewer had fallen for Hotson's nonsense about 'the mortal moon' being the Spanish Armada — when all sensible persons know that the phrase always refers to the Queen — and so pushing the Sonnets absurdly back to 1588! These literary folk have no idea of the decisive significance of a date — as historians know — and are all over the place in dating the Sonnets from the Spanish Armada to the death of Elizabeth and beyond.

When it came to my biography, the book was treated to a full-page diatribe by one John Crow. I never knew him, though he lived somewhere in the suburbs of Oxford. He was not a biographer but a bibliographer; moreover he had never written a book himself and so was possessed with envy of those who can and do. This is all too boringly recognisable — one can smell it a mile off — and it is in fact a sociological symptom of our time. An egalitarian society releases envy of every kind and at every level.

The reception of the big book in America, by a large audience of a thousand Eng. Lit. professors at the Modern Language Association, was open-minded and encouraging. There had preceded me one McManaway, of the Folger Shakespeare Library, always supposed to be going to write *the* biography. After the friendly reception from the audience, all I got from him was a grumpy 'Still I shall always think we shall never know who the Young Man was or who the Rival Poet was.'

There you have the old Shakespeare Establishment in a nutshell: 'The problems of Shakespeare are insoluble, therefore they are insoluble.' Anybody who solves them for them is offending against their religion. Or, as a friend said, it is like taking a bone away from a dog.

I noticed later that I was described as 'using my prestige as an Elizabethan historian' to advance my views on Shakespeare. But I do not think in terms of 'prestige', or value it, I only want to get at the truth; what I am using is my *knowledge* of Shakespeare's Age to advance our knowledge of his real background.

This leads me to a second sociological point of some significance. People in a demotic society are led to believe that anybody's opinion is as good as anybody else's about anything. This, of course, is quite untrue. If you have something seriously wrong with your insides, you ask a (medical) specialist; if there is something wrong with the electricity, you ask an electrician. If there is something wrong with your motor-car, there is no point in asking me: I am an ignoramus in such matters, ask somebody who knows. But if it is something about the Elizabethan Age, you would do well to consult the historian.

There is even a third sociological point. When I got back to Oxford after the Shakespeare biography was published, I heard that there had been quite a rumpus. John Bayley, Eng. Lit. don but a highly intelligent one, greeted me with 'Hi! You've been offending against trade union regulations!' And that was the long and the short of it. But how short-sighted, how much without a sense of strategy, not to welcome the clearing up of these problems, by an Elizabethan historian, really their effective ally in our common struggle against the crackpots in the field. It is totally unlike the Elizabethans, where a Ralegh could be soldier and poet, sailor and chemist, historian and politician; or a Bacon could be lawyer and scientist, politician and philosopher. I have never respected the over-specialisation in the academic life of our time; I have always favoured the cross-fertilisation of studies. Besides, I had come to Oxford with a scholarship in English Literature and expected to take that School. (The dons at Christ Church thought that English Literature was a soft option, and made me do the Modern History School — for which I have been insufficiently grateful to them.)

I did not say to these people that all my life I have been as deeply attached to literature as to history, that I had been

writing poetry far longer than I had history, had in fact
published several volumes of verse, which was more than they
were ever likely to do. Other *real* writers saw the point and
were generous in their reception of my Shakespeare work:
Priestley, Cyril Connolly, André Maurois, Rebecca West,
Elizabeth Jenkins. C. P. Snow wrote: 'This is a wonderful
work. It shows what a first-class historian can do when he
turns to literature.' J. I. M. Stewart saw the particular point
of it: 'Dr. Rowse is a poet as well as an historian – and it is
really the poet who has written a very good book about
Shakespeare. Not only does he draw a splendidly rich and
vivid background for the dramatist; he also shows, again and
again, how the passion and excitement of the Age pours into
the plays.' And there were similar tributes from other
fields – John Gielgud, Harold Macmillan, and even a personal
letter from de Gaulle.

A young American professor, a leading authority on
Elizabethan stagecraft, said, 'I think if you had come to the
Eng. Lit. professors with your cap in your hand and said "I
put forward this theory for your better judgement", they
would have been better pleased.' I reacted to this, quite
simply and honestly: 'But I couldn't say that: this isn't a
theory, it is the answer. Besides it is the right one.' My friend
replied: 'That is the trouble: you are right. But think what
they would have done to you if you had been wrong!'

I made no reply, though a Swiftian or an A. E. Housman
reaction came into my mind: it is not for the first-rate to
take their opinions from the third-rate; it is for the third-rate
to learn from the first-rate. Anything else is a reversal of the
order of nature – how else can they learn, poor things?

And what about the last phase in my work, not only with
regard to the Dark Lady, but the new light I have been able
to throw, from Forman's Case-Books, on Shakespeare's
known landlady, Mrs Mountjoy, and putting the record right
about Mary Fitton.

I don't claim any credit for any of this – credit from such
people today is not worth having. I write for myself alone,

my aim to recall the dead to life and get the record straight. And yet people respond in the most extraordinary manner. Four of my books have each of them sold over 300,000 copies; which means that my books altogether must have been read by at least a couple of millions. I never thought of that before — it doesn't seem to give unadulterated pleasure to the poor Crows of this world. But they might as well reconcile themselves to the unpleasant fact that, a most unpopular writer with them, I must be a popular writer with people in general. There is a curious paradox here they would do well to reflect on.

In my article about Mary Fitton I managed to put that piece of nonsense straight and cleared her out of the way once and for all. There had been dozens of books and articles, colour supplements and all, featuring her as the Dark Lady. It always was nonsense — the real scholarly reason being that she was Pembroke's mistress, that Pembroke had nothing to do with the Sonnets which are years before his affair with her in 1600. Dating is decisive. Of course, with the simple and innocent, what settled the matter was that she was not dark but had grey-blue eyes and auburn hair. Anyway, I have succeeded in bundling her out of the way for good and all.

Next, from Simon Forman's Case-Books I have uncovered some new information about Mary Mountjoy. Not a great deal; but anything that lights up information — as opposed to useless conjectures — about Shakespeare's real background and the people he lived with is of value. If Shakespeare's known landlady came to consult Forman, there is nothing improbable in Shakespeare's mistress turning up there too. Especially when she was the discarded mistress of the Lord Chamberlain, the official head of Shakespeare's Company. That was what made me prick up my ears and forced itself on my attention, rather reluctantly and belatedly, when I certainly wasn't looking for her.

I never thought she would be found. Yet Forman's papers offered the one place where she might turn up. Hundreds of

women and men of all conditions in Elizabethan society
came to consult Forman, from the grandest Court-ladies
downwards. The real difficulty is identification – you need
to have an Elizabethan Who's Who in your head to make
them out.

I had already made new contributions throwing light on
the nature of *Love's Labour's Lost*, as a skit on the
Southampton circle by its poet and on the familiar Southampton theme of not responding to the love of women; as
also on the dating and occasion of *A Midsummer Night's
Dream* to 2 May 1594, for the marriage of Southampton's
mother to Sir Thomas Heneage; with the suggestion for
*Romeo and Juliet* as prompted by the feud down in
Southampton's neighbourhood between his friends, the
Danvers brothers and the Longs, whose son and heir they
killed. John Florio, Southampton's tutor, turns up in the
affair. One does not have to look far for the Italian flavouring
of the plays.

No notice was taken of this by any of the obtuse
Shakespeare Establishment, going on in their old ruts, with
little idea of what was going on at the time Shakespeare was
writing the plays. Only the other day a popular journalist
wrote an abusive article on my *Shakespeare the Man*, knowing
nothing whatever about the subject, of course. But he called
in aid an aged professor, who repeated all the old nonsense
about Mr W. H., still not having grasped the elementary point
that he was Thorp's man, not Shakespeare's. He couldn't see
that the characteristics of the young Lord in the Sonnets
were absolutely those of the obvious person, the patron
Southampton, personality, circumstances, refusing to marry,
dating and all. He thought the likeliest 'candidate' to be
William Hatcliffe, Prince of Purpoole, evidently unaware that
everybody recognises the suggestion as absurd.

This leads me to a strategic point. As the result of the
needless confusion created by these people, creating
'problems' where they don't exist, leaving open questions
which can be settled, thousands of people in Britain and

America don't know whether Shakespeare wrote his own
plays or whether he ever existed. All this is crackpot
nonsense, we know. The Shakespeare Establishment are
largely responsible for it, by confusing the issues, and leaving
the gates wide open for all the crackpots to gallop through all
over the field.

I blame the Establishment – and they never have been
able to deal with the crackpots they have let in (Baconians,
Marlovians, Oxfordians – sheer lunacy of course). If I have
accomplished one thing I am not at all proud of – I have
certainly dealt these lunatics a more effective blow than the
Shakespeare professors ever could. They have not been a bit
grateful for it: too purblind to see that in the leading
Elizabethan historian they have their most effective ally,
bringing the background to Shakespeare, both life and work,
into the light of commonsense knowledge of the age as no
one else can.

Why do they dislike it so much? That is the amusing
problem. (I like being told what I don't know about, am
anxious to learn.)

So far from proper recognition of the remarkable amount
of work accomplished, the new light thrown on Shakespeare,
the new material brought out, the new impulse given when
Shakespeare scholarship was at a dead end, become a dead
scholasticism repeating all the old abracadabra – 'the
problems of Shakespeare's Sonnets are insoluble' – when I
solved them for them, anyone would think I had committed
a crime.

The Oxford University Press published a fat book on
*Shakespeare's Lives.* It described my work as merely 'a
triumph of promotion', dragging in a reference to my poetry
as that of 'a poetaster'. When I protested at this disgraceful
treatment by my own university press of original work by
one of the university's leading historians, I could get no
redress – all they would do was to withdraw the insulting
word 'poetaster'. (It is of no consequence to me, merely
ironical, that the poetaster appears in their own *Oxford Book
of Twentieth Century Verse.*)

Envy and spite are such familiar phenomena in contemporary literary life as to be boring, rather than hurtful. So used to them, I can smell them from a mile away. They should try something else for a change – let them try learning from someone who has got fascinating things to tell them about a far more rewarding age than this. As for the beautiful Schoenbaüme and Levins, they will be forgotten five minutes after they are dead or have ceased to go through their hoops in the newspapers. The historian takes longer views and can afford to wait.

Nor am I the only person who has reason to complain of the obstinate obtuseness of these people. A younger scholar, Roger Prior, discovered that two years after the publication of the Sonnets, Emilia Lanier published a volume of verse bitterly refuting men's denigration of women. Mr Prior also discovered something significant about George Wilkins, who cashed in on the success of Shakespeare's *Pericles* with a prose-tale on the subject. Hitherto, no one was certain of the relationship between Wilkins' novel and the play. Mr Prior further found that Wilkins kept a not very respectable tavern. The daughter and son-in-law of the Mountjoys with whom Shakespeare lodged in Silver Street – and he performed the betrothal of the young couple – went to live in Wilkins' tavern. It is a genuine link, that indirectly reinforces the connection with the author of *Pericles*.

When an old professor read Prior's article, with its new information from the documents, he exclaimed, 'We do not wish to think that William Shakespeare was connected with such people.'

There you have it in a nutshell: this blimpish attitude of not wanting to know, a conventional *bien-pensant* view of Shakespeare, totally alien to the nature and conditions of Elizabethan life, ignorant and as opposed to real scholarship as it is to perception and creative understanding.

To sum up: I think something more hopeful may be indicated for the future. It is perfectly true that the old Shakespeare Establishment, at a dead end, has nothing more to offer than its wearisome academicism, infinitely boring, incapable of taking in, let alone absorbing, a new idea, a new approach. Some of the old men did good work — Chambers erected a strong and massive structure on which to build. Even Dover Wilson did good work, though notoriously erratic. The work that I find most illuminating is that which sees Shakespeare first and foremost in terms of the theatre — Granville Barker, Nevill Coghill, G. E. Bentley. The theatre is the best place in which to study Shakespeare, not the lecture-room.

For my own work, it is alive and kicking, where most of the professors are dead from the neck upwards. As for its reception — it is quite simple and what you would expect: a first-rate response from the first-rate, second-rate reactions from the second-rate, and third-rate from the third-rate. You can always tell what people are from the reviews they write.

Why am I then so contemptuous of them? I think it is partly, as a woman writer of distinction saw, that I love Shakespeare so much that I cannot endure to see him made such nonsense of by people with second-rate perceptions. But I see a gleam of light. At the very least I shall have given this Elizabethan subject a new impulse. And this will work in two ways. Younger scholars will follow up the trails I have started and they will yield us new and solid information about the people Shakespeare knew and lived and worked with — the real thing as against the conjectures of the dull and inferior.

# Popular Misconceptions about William Shakespeare

Much of the nonsense written about Shakespeare comes from people who know nothing of the Elizabethan Age in which he lived. A good deal of the confusion in people's minds about our greatest writer has come from literary scholars leaving open questions about his life and associations – quite superfluously, for they can be settled. The result is that thousands of people in Britain and America do not know whether he ever existed or wrote his own plays, or whether Queen Elizabeth wrote them under an assumed name.

Let me answer a few questions that have come up to me from audiences all over the country, and help to clear people's minds of misconceptions. The first is that people think we do not know much about him. The truth is, we know more about him than about any contemporary dramatist – except for the later career of Ben Jonson, about whose early life we know hardly anything.

In the Elizabethan Age people didn't bother much about the lives of mere writers, let alone playwrights and actors. It is remarkable how much we do know about this Elizabethan actor-dramatist.

People are apt to think that only a grandee, some earl or other, must have written his plays. Snobbish nonsense: earls are just the people who do not write poems and plays. They are almost always written by clever grammar-school boys – like Milton or Wordsworth, Marlowe or Ben Jonson, Dr Johnson, Southey, Coleridge, Tennyson or whoever – usually middle class, rarely aristocrats.

As a matter of fact, there is more about grammar-school

education, schoolmasters, the process of instruction, the
textbooks used, the Latin tags, in Shakespeare's plays than in
any other dramatist's.

There is a special reason for this — the information has
come down from a reliable source that he taught school for a
bit in the country, during the so-called lost years. Then how
did he know so much about the life of the Court, and
upper-class life?

Quite simply, from performing so frequently at Court —
that gave him a close-up view of people and happenings there.
Then, too, his association and friendship with his young
patron, the Earl of Southampton, was a tremendous advantage in opening up a world of greater refinement and culture
to the actor. Actors are naturally good at this sort of thing
and moving up in society.

It is significant that the greatest of English dramatists, like
Molière, the greatest of French, was an actor. We are told by
John Aubrey, who knew, that Shakespeare was a very good
actor. The plays, as well as the Sonnets, are full of revealing
passages about acting, from the actor's point of view. The
author of the plays was an actor, though in the Sonnets he
regretted that he had to earn his living this way. He would
have preferred to be independent; he was very insistent on
being regarded as a gentleman, and in the end achieved it.

The connexion with Stratford? Shakespeare's loyalty to
Stratford and Warwickshire is obvious, and quite exceptionally strong.

All the other theatre-folk who made money in London
invested their gains in London property or nearby. Not so
Shakespeare: he was determined to cut a figure in his native
town. The moment he had some money to invest, he bought
the finest house there, and later made two considerable
investments in Stratford property, over a hundred acres of
Old Stratford and later tithes in the villages roundabout.

His will gives a perfectly clear picture of his situation. Most
of what he was to leave is property in Stratford; but he also
owns a property conveniently in Blackfriars for the theatre,

and leaves money for mourning-rings to three of his fellow-actors in his Company.

There you have it: the Stratford man who went to London, made good in the theatre, invested the proceeds in his native town, and retired there, to die and be buried where his family were.

Of course, the plays themselves give Warwickshire and the Cotswold country an exceptionally good deal, in *The Taming of the Shrew*, in *Henry VI* and *Henry IV*; while in *As You Like It* the Forest of Arden is itself brought on to the stage. Both Shakespeare's parents were Forest of Arden folk; Shakespeare's mother, of superior social standing to the father and a bit of an heiress, was Mary Arden. A few years after Shakespeare took out a coat-of-arms in his father's name — so that he should have been born a gentleman — a draft was prepared for quartering the Arden coat with it.

Did Shakespeare die a Catholic? No. There was a vague rumour to that effect later in the century; but his will makes it quite clear. Elizabethan Catholic wills all include in the formula bequeathing the soul to God, the Blessed Virgin and all the Holy Company of Heaven; such are adherents of the old Faith. Shakespeare's recites the regular Protestant formula, 'hoping and assuredly believing through the only merits of Jesus Christ, my Saviour, to be made partaker of life everlasting'.

There is the regular Protestant doctrine of merit — faith as against works. The whole of Shakespeare's work as well as his life reveals him as a conformist — all his family baptised and buried in church; he was not the one to stick his neck out and ask for trouble, unlike Ben Jonson, who became a Catholic for a time, or Christopher Marlowe, who was an unbeliever, dangerously heterodox. Both of them obstinate types, self-willed and arrogant, unlike the courteous, in-gratiating Shakespeare, described as 'gentle', by which the Elizabethans meant gentlemanly.

Do we know what he looked like? Of course, we do. Almost everybody in the country recognises that immense,

bald brow; have you ever seen such a dome of St Paul's as
that on any man's head? The Folio engraving and the bust at
Stratford are at one on that – a noble span of brain sufficient
to contain the plays.

How could he have written so many plays? Again people
don't know the facts about the Elizabethan dramatists. John
Fletcher, who succeeded Shakespeare as the Company's
dramatist, wrote or collaborated in 69; Thomas Dekker wrote
at least 64; Massinger wrote or largely wrote 55.

Shakespeare wrote 38, with a hand in one or two more. So
again we see that there is no problem.

As with all these points that occur to some people's minds,
they all have a simple answer, and there is no reason whatever
for any confusion about our greatest writer, or the nonsense
written about him by people who know nothing of the
circumstances of the age he lived in.

# Southampton's Quatercentenary: What Shakespeare Owed to Him

Four hundred years ago, on 6 October 1573, Shakespeare's
Southampton – his patron and friend to be – was born at
Cowdray House in Sussex, his mother's home. His own home
was Titchfield in Hampshire, where one can see him as a boy
on the splendid pile of the family tomb.

Why should we remember him today? We shall see that both
English and Americans have special reason to do so – or,
rather, people all over the world.

First, for what he did for Shakespeare.

He became the actor-dramatist's patron at the decisive

moment in his career — as it happened, during the most critical years of his life, 1592-3, the plague years which saw the disappearance of Marlowe and his friend Watson, Robert Greene and Thomas Kyd. Shakespeare might well have gone under, in those years when the theatres were mostly closed, with no visible means of support. As he himself says:

And life no longer than thy love will stay,
For it depends upon that love of thine.

Shakespeare owed everything, at this juncture, to this generous young peer with the golden nature. What he owed to his patron he expressed in the dedications of the two long poems he wrote at this same period, *Venus and Adonis* (1593) and *The Rape of Lucrece* (1594), the second of which is of exceptional warmth and affection — the poet had indeed reason to be grateful.

We need not argue the matter any more, for it is now perfectly clear that the obvious person, the young patron, was the inspiration of the Sonnets too in these same years. (All the fuss about Mr W. H. is beside the mark: he is merely the publisher's dedicatee years after, not Shakespeare's young Lord at all.) Shakespeare wrote for no other than his young patron, as he himself tells us:

Since all alike my songs and praises be
To one, of one, still such, and ever so.

What is more interesting, and more original a theme to pursue, is to estimate all that Shakespeare owed to the acquaintance, socially, personally, emotionally. I think it would be difficult to overestimate what Shakespeare owed to it.

In the first place, it opened cultural vistas hitherto closed to him; it gave him the entry to a cultivated circle, of greater refinement and sophistication than anything he had known. To this his whole nature ardently responded, for this was what his own nature truly was — aristocratic in its tastes and values (though never losing touch with the people he came

from). Everybody notices his instinctive courtesy and gentle-
manliness; Miss Spurgeon showed years ago the greater
refinement of the senses reflected at once in his imagery.

Emotionally, the experience deepened Shakespeare's conception of friendship, while the triangular relationship with
the dark Italianate mistress plumbed depths of emotion and
anguish, created the critical experience that great creative
writers often have to go through. Before it, works of talent
like *The Comedy of Errors*; after it, works of genius like *A
Midsummer Night's Dream* and *Romeo and Juliet*.

Southampton was as much involved in this dramatic side:
*A Midsummer Night's Dream* celebrated his mother's second
marriage in 1594, to the grave councillor Sir Thomas Heneage:
while *Love's Labour's Lost* was a skit on the Southampton
circle by its poet. That this play had a personal association
for Southampton may be gathered from his choosing it for
representation at Southampton House before James I years
afterwards, when he came to the English throne.

There is Southampton's last service in making it possible
for his poet to buy a share in the Lord Chamberlain's
Company on its foundation in 1594. (The Italianate Emilia
Lanier was the discarded mistress of the Lord Chamberlain.)
After that Shakespeare was on firm ground, achieved security
at last to go forward with his career independently in the
theatre.

It was the young Southampton who failed to achieve
security, who staggered forward on a most uncertain course.
Something of a delayed adolescent, with an over-loyal, too
confiding nature, he was mesmerised by Essex and followed
him on land and at sea, eventually into dangerous opposition
to and conspiracy againt the Queen.

When only seventeen Southampton had slipped across the
Channel, without permission, hoping to serve in Essex's
campaign of 1591 in Normandy. Physically brave, though
feminine in looks with his golden tresses and fair complexion — as in the Sonnets — he tried again and again to

serve at sea, but was frustrated by the Queen. In 1597, however, he commanded the *Garland* in Essex's expedition to the Azores. (Emilia Lanier's husband served in that too — and we learn later that he knew Southampton.)

In 1599 Southampton served in Ireland under Essex, though the Queen refused to allow him to be General of the Horse. Two years later Southampton joined Essex in his armed outbreak into the City, for which Essex was executed. Condemned to death, Southampton was reprieved and spent the next two years in the Tower of London, from which he was liberated on James I's accession, to become something of a favourite. He was always popular and well-loved.

While in the Tower, in 1602 he promoted Captain Gosnold's voyage to prospect the uncharted New England coast, which reached Maine, naming Martha's Vineyard on the way. But the effective colonisation of North America started with the formation of the Virginia Company, especially with the second Charter of 1609, in which Southampton eventually played a leading part. In that roll-call of Jacobean society which started Jamestown, Southampton's name came third on the list with a large venture in the Company.

We find him taking an interest in its affairs, recommending sea-captains, sending bucks for the Company's feast — as Sir Thomas Roe sends him also journals of his early embassy to India. In 1610 Southampton put down money for Hudson's voyage to Hudson's Bay, hoping to find the North-West Passage. Two years later Southampton became a member of the North-West Passage Company, and we find him subscribing to Harlow's voyage to the New England coast, not yet fully explored.

But Southampton's main work fell later as Treasurer, or official head, of the Virginia Company in its last four years, 1620—4. Those were the years that covered the crisis of Virginia's existence with the Indian Massacre of 1622. We cannot go in detail into all his work for Virginia here; suffice

it to say that it is his name that is commemorated there in
Hampton Roads and Hampton River, and that Chickahominy
Hundred was originally Southampton Hundred.

An elderly man he died in 1624, while on campaign for the
Dutch in the Netherlands; like Essex, he had always
supported popular causes and been beloved by the people:

Grant, if thou wilt, thou art beloved of many.

# Mr W. H. and Who He Was

I have sometimes been asked what the importance is of
knowing who Mr W. H. – of Thorp's dedication of
Shakespeare's Sonnets – was. Why does it matter? Why
should we bother?

Apart from the historian's interest in getting it right, and
apart from the unceasing public interest in the matter, if we
do not get it right we make utter confusion of the biography
of our greatest writer at its most revealing spot: his relations
with his young patron Southampton, to whom Shakespeare
dedicated his two long poems – his only dedications – and
to whom and for whom he wrote the Sonnets.

That has been the traditional view of Shakespeare scholars
from Malone downwards, and there is no doubt that it is
correct.

There has been a small minority who have thought,
without feeling certain, that the young lord of the Sonnets,
was Lord Herbert. They were completely wrong. But what
misled them?

They failed to notice the importance of the fact that it was
Thomas Thorp, the publisher, who dedicated the Sonnets to
Mr W. H., not Shakespeare. So Mr W. H. is Thorp's Mr

W. H., not Shakespeare's. And Mr W. H. is *not* the young man of the Sonnets, who is obviously Southampton, identifiable by all his known characteristics and circumstances.

Mr W. H. and the young man of the Sonnets are two totally distinct persons. Hence the indescribable confusion that has resulted, with whole libraries of superfluous nonsense written around and about it. I greatly blame the English Literature faculties and the Shakespeare 'experts' of the English-speaking world for leaving the gate wide open for all. the crackpots to canter through. It is nothing short of wicked that the biography of the greatest writer in our language should be made such nonsense of. This is the importance of getting it right. What I have to say is not at all radical or eccentric – there is nothing I hate more; it is completely conservative and traditional, but it is firm and certain, the historian's commonsense of the matter.

It is the dedication that is partly responsible for the confusion, and it does offer a problem. It has to be worked out in accordance with commonsense, a completely commonsense explanation, nothing fanciful or silly. Let us look at it freshly, as if we were looking at it for the first time. What most people will not know is that Thorp usually wrote in this flowery, slightly inflated fashion. A study of his dedications, such as few have made, reveals that this was characteristic of him: he just wrote like that – 'wisheth the well-wishing adventurer in setting forth'!

To the only begetter of these ensuing sonnets
Mr. W. H. all happiness, and that eternity
Promised by our ever-living poet
Wisheth the well-wishing adventurer in setting forth. T.T.
(i.e., Thomas Thorp).

Now note that the phrase 'the only begetter' which people have mulled over *in vacuo* and prostituted for every kind of silly purpose, does not, in this case, mean 'the only inspirer' of the Sonnets. There are two inspirers of the Sonnets; the

Dark Lady, Shakespeare's mistress, is almost as important an inspiration as the young lord.

Note also that no Elizabethan would ever refer to a Lord as Mr W. H. So it cannot be Herbert or Southampton who is being referred to.

We can dispose of Lord Herbert at once. There is nothing whatever to connect him with the Sonnets. At the time they were being written, between 1592 and 1594-5, he was a boy aged twelve to fourteen. One does not write sonnets to a boy of twelve urging him to get married right quick and do his duty by the family by having children – which is what Shakespeare was urging young Southampton to do, quite rightly, from nineteen to twenty-one. Secondly, when the boy Herbert grew up he was an unadulterated hetero-sexual – quite different from the ambivalent, rather feminine young lord of the Sonnets, who will not do his duty and get married: precisely Southampton's case.

So let us hear no more about Lord Herbert: it makes no more sense than William Hatcliffe, Prince of Purpoole, or Windsor Herald, or Oscar Wilde's invented Willie Hughes or, for that matter, the Mad Hatter. They are all equally nonsense, and in the realm of nonsense there are no comparatives.

The next point to observe is a little more special. Though you could not address a lord as Mr in the sixteenth century, you could so address a knight. Many will recall 'Master More' for Sir Thomas More, 'Master Bacon' for Sir Francis Bacon.

Who, then, was  Mr W. H.?

He is, naturally, to be found in close association with Southampton: he was, in fact, Southampton's stepfather.

Southampton's mother, the Countess, took for her third husband a much younger man, Sir William Hervey. She died in 1607, leaving him her household goods and chattels – it would be a mere conjecture to suppose that the Sonnets were among them, though there is nothing against it. Anyway, Thorp was very grateful to Sir William Hervey for getting him the manuscripts, the only person to have got them. In the very next year, 1608, Hervey married a young wife, Cordelia Annesley: this is why Thorp, in 1609, is wishing him 'all happiness and that eternity promised by our ever-living poet', i.e., the continuance that Shakespeare, still alive, had promised his young patron in the Sonnets years before if only he would marry and carry on the family to all posterity.

That is all; that is the answer to the puzzle that has bred such confusion for decades.

The 'well-wishing adventurer in setting forth' is just another of Thorp's flowery phrases, but it reflects the enthusiasm for becoming adventurers to Virginia, i.e. taking shares in the Virginia Company, that swept London in 1609.

When I wrote my biography of Shakespeare and did my edition of the Sonnets I did not know that Sir William Hervey was a scion of the Herveys of Ickworth in Suffolk, that family that was to become so celebrated in English history and literature. He was the younger son of Henry Hervey by a Welsh wife, Jane Thomas of Llanvihangel; his elder brother succeeded at Ickworth, so young William had to look out for himself – which he did very well by marrying Southampton's elderly mother, the Countess.

Southampton did not like the prospect of this marriage at all – after all Hervey was much his own age and it might well damage his inheritance. The Earl's protests held it up for a time, but Hervey was a gallant and spirited soldier, well able to speak up for himself, and some time before the end of January 1599 he married the old lady. (The Countess kept her second and third weddings private: we only know of her second marriage to Sir Thomas Heneage – she always referred to him as Master (Mr) Heneage – on 2 May 1954, that it was celebrated with *A Midsummer Night's Dream* for the occasion.)

Hervey served against the Spanish Armada when young, was knighted at Cadiz in 1596, served along with Southampton in the Azores in 1597, and again with him, and after him, in the Irish wars.

But it is in regard to his second marriage to Cordelia

Annesley that a curious story hangs. She was one of the three daughters of Brian Annesley who, as a gentleman-pensioner of the Queen, could well have been known to the dramatist in and out of the Court with performances of his plays. This old gentleman in the decline of his faculties was fought over by his three daughters. The second of them, married to Sir John Wildgoose, wanted to have him declared a lunatic so as to get hold of his inheritance.

Cordelia, the youngest daughter, would have none of this and wrote to Lord Cecil in October 1603 on behalf of her father 'whose many years service to her late majesty deserve a better agnomination'.

The interesting thing is that this was only a couple of years before *King Lear* was written.

What happened to the posterity Thorp promised Hervey — as Shakespeare had his young patron — upon his marriage at last to a young wife?

They had three sons and three daughters. Two daughters, Dorothy and Helen, died unmarried; the youngest son, Henry (named for Southampton?), died a child; the second son, John, died in Ireland. There remained the eldest son, William, and Elizabeth.

In 1620 Sir William was made Baron Hervey of Ross in Ireland for his services there, and in 1628 Baron Hervey of Kidbrooke in Kent. But in 1632 we hear sad news of the eldest son, upon whom rested the father's hopes of continuing his family in the peerage. 'My wandering son being returned from Asia into Italy, he gave me to understand from Zürich he would see the king of Sweden [the famous Gustavus Adolphus] and his army. Here is a report that he should be miscarried about Nuremberg. If it be true, as I fear it is, I may then swallow up my grief at once and live a comfortless man the small remainder of my life.' Thus ended Hervey's hopes of founding a family in the peerage. *The Complete Peerage* comments soberly: 'It has been supposed by some that he was the W. H. to whom Shakespeare's Sonnets were dedicated.' He was indeed!

There remained Elizabeth, who married her cousin, John Hervey of Ickworth, head of the family.

Four years later, Cordelia died and was buried with her daughter, Dorothy, in St Martin-in-the-Fields: 5 May 1636, *'Domina Cordelia Hervey, in cancella'*.

Lord Hervey lived on to a good old age, not dying until 8 July 1642, amid all the excitements of the Long Parliament and the approach of the Civil War. We know that he was buried in Westminster Abbey, but where? For, because of the Civil War, no monument was placed over him and even his will was not proved for six years.

But I have tracked him down to his last resting place in the chapel of St Edmund and St Thomas the Martyr. When his daughter, Helen, died, in 1648. the registers state that she too was buried there, no doubt in the same grave, 'between Lord Russell's monument and the step'.

It is not far from Poet's Corner. When you go from the South Transept to the second chapel in the south ambulatory, pause at the step as you look across to the Elizabethan Russell monument. Mr W. H. lies there in the space between. When you go into the abbey remember Mr W. H.: Thorp had reason to be profusely grateful to him for getting the Sonnets together for publication. Without that they might have been lost. He thus has a better claim to enduring fame than the peerage that did not continue.

# Shakespeare's Landlady in Silver Street

Any factual information that illuminates Shakespeare's background is of value, revealing him as an Elizabethan among other Elizabethans — as opposed to the useless conjectures about him in many volumes and many languages, which have created only confusion and can now go on the scrap-heap.

Actually it never occurred to me that I should make the discovery of who the Dark Lady was, bearing so directly upon him — Emilia Bassano, the musical, Italian girl who had been the mistress of the Queen's first cousin, Lord Chamberlain Hunsdon, the official head of Shakespeare's company of actors.

Another piece of direct information, discovered (by a Canadian scholar) only this century, illuminated for us the family and household in which Shakespeare was a lodger about 1602. The family was a French one of fashionable wig-makers — and the interesting thing is that not long before, while he may have been in residence there, he was writing the French scenes in *Henry V*.

The couple were Christophe and Marie Montjoie — we will call them Mr and Mrs Mountjoy. First, what is known about their relations with Shakespeare must be summarised, to put in perspective what I have to add about Shakespeare's landlady that is totally new — from the Forman manuscripts where the Dark Lady was lying in wait for me.

In 1612, four years before he died at Stratford, Shakespeare travelled from there to London to give evidence in a law-suit brought by the Mountjoys' son-in-law, Stephen Bellot, for the dowry promised when he married their daughter.

Shakespeare's evidence in the case was crucial, as he had taken a leading part in promoting the marriage on behalf of Mrs Mountjoy and had actually betrothed the young couple in the regular way by handfasting.

Shakespeare could not remember all the details of the affair after the lapse of ten years. We do not know whether his memory was beginning to fail — after 1612 he wrote no more plays, and he had had an exhausting life. He is described in the documents as 'gentleman', the status he had won the hard way, his age as forty-eight: correct, he was born in 1564.

Examined on oath he said that Mrs Mountjoy 'did solicit and entreat' (a favourite Shakespeare word) him 'to move and persuade the said complainant' — Bellot, formerly Mountjoy's apprentice — 'to effect the said marriage'. In accordance with her wish he had done so, and while he was dwelling in the house 'they had amongst themselves many conferences about their marriage'.

He said that he thought Bellot 'a very good and industrious servant', but he could not remember what the dowry was to be or whether a portion of household goods was to go with the daughter. Another witness recalled that Master Shakespeare — as he is respectfully referred to throughout — had told him a good deal more at the time.

So another set of interrogatories was designed to press Shakespeare's memory further on a second hearing, but the elusive dramatist never turned up to answer them.

Evidently he had been on a rather intimate footing in the Mountjoy household at the time. We learn that, in the eyes of the authorities of the French Huguenot church in London, Mountjoy was of licentious life and both father and son-in-law 'debauched'.

This may be a rather harsh judgement, coming from Calvinists; for Forman's case-books show us that Elizabethans were very free and easy, and not all that respectable. It is from Forman that we derive our new information about that household a few years before, particularly about Mrs Mountjoy.

We are fortunate to have a depiction of the site of these happenings, the surroundings of Shakespeare's daily life, and even, as so rarely, of the house.

It is in Agas' map of the city, the house with the twin gables — perhaps one of them housed the dramatist — and the pentice of the Mountjoys' shop-front, at the corner of Silver Street with Mugle Street. Silver Street, with its little parish church of St Olave, was obliterated by the barbarian blitzes of the last war.

In Shakespeare's time it was a quiet enclave within the north-west angle of the City wall. Near by were Haberdashers' and Surgeons' Halls, and the celebrated surgeon, John Banister, was a neighbour in Silver Street. Business would take Shakespeare down Wood Street to Cheapside or St Paul's Churchyard, where the publishers had their bookstalls with frequent quartos of his plays on sale for sixpence.

Through Mrs Mountjoy coming to consult the astrologer and medical practitioner, Forman — the two subjects were closely allied then — a shaft of light penetrates beyond the shopfront. As Mrs Mountjoy went along Silver Street on 16 September 1597 she lost out of her purse a gold ring, a hoop ring, and a French crown. (We recall Shakespeare's bawdy jokes about French crowns.) Mary Mountjoy was then thirty; so she was three years and a half younger than her later lodger.

Next time she comes to consult Forman medically. She is suffering from pains in head, side and stomach. Forman diagnosed that 'she seems to be pregnant for 11 weeks — seven weeks more and then it will come from her, or stay hardly', that is with difficulty. This is an astrological forecast.

Early the next year, in March 1598, she comes to know whether her husband will be sick or no. She evidently had someone else in view; for the next we learn is that a certain Mr Wood put the question, on her behalf, 'whether the love she bears will be altered or not'.

Then Mrs Wood went to Forman for advice whether to keep shop with Mrs Mountjoy. The sage astrologer's reply came: 'they may join, but take heed they trust not out their wares much, or they shall have loss.'

A tantalising note reads: 'Mary Mountjoy alained' – which means concealed. What was going on in the house in which Master Shakespeare was to lodge but a year or two later? Evidently the lady's affections were straying from her husband.

In the same month he went to put questions concerning his apprentices. Forman did not know French – though he did Latin – so that his rendering of their names looks odd: Gui Asture and Ufranke de la Coles. Evidently French apprentices to the fashionable art of wig-making, like Stephen Bellot whom Shakespeare knew and approved of as a fit husband for the Mountjoys' daughter.

And who was Mr Wood, Mary Mountjoy's lover at this time? Fortunately he, too, was a client of Forman – it is astonishing, and very revealing, how many denizens of Shakespeare's London turn up in Forman's books.

Henry Wood was a mercer and cloth-trader, who lived in Swan Alley off Coleman Street, and was engaged in cross-Channel trading. So he was anxious about his cargoes and ships carrying his goods – like Antonio in *The Merchant of Venice*.

Actually Mr Wood was a client of Forman before Mary Mountjoy was – so he may have suggested to his lady-friend to consult the astrologer when she lost rings and money out of her open purse. In December 1596 Wood went for the horoscope to be cast concerning two overdue Dutch hoys carrying his goods. In January 1598 he put the question whether it was 'best to buy bay-salt now', that is salt from the Bay of Biscay. Mr Wood consulted Forman several times that year, for he was worried, not only about business: Mrs Mountjoy was on his mind.

In April, he was there to question the planets – was there ill coming to him? In May – in Latin, for security sake – was there trouble threatened against him? In August – again in Latin – what would happen to him after this? The answer revealed that the worry was about business. 'It seemeth that his goods shall be attached [i.e., detained], some great enemy shall proffer him fair friendship, but treachery will follow.'

Living in Swan Alley, Mr Wood was conveniently placed for paying Mrs Mountjoy a visit: all he had to do was walk up Coleman Street, along the City Wall and down to little Silver Street. Mrs Wood does not appear to have joined forces with Mrs Mountjoy to set up shop. But it seems that she kept her husband, for it was she who went to Forman, when Mr Wood went over with his goods to Flanders, to put the question whether he had been captured by the Dunkirkers – for the Channel was alive with privateers at the end of the Elizabethan war. Forman was able to assure her that 'he was passed over and not taken, but well'.

Meanwhile we have seen that the household in Silver Street held together, to receive its lodger a year or two later.

# Shakespeare, Bacon, Marlowe, Oxford - and Sex

### 1

Shakespeare is the sexiest great writer in the language – quite as much as, if not more than, the reprobate Restoration dramatists. His mind, quite naturally and effortlessly, dripped sex at every pore. Of course, Elizabethan England was far freer in matters of sex and accepted all the physical facts and functions of the body more easily than at any time since. In between came two victories of the Puritans – when they won in the Civil War and again in the Victorian Age.

In spite of the reaction from the Rule of the Saints with

the Restoration of naughty Charles II, the middle classes always remained a more Puritan element in society than either the upper or lower classes. (There *is* something ineffably middle-class about Puritanism.)

When I wrote my biography of Shakespeare, at the time of the Quatercentenary, I rather overlooked this characteristic and constant side to him: it is my own chief criticism of the book today.

At that time I had not read, or properly taken in, Eric Partridge's *Shakespeare's Bawdy: A Literary and Psychological Essay and a Comprehensive Glossary.*[1] It appeared first in a limited edition and, an academic, I missed it. In fact it is a scholarly performance, though even so it is not quite complete — I could add, for example, the suggestive subsidiary meanings the Elizabethans gave to words like 'hell' (still in use in the sexual underworld today), 'will' and 'fire'.

Mr Partridge gets the full force of the phrase to 'flesh one's will', but he doesn't get the meaning of the reference in Sonnet 144 to Shakespeare's young friend and his mistress, the dark lady:

> But being both from me, both to each friend,
> I guess one angel in another's hell.
> Yet this shall I ne'er know, but live in doubt,
> Till my bad angel fire my good one out.

Or, in Sonnet 129:

> All this the world well knows, yet none knows well,
> To shun the heaven that leads men to this hell.

There are two notorious Sonnets, 134 and 135, entirely given up to naughty play on the word 'will', (it meant in Elizabethan English, in addition to passion, desire, specifically the sexual organs). The heavy weather Victorian editors made of these sonnets has to be seen to be believed! — confused, in both senses of the word, they are really quite comic. My edition of the Sonnets is the only one to make

---

[1] (Routledge and Kegan Paul, 1968.)

sense of these, and other, reprehensible sonnets – a good reason for the Eng. Lit. people to discourage the use of it among students!

Actually in these permissive days it is possible to come clean about the whole subject, without Victorian embarrassment. It is a most important element in Shakespeare's mind and make-up, the salty element that acts along with the rest as a preservative of his work (as also with Chaucer). As Partridge says, Shakespeare not only very much enjoyed sex but took a lively, curious interest in it. 'He was no mere instinctive sensualist, but an intellectual voluptuary and a thinker keenly, shrewdly, penetratingly probing into sex, its mysteries, its mechanism, its exercise and expertise, and its influence on life and character.' We know that Ovid was Shakespeare's favourite (with Chaucer) among poets, and Mr Partridge is quite right when he says, with some enthusiasm, that 'Shakespeare was an exceedingly knowledgeable amorist, a versatile connoisseur, and a highly artistic, an ingeniously skilful, practitioner of love-making, who could have taught Ovid' a thing or two.

All this is obvious enough in the sonnets about (not written to) his mistress. But all through the Plays there is the constant refrain of sexual reference – such as comes readiest to mind in and around Falstaff, the brothel-scenes of *Pericles*, throughout *Troilus and Cressida*, or in the very essence of *Hamlet*. There is not only plain bawdy which we can all recognise, but there is the continual fountain-play of innuendo which not all nice minds can grasp at first sight. Over and beyond this, a knowledge of Elizabethan English opens up another whole realm of double-meanings, further suggestiveness: you need to be pretty familiar with the Elizabethans to catch it all. Another reason, no doubt, why he never ceased to be their favourite playwright: one can hear them roaring at it all, not missing much – as we have been apt to do.

There is, of course, complete consistency between what we know of Shakespeare's life and his work. He refers, once and again, to his own 'sportive disposition'; in the Sonnets he is utterly candid about his own highly-sexed nature, and his adulterous relation with his mistress; he offers no apology, he cannot help himself, he has an absolute fixation upon sex with her — in contrast to the sonnets to the young man, in whom he has no sexual interest whatever: an ideal, a platonic friendship. We know that at the age of eighteen or so young Shakespeare got the much older Ann Hathaway with child, and twenty months later gave her twins. Moving to London and the theatre, touring the country, it is obvious that he lived a double life.

His fixation on women, his fascinated adoration of them, his sympathetic understanding of all varieties of feminine nature, his unquenched ardour, his undying love of women — all this is utterly obvious from beginning to end of his work. Hence the most marvellous gallery of female characters in literature. Shakespeare had an infatuation, rather endearing in its way — though his persistence evidently was often a bit of a nuisance to the Dark Lady.

Mr Partridge pinpoints the area of Shakespeare's fixation: this 'was, to Shakespeare, of considerably greater importance and significance singly than all the rest of woman's sexual features collectively: it would appear to have been the one unfailing lodestar, the one sexual objective.' This is correct and undeniable — obvious throughout his work, the Plays and the more personal poems, and — most personal of all — the Sonnets.

There is no homosexuality in Shakespeare whatever. There is, indeed, only one reference to the subject throughout the whole of his work: the relationship between Achilles and Patroclus in *Troilus and Cressida*, which could hardly be avoided since antiquity recognised the fact. And Shakespeare treats it with disapprobation. There is plenty about men's friendship in the earlier plays, particularly in those associated with the Southampton circle at the time of Shakespeare's dependence upon and grateful friendship with his young patron. But it is visibly not sexual. Shakespeare, with his fixation on woman, was not interested in his own sex that way.

This is the point that is crucial for Shakespeare scholarship and for understanding the man: he was highly, passionately heterosexual — perhaps more than normally, for an Englishman.

Now let us see in what a marked contrast he stands with those contemporaries of his, Francis Bacon, Christopher Marlowe, Edward de Vere, Earl of Oxford.

<h2 style="text-align:center">2</h2>

It was quite well known in his own day that Francis Bacon was a homosexual, in fact a paederast. Today we can speak quite openly about the little foibles of the great and, with the advantage of being post-Freud, can understand how these illuminate their work. It is all too obvious that Victorian Baconians (New England Delia Bacon, who invented it all, ended in a lunatic asylum) had no such understanding.

John Aubrey was in a good position to know about Bacon, for he was a friend of Thomas Hobbes, the great man's amanuensis. Aubrey writes of Bacon in his *Brief Lives*, that he was, in Greek characters, 'a *paiderastes*. His Ganymedes and favourites took bribes'. When Philip II's brilliant Secretary of State, Antonio Perez — he was a well-known homosexual — took refuge in England, young Francis Bacon had him to stay with him in his chambers at Gray's Inn. This much worried his mother, Lady Bacon, who wrote to her elder son: 'though I pity your brother, yet so long as he pities not himself but keepeth that bloody Perez, yea as a coach-companion and bed-companion . . . whose being about him I verily fear the Lord God doth mislike and doth less bless your brother in credit, and otherwise in his health.'

This may have been a factor in Queen Elizabeth's reluctance to give Bacon office or preferment, but it was no impediment to his rise under the homosexual Stuart, James I, who was surrounded by such and with whom it would have been a further recommendation to favour. But at the time of the Lord Chancellor's fall from power, got down at last by his enemies, it added to his danger – I have always thought it may have been a powerful factor in his sudden (and otherwise, rather craven) submission. Sir Simonds D'Ewes tells us, contemporaneously:

> Upon his censure at this time his ambition was moderated, his pride humbled ... yet would he not relinquish the practice of his most horrible sin of sodomy; keeping still one Goderich, a very effeminated youth, to be his catamite and bedfellow ... Men generally after his fall began to discourse of that his unnatural crime, which he had practised many years, deserting the bed of his lady – which he accounted, as the Italians and Turks do, a poor and mean pleasure in respect of the other.

D'Ewes tells us that rhymes were fixed up on York House in the Strand, Bacon's residence, attacking his tastes and that it was thought that he would be brought to book for them. But James I would not have allowed that, and Bacon continued in his old ways: 'nor did he ever, that I could hear, forbear his old custom of making his servants his bedfellows so to avoid the scandal that was raised of him.'

Bacon's works are consistent with this. There is no amorousness, nothing erotic in them, no favour to women, hardly any mention of them: he was just not interested in the subject. He does, however, write warmly – so far as such a cold nature could – of male friendship, and commends the works of the celibate state.

So much for the lunacy of supposing Bacon as the author of Shakespeare's Plays.

### 3

Shakespeare exemplified that constant bubbling up of bawdiness which is often characteristic of the normal, highly-sexed heterosexual. Psychologists know that this is not characteristic of homosexuals: with them there is noticeable a certain chasteness of expression, if only because they are

not amused by the subject. We could go further into the
subject psychologically: it is more than likely that heterosexual 'fun' is distasteful to them.

I am not the first person to notice that this is characteristic
of Marlowe's work — one other person got that point before
me. It is true, and rather striking for an Elizabethan
dramatist, how little bawdy there is in his plays, in marked
contrast to Shakespeare's.

In his own day people knew quite well that Marlowe was a
homosexual, indeed a rather aggressive propagandist for the
art. A saying of his was brought up against him, that 'all they
that love not tobacco and boys were fools' — one hardly
knows which was held more reprehensible in the Elizabethan
Age. (Marlowe's atheism was actually more dangerous.) His
fellow-dramatist, Thomas Kyd, gave evidence that 'he would
report St. John to be our Saviour Christ's Alexis', and more
to the same effect. (Quite recently an English divine has been
developing this line of thought.) Kyd further witnessed that
the unknown Lord for whom they were both writing plays
could 'never endure his [Marlowe's] name or sight, when he
had heard of his conditions', nor did Kyd consider that the
'divine prayers used daily in his lordship's house' square with
such thoughts.

Marlowe's work is completely consistent with all this: the
homosexual strain runs throughout it from beginning to end,
there are references to it again and again, always with
sympathy. His last and most mature play, *Edward II*, takes
the theme for its main subject, the relations between the king
and his favourite, Gaveston.

We do not need to traverse the whole material here, indeed
it is too obvious. Marlowe's early play, *The Tragedy of Dido*,
begins with the well-known theme of Jupiter's relations with
Ganymede and Juno's understandable jealousy: when the
curtains are drawn, 'there is discovered Jupiter dandling
Ganymede upon his knee', and so the play proceeds.
Marlowe's last poem, 'Hero and Leander', has delighted
descriptions of Leander's young body, with Neptune fondling

it beneath the water. It has been observed that, when
Marlowe describes the attractions of male beauty, it is all
about arms and chests, thighs and buttocks, and the rest;
with Shakespeare, it is eyes and hair, colouring and complexion: he is no further interested.

There is no doubt whatever that Marlowe was the Rival
Poet of the Sonnets, rivalling Shakespeare for the patronage
of his patron, Southampton. That this was Marlowe's
'condition' must have added to Shakespeare's anxiety over
the growing relationship, for young Southampton, as we
know, was ambivalent — Shakespeare not.

We need go no further into the matter, except to say that
women play a noticeably small part in Marlowe's plays, in
contrast to Shakespeare's. There is a lyrical apostrophe to
Zenocrate in *Tamburlane*; not much of a part, when all is
said, for the Jew's daughter, Abigail, in *The Jew of Malta*. In
*Edward II*, where Queen Isabella inevitably has more of a
part — for she is party to the murder of her husband — the
wife takes second place to Edward and his lover, Gaveston,
and also to her paramour, Mortimer. In *Dr. Faustus* Helen of
Troy hasn't even a speaking part: she merely walks across the
stage.

I think we may fairly conclude that Marlowe, in utter
contrast to Shakespeare, was not much interested in women.
And yet an Eng. Lit. professor who is a friend of mine simply
wouldn't admit that Marlowe was a homosexual. It is
impossible, and fortunately unnecessary, to respect most
people's thinking: they don't know how to think. The joke is
that they don't know it.

So much for the lunacy of supposing Marlowe to be the
author of Shakespeare's Plays.

### 4

And what of the Earl of Oxford?

A great deal is known about this gifted, but deplorable,
creature. Here we need only confine ourselves to the subject
in hand. This young scapegrace was married by his guardian,

Lord Burghley, to his unfortunate daughter Anne, and a
miserable life of it the young Earl proceeded to give her. At
length he went to Italy, and returned with what old-
fashioned Protestants, like Roger Ascham, regarded as
Italianate tastes. The young Earl refused to cohabit with his
wife, and publicly asserted that, if she had a child, it would
be none of his.

Oxford then quarrelled with his former friends, Lord
Henry Howard and Charles Arundel, who proceeded to delate
him to the government for his addiction (though they were
no better themselves). The evidence is in the State Papers, in
the Public Record Office. When Miss B. M. Ward wrote her
biography of Edward de Vere, *The Seventeenth Earl of
Oxford*, in 1938 she omitted it, though she knew of it;
perhaps it was hardly possible to publish it then. Here I give
extracts for the first time in print.

Furious with his former friend for betraying their conversion to Catholicism, Charles Arundel deposed: 'I will
prove him a buggerer, of a boy that is his cook', by Oxford's
own confession as well as by witnesses. 'I have seen this boy
many a time in his chamber, doors close-locked, together
with him, maybe at Whitehall [i.e. at Court] and at his house
in Broad Street. Finding it so, I have gone to the backdoor to
satisfy myself, at the which the boy hath come out all in a
sweat, and I have gone in and found the beast in the same
plight. But to make it more apparent, my Lord Harry
[Howard] saw more, and the boy confessed it unto
Southwell and himself confirmed it under Mr William
Cornwallis.'

We need not go into disagreeable detail with Lord Henry's
corroborative evidence, but in addition to the cook's boy
there was 'Orache', an Italian boy, and others of Oxford's
pages. The Earl of Oxford had often expressed the kind of
view that Marlowe was known to hold, that 'Englishmen were
dolts and nidwits' not to realize that there was better sport
than with women.

It is all exceedingly unlike the views and life of William

Shakespeare: so much for the lunacy – in this case appropriately invented by a Dr Looney – of supposing Oxford to have written Shakespeare's Plays.

5

And yet, a few years ago the American Bar Association published a book endorsing this rubbish!

It is as the historian Lecky said: people (including lawyers) will believe anything without evidence, will believe things against the evidence, but will hardly ever believe because of the evidence.

The explanation is quite simple: the bulk of human beings simply don't know how to think. If they were rational, there would be an end of this nonsense; but, of course, few are.

# The True Story of Mary Fitton

We can now be certain who the Dark Lady, Shakespeare's mistress, was – Emilia Bassano, the musical and proud Italian girl, the discarded mistress of Lord Chamberlain Hunsdon, first cousin of Queen Elizabeth I and head of Shakespeare's famous Company of players.

It always was nonsense to think of Mary Fitton in the role; she wasn't dark at all, nor do dates or circumstances correspond.

But Mary Fitton's true story is quite fascinating – we know a great deal more of her than we do of most of Queen Elizabeth's maids of honour, if that is the word for it – they were apt to be frail creatures.

There is no mystery about Mary; she was not a frail creature, but a decidedly tough one; she survived a lifetime of scandal and trouble to be an old lady, who outlived family, husbands and her various lovers. She was a brazen hussy (as some thought) – or a woman made for love, more than usually capable of giving and receiving it – according to taste.

She was the daughter of a Cheshire knight of old family, Sir Edward Fitton, and his wife who was a bit of a Lancashire heiress. At Gawsworth – that attractive village with several ancient houses grouped around the mere – their old half-timbered Hall still stands. So does the monument to Sir Edward and his wife in the church, with the two little girls, Anne and Mary, kneeling piously at the foot.

Sir Edward used his friendship with Sir William Knollys, who was Comptroller of the Household to Queen Elizabeth, to secure for his younger daughter a much-coveted post as maid of honour. There was tremendous competition for this opening, for it could lead to a grand marriage, or at least a good catch. For Mary it led to a gamble – and social disaster.

Anne had been safely married at twelve to a boy of sixteen, John Newdigate, in whose family the letters have come down from which we can reconstruct the story. At Arbury in Warwickshire, their family house, is a charming double portrait of the two girls, Anne plumper, Mary slim, both with nut-brown hair.

Mary was seventeen when she got her chance at Court in 1595, and at first all went well. But there was an element of danger, with so vivacious and attractive, so temperamental, a girl. She was not dark but fair, fair complexion, brown hair, grey eyes, narrow pointed face, long, sexy nose. She had one of the Queen's horses to ride: a fine big bay, known as Bay Fitton. Her father's old friend, Sir William, promised to look after the girl. His father was a cousin of the Queen, and the Knollyses were tinged with Puritan ideas. Listen to Sir William's self-righteous language:

> I will not fail to fulfil your desire in playing the Good Shepherd, and will to my power defend the innocent lamb from the wolvish cruelty and foxlike subtlety of the tame

beasts of his place. . . . I will with my counsel advise your fair daughter, with my true affection love her, and with my sword defend her if need be. Her innocency will deserve it and her virtue will challenge it at my hands. And I will be as careful of her welldoing as if I were her true father.

Alas, things did not fall out like that. The elderly gentleman fell in love with the girl in his charge. It was not the part of the Good Shepherd that he wished to play, nor the sword that he wished to take out of its scabbard. Though he spoke in parables, his intentions were plain: he wanted the girl, and to marry her. Unfortunately, he was himself married to a rich old dowager who obstinately remained above ground. He wished her under it, and said so in no very polite language:

The fairest flowers of our gardens be blasted . . . mine in the leaf by the hoar frost. By reason of the continued frosts, my looking for any fruit of my garden is in vain — unless the old tree be cut down and a new graft of a good kind planted.

What a way to write of his wife! Thus he confided his hopes of Mary to her sister. Constantly in her company, in charge of these frisky young ladies in waiting, he felt himself

cloyed with too much and yet ready to starve for hunger. My eyes see what I cannot attain to, my ears hear what I do scant believe, and my thoughts are carried with contrary conceits. My hopes are mixed with despair and my desire starved with expectation.

The hoity-toity young lady had gone off to bed without bidding him good night, he wrote querulously to her sister, and this had given him toothache, at least some kind of ache. But he would endure purgatory, if only he could reach his desired heaven at last. The obstacle of his old dowager had, however, no intention of removing herself.

My constant desires no sooner bud by the heat of the
morning sun but they are blasted by an untimely frost, so
as in the midst of my best comforts I see nothing but dark
despair. Continue, I earnestly entreat you, your prayer for
my delivery.

It sounds a rather odd request from an upright Puritan, to
write to his mistress's sister to pray for his delivery from the
burden of his wife! However, we may be sure that Mary was
only the mistress of his affections, and that she was playing
him up, blowing now hot, now cold. 'Arrant coquette', the
Victorian Lady Newdigate-Newdegate, of sister Anne's
family, calls her.

Anne called on Sir William to be godfather to her baby,
and to name the girl. He returned:

Imagine what name I love best, and that do I nominate.
And if I might be as happy as to be a father as a
godfather. . . .!

But that would never be until he was free and Mary was
willing. . . . The child was, of course, called after her. Now
Mary was blaming him for the melancholy into which his
predicament was plunging him, and teasing him with having
small regard for her. So far from that being true, she is 'the
only comfort of my heart.'

Sir William wrote, in the midst of Essex's final troubles
with the Queen, that Mary

is now well and hath not been troubled with the mother
(i.e. nerves) of a long time. I would God I might as
lawfully make her a mother as you are . . .

Meanwhile, Mary was having a gay time at Court, in favour
with the Queen, and much noticed among her young ladies as
the most spirited, taking the lead in the masks and dances the
ageing Elizabeth delighted in. In June 1600 there was a
strange new mask, danced by eight of them, each in cloth of
silver, 'a mantle of carnation taffeta cast under the arm, and

their hair about their shoulders curiously knotted and interlaced.'

On 16 June 1600, there was a grand entertainment in Blackfriars for the marriage of Anne Russell, one of Mary's companions as maid of honour. The Queen graced it with her presence: this is the occasion portrayed in the famous picture of her dressed all in white as the Virgin she was, borne high in her litter like a painted idol by the nobles and gentlemen of the Court — Sir William would have been one. After supper there was a mask, danced by the Queen's ladies.

> Mistress Fitton led. After they had done all their own ceremonies, these eight lady maskers chose eight ladies more to dance the measures. Mistress Fitton went to the Queen, and wooed her to dance. Her Majesty asked her what she was.
> 'Affection,' she said.
> 'Affection,' said the Queen, 'Affection is false.'

This is a reference to the heartache the Queen was suffering from her sense of betrayal by Essex. Yet the gallant old girl rose and danced with Mary.

June 1600. Mary had been at Court five years — and there was no marriage yet on the horizon for her. That month she would be twenty-two — more than high time for an Elizabethan lady to have got a husband. At Arbury there is a portrait of her from this time in all her Court finery: immense lace ruff and puffed sleeves, hooped farthingale and jewelled head-tire, very low neck-line as was usual to display her virgin-condition (as with the Queen herself), a cameo placed over her heart. I descry no demure look upon her features, but one of sulky discontent, a sultry look in the eyes. What was she to do? Sir William was not even yet free of his encumbrance:

> I live in doubt ever to enjoy the sweet fruit of my summer's harvest. My ground is covered with the bramble and the briar, which, until it be grubbed and cut up, there is no hope of good.

And yet again:

> I must live in frost and snow, subject to blasts and all ill winds, and shall, I fear, never be so happy as to possess the fair flower of the summer's garden.

What a bore he was! And even worse that he could not offer her marriage, and to make her a mother lawfully — for he was a Puritan. Mary was clearly beginning to worry.

> Her greatest fear is that, while the grass groweth, the horse may starve. And she thinketh a bird in the bush is worth two in the hand —

— Sir William was so upset that he seems to have got the old proverb the wrong way round. He kept preaching patience — 'that will bring peace at the last.' But the time was passing for that.

In this dilemma there were dazzling examples of how maids of honour had resolved it, taking the bull by the horns. By risking everything, putting her 'honour' on the throw, only a couple of years before, Elizabeth Vernon had captured her man, the handsome but ambivalent Earl of Southampton — the effeminate young Lord of Shakespeare's Sonnets. A few years before, another maid of honour, Elizabeth Throckmorton, had wrested the Queen's favourite, Sir Walter Ralegh, away to herself. What a catch, for a dowerless girl! — Ralegh paid the penalty in his frustrated career.

The young man whom Mary fancied for herself was the Earl of Pembroke's heir, Lord Herbert, who would have been a great catch indeed — and Mary risked everything to catch him. In this year 1600 when they became very intimate together (years after Shakespeare's Sonnets, which have nothing to do with them), Lord Herbert was twenty, Mary twenty-two.

Young Herbert — totally unlike Shakespeare's Southampton — was, as Clarendon describes him, 'all his life immoderately given up to women.' He was, by the way, present that night in Blackfriars, when Mary led the dance with the Queen. We learn later that

> during the time that the Earl of Pembroke favoured her she would put off her head-tire, tuck up her clothes, take a large white cloak and march as though she had been a man, to meet the said Earl out of the Court.

That high summer, it would seem in July, she became pregnant.

The whole question now was whether Herbert would make an honest woman of her — as Southampton and Ralegh had done with their maids of honour, if each with understandable reluctance. In January 1601 young Herbert succeeded as Earl of Pembroke. In February, the great little Secretary of State, Sir Robert Cecil, wrote to a crony from Court that

> there is a misfortune befallen Mistress Fitton, for she is proved with child. The Earl of Pembroke, being examined, confesseth a fact but utterly renounceth all marriage.

The Queen was furious, as usual, at such happenings, and threatened to send the offenders to the Tower. Actually she sent Pembroke to the Fleet prison, and committed Mary to the care of Lady Hawkins — widow of the great seaman — for her confinement. In March, Mary was delivered of a boy, who died.

But the Earl was not going to marry her, for all the pressure put upon him. He was banished from Court into the country, whence he wrote unrepentantly to Cecil that rural life would turn him into a clown, and that he could not frame himself to turn JP. We have a pathetic letter from Mary's father:

> I can say nothing of the Earl, but my daughter is confident in her chance before God, and wisheth my Lord and she might but meet before indifferent [impartial] ones.

But poor Sir Edward expected no good from the young man, who 'in all this time hath not showed any kindness.' Then

I count my daughter as good a gentlewoman as my Lord is, though the dignity of honour be greater only in him which hath beguiled her, I fear – except my Lord's honesty be the greater virtue.

It did not prove to be so, and Sir Edward had to take his daughter back home to Cheshire in some secrecy, and public disgrace. Evidently the Earl did not think her a good enough match. Three years later he made a great marriage to Lady Mary Talbot, daughter of the Earl of Shrewsbury and a co-heiress to his vast estates. The lady was stunted and deformed, and gave him no children: Clarendon wrote unkindly, 'he paid much too dear for his wife's fortune by taking her person into the bargain.'

Mary Fitton had played for the highest stake, and lost. No more Court grandeur for her, henceforth she was rusticated, to make a life as best she could in the country. The irrepressible Sir William pipes up once more, still not free to offer her marriage.

I must confess the harvest was overlong expected . . . But the man of sin [Pembroke] having in the night sowed tares amongst the good corn, both the true husbandman was beguiled and the good ground was abused . . . God knows I would refuse no penance to redeem what is lost.

It seems that Mary rejected his handicapped suit – 'I may boldly say that Mary did not choose the better part.' When at length free of his encumbrance he rushed straight into matrimony with a girl of nineteen, himself then being sixty-one. Mary made a mistake, for Sir William lived on to become an Earl himself – one sees him on the very grand monument that fills the Knollys chapel at Rotherfield, near Henley. She would have been a countess – of Banbury – if not of Pembroke.

What fortune was there now for Mary Fitton? A very rum one, we shall see. At a loose end, unprovided for, still young, she came under the protection of a well-known commander,

Vice-Admiral Sir Richard Leveson, whose bronze figure we
see in the church of Wolverhampton, celebrating his part in
the sea-actions of the time. His marriage to the daughter of
Lord Admiral Howard of Effingham had turned out unfortunately; she became insane, so unable to remarry, he had
need of a woman to take her place. A fine portrait at Arbury
shows him an upstanding fellow in black silk doublet and
wide pantaloons, a bushy beard and a battered look about
the eyes. He was only thirty-five when he died in 1605,
leaving provision of £100 a year under private instructions
from himself – for whom?

He had a close friend in the Cornish sea-captain, William
Polwhele, who had served under Leveson abroad as captain of
the *Lion's Whelp*. These gallant fellows seem to have shared
an interest in Mary. The next we hear of her is that she is in
disgrace again over the birth of a boy. In the winter of
1606–7, her mother, now widowed, is writing:

> I take no joy to hear of your sister, nor of that boy. If it
> had pleased God, when I did bear her, that she and I had
> been buried, it had saved me from a great deal of sorrow
> and grief and her from shame – and such shame as never
> had Cheshire woman, worse now than ever. Write no more
> to me of her.

The women of the family were characteristically more
censorious than the men, and seem to have taken against
Captain Polwhele for making Mary at least a married woman.
Lady Fitton wrote:

> Polwhele is a very knave, and taketh the disgrace of his
> wife and all her friends to make the world think him
> worthy of her, and that she deserved no better.

Very grand Lady Frances Stanley, who as Countess of
Bridgewater became the patroness of Milton's *Comus*, said
that Mary was 'the vilest woman under the sun.'

They all thought that Polwhele was not a fit marriage for a
Fitton; but in fact the Polwheles were as old a family as the

Fittons, going back to the fourteenth century in Cornwall. The menfolk were kinder and recognised his friendliness. Old Francis Fitton, Mary's great-uncle, left him his best horse and equipment, 'as a remembrance and token of my love for him.' Mary's marriage lasted only three years, for Polwhele died in 1610; leaving her with a son and a daughter. The property upon which they lived, Perton in Staffordshire, had come from Sir Richard Leveson.

Through all these troubles Mary's sister remained faithful to her, and she seems always to have had a refuge open to her in beautiful Arbury of the Newdigates in Warwickshire. Anne, now herself a widow, had an elderly admirer in Francis Beaumont, who found an ally in Mary in pressing his suit. Francis was fond of Mary, too, who was evidently all for love — and the menfolk reciprocated:

> I must entreat you when you see my counsellor to command my heartiest love unto her, and to tell her that, though she be a married wife, yet I will take leave to love her for ever, while I carry within me a heart that can love.

From this we learn that Mary had found someone else to marry her, a Captain Lougher, of a Pembrokeshire family. For when she died in 1647 — her second husband having died in 1636 — she had a little property there which she bequeathed to their daughter. I do not know if her son by Polwhele had children, but their daughter had. So that Mary Fitton left descendants, through the Gattacres and the Chernocks, when, an old lady in her seventieth year (like the great Queen she had served all those years ago), she was buried in the church at Gawsworth, where she had been baptised and where one sees her still as a girl upon her parents' tomb.

# Shakespeare at Work

Gerald E. Bentley is our leading authority on the Elizabethan
and Jacobean drama, and he has written a valuable book on
the professional dramatist which throws new light on these
writers, Shakespeare included.[1] This is rare; however, he is
not only the foremost scholar in the field, but has the
perception and the commonsense to see what is significant,
and what is not. On Shakespeare he says, in forthright
fashion:

> Most studies tend to take Shakespeare's plays out of the
> theatres for which they were created and to analyse them
> in the milieu of the lyric and philosophical poet, and not
> in the milieu of the hard-working professional playwright,
> devoted to the enterprise of the most successful and
> profitable London acting company of the time – or
> perhaps of any time.

This, of course, is the proper perspective in which to see
Shakespeare's work. No one was ever more completely a man
of the theatre – actor, playwright, producer, sharer in the
profits, eventually part theatre-owner. And the conditions of
the theatre defined the layout, and more, of the plays.

No art is more of a co-operative one than the theatrical.
The professional Elizabethan dramatist working for a reper-
tory Company – as all the real professionals did –

> knew that songs could be written into the parts of only
> those actors who sang well; he knew that the roles of
> women and children must be limited to the number

---

[1] G. E. Bentley, *The Profession of Dramatist in Shakespeare's Time* (Princeton
University Press; Oxford University Press, 1972).

which could be handled by the boys presently in his
company. He knew that if he wanted more adult male
characters than the number of sharers and hired men in his
troupe (as he generally did) he must plan the structure of
his play to allow for doubling. He knew he must take into
consideration the characters of the audience for which he
was writing: at the Red Bull it was notoriously vulgar, at
the Blackfriars it was notoriously sophisticated.

How many of the professors writing about Shakespeare take
these conditioning facts of the theatre into consideration?

The regular professional dramatist provided almost a half
of the known plays in the period 1590 to 1642. They were
less than a dozen in number, and they were very prolific.
Some of them wrote or collaborated in fifty or sixty
plays — John Fletcher in sixty-nine, nearly all of them for the
King's Company — as Shakespeare was the leading dramatist
of the Chamberlain's from its formation in 1594 to his
retirement about 1613. He was succeeded by Fletcher till his
death in 1625, Fletcher by Massinger, and he by Shirley,
when the theatres were closed down by Parliament.

Altogether there were some eight men who were the
complete and regular professionals — Heywood, Shakespeare,
Dekker, Fletcher, Rowley, Massinger, Shirley, Brome.
Beyond these was a margin of writers who sometimes wrote
for the Companies or were even attached to them regularly
for short periods — such men as Ben Jonson, Beaumont,
Ford, Webster, Chapman. But they regarded themselves as
essentially independent, and writing for the theatre as
beneath their literary work.

The regular professionals contracted to write about two
plays a year for their Company; the plays were read over for
approval, often at a tavern over some wine. These dramatists
were fairly well rewarded — better than the school-mastering
profession with which they had some connections. An
Elizabethan schoolmaster was often paid £10 p.a.; the Stratford grammar schoolmaster was exceptionally well-paid at
£20 p.a. The professional dramatist made over £30 p.a., and
there was usually a benefit performance for a new play.

Naturally the professional dramatists did not publish their plays: they were the property of the Company, which kept good hold of them for performance. It was Ben Jonson who was the exception by publishing his plays as his Works in 1616, one more evidence that he regarded himself primarily as an independent writer. There was nothing exceptional in Shakespeare not publishing — that was the normal rule, like his rate of production; nothing exceptional in his writing thirty-eight plays either, Dekker wrote sixty-four, Massinger wrote or collaborated in fifty-five. When Shakespeare's plays were published it was a tribute to him by his Fellows in the Company.

All this salutary sense and more we learn from this book by a master of the subject.

Professor Kenneth Muir's book is a collection of previously published articles.[2] As such there is a good deal of repetition. On p. 9 there is a remarkably fatuous passage:

> As Professor Bradbrook suggested long ago, the breast-feeding images in *Macbeth* may have been prompted by the account given in the *Chronicles* of the way in which Scottish women preferred to nurse their own babies. Or it may rather be prompted by the subject proposed for debate before James I, whether a man's character was influenced by his nurse's milk — or, indeed, by a combination of the two.

This is thought so original an observation that we get it again on p. 135:

> It has been suggested by Professor M. C. Bradbrook that Shakespeare may have noticed ... in Holinshed's *Chronicles* that every Scotswoman 'would take intolerable pains to bring up and nourish her own children ... Whatever the origin of the images in *Macbeth* relating to breast-feeding, Shakespeare uses them for a very dramatic purpose.

---

[2] K. Muir, *Shakespeare the Professional* (Heinemann, 1973).

Really! one would have supposed that Professor Muriel Bradbrook, though a lady-professor, would have known the function of a woman's breasts without having to look in Holinshed to find it.

The book is written in wearisome professional *clichés*. Professor Bradbrook, whatever else she may or may not know, has 'plucked out the heart of the mystery' for Professor Muir. The plays of Tennyson, Browning and Bridges were 'never clapper-clawed by the palms of the vulgar'; on the other hand the Professor is 'with it' with Pinter, whom he admires 'on this side idolatry as much as any'. One wonders whether the Professor is not going a little far with 'The painted cheek of the harlot is an image of hypocrisy'; it is very bold.

But the Professor is bold: he thinks that the poem printed as Shakespeare's along with the Sonnets, *A Lover's Complaint*, was really written by Shakespeare. Now Professor Mackail didn't think so: 'its preciosity, its strained rhetoric, its parade of learned words' would rather suit the Rival Poet. No idea on the part of the obtuse Victorian Mackail that, of course, *A Lover's Complaint* was early prentice-work, its defects just what you expect.

These people have no idea how real writers write. What are they professors of literature for? They should learn.

Professor Muir, having accomplished the feat of recognising that Shakespeare's *A Lover's Complaint* was written by Shakespeare, proceeds to get the dating all wrong, suggesting that it was years later than his poetic apprenticeship. Completely contrary to commonsense and all the indications that the poet's young patron, Southampton, sat for the portrait of the naughty young man in the poem. Moreover, when the poem was published, it was published along with the Sonnets, obviously out of the same Southampton *cache*.

No idea of dating, no idea of writing (this Professor boasts of having written thirty books), little sense of literature — what is one to think?

I am being forced to agree with Mr Auberon Waugh that

these Eng. Lit. professors inhabit a crustacean world of their own: their books written by professors for professors largely about other professors. I suppose they have to lecture, but why write?

# The Shakespeare Industry

It is a solemn thought that there is a Shakespeare Industry — as there is a Milton Industry, a Spenser Industry, etc. — supporting hundreds of academics, if not thousands, churning out their contributions to justify their existence. What would Shakespeare, or Milton, or Spenser have thought of it? The imagination boggles at it all; the only way to hold on to sanity on the subject is to reflect that most of the people engaged in the industry have nothing of any value to say, and that ninety-nine per cent of what they say is not worth reading.

Of course there are age-old ways of keeping the treadle going: Professor X will put forward some perverse nonsense by way of 'criticism' or 'interpretation', which will then give Professors Y and Z something to chumble over or tangle with each other about. Or some lines of the poor dramatist may provide a text for a professional exercise in ethics or metaphysics, or just 'criticism'. And so the game goes on — as with a good deal of modern art-criticism, it is highly unlikely that the artist ever thought in the terms imputed to him, or sometimes even would recognise his work from the discussion of it.

The first two works under view illustrate these observations, their various writers at issue with each other on the point.

This is the twenty-fourth number of the Annual *Shakespeare Survey:*[1] one is not so much surprised by what is said in it as that there is anything left to say at all. Except for the account of new Shakespeare productions, it has practically all been said before. Let us concentrate on our theme.

Mrs Rees writes, in the best article in the book:

> The tendency of these studies often seems to be to encourage the notion that Shakespeare worked in each play according to a preformed and carefully articulated scheme which study can identify. This seems to me to be a false position.

Well, of course. Yet this is what most of her colleagues, the scholastics, do. She puts her finger right on their silliness when she goes on: 'To derive the creative act primarily from a conceptualising power is to turn the situation back to front'. Exactly: it is to turn Shakespeare into a Professor – the last thing he was!

> All the evidence would seem to show that Shakespeare hunted for plots rather than for themes. He would not have decided to write a play about Justice and Mercy, or about Jealousy, or Ingratitude or Ambition; but he would read ... the old play of *King Lear* and decide how best to dramatise the material, what theme he could extract from it.

This is mere sense. But you wouldn't think so from most of the 'critical' articles in the book. Nor from Professor Hobson's whole work, which completely exemplifies what Mrs Rees succinctly called getting the situation 'back to front'.[2]

---

[1] Kenneth Muir, *Shakespeare Survey 24* (Cambridge University Press, 1971).
[2] Alan Hobson, *Full Circle: Shakespeare and Moral Development* (Chatto and Windus, 1972).

Here is Professor Hobson on *The Tempest:*

> *The Tempest* makes us think about the proper exercise of power, the relation between love and power, between love and duty, between authority and freedom, between service and slavery. It is about wisdom and choice, about charity and equality, about deprivation and destructiveness and hate, about answerability, about punishment, vengeance and forgiveness, etc.

Do you suppose that that was how Shakespeare thought about his play? If he had, he would have written a treatise on Ethics, and been Professor Shakespeare. What these people should remind themselves every day is that *A play is a play is a play.*

A prime reason why these professors of Eng. Lit. go so far astray is that – in the increasing specialisation and scholasticising of their work – they have no sense of history. This means that they lose all touch with the groundwork of reality, the actuality of life, the way that Elizabethans lived and thought and worked.

This is why I find the modest little colour paperback, *The Age of Shakespeare*, describing and illustrating the way people lived, altogether less pretentious but more satis-factory.[3] It even has a revealing illustration I did not know: a carved and gilded panel, featuring a coat-of-arms with scrolls and swags and cartouches, expressive of the family-pride of the Age.

[3] Nathaniel Harris, *The Age of Shakespeare* (Hamlyn 1971).

# The Shakespeare Trade Union

'Hi! You've been offending against trade union regulations,' said an Eng. Lit. don to me on returning to Oxford from the Huntington Library after the publication of *William Shakespeare: A Biography*. Can you imagine anything more small-minded or, for that matter, more un-Elizabethan? Elizabethans did not suffer from a dispiriting and counter-creative specialisation. The fact is that, having written biographies of Grenville and Ralegh, a good deal about the Queen and other Elizabethans, what was there surprising in a leading authority on the Age writing the biography of its greatest writer?

I always intended to do it – only I didn't ask leave of them, the Eng. Lit. Trade Union. This is what has infuriated them. Maurice Bowra, as a superior classic; always regarded them as second-rate; more kindly disposed – after all, I started as an Eng. Lit. scholar and have published half-a-dozen volumes of verse (which they choose to ignore) – I didn't wish to think that. But their attitude ever since has shown that Bowra was right. There they go on in their old ruts, nothing new to say or think, refusing to make use or even to take notice of the new facts and findings brought up by the historian of Shakespeare's time. The shocking thing – to anyone who cares for knowledge – is that *they think they have nothing to learn*. That is a sure sign of the second-rate. Myself, avidly curious, wanting to know everything, I am learning all the time, taking tips from everywhere, even from them.

Why do they not learn from the historian of Shakespeare's age and time?

Because they are too inhibited, too apprehensive and unimaginative: safer to stick together and repeat the same old worn-out clichés and confusions of mind. It is precisely the attitude of a trade union: nobody must stand out from the mob by being too bright, or working too hard, let alone challenging the received ideas of the second-rate, when not third-rate.

Everything shows that this is their attitude, including what happened over this edition of Shakespeare.[1] Twelve years ago I was asked to write the General Introduction to it, the background to Shakespeare in his age and the life of the time. When the contributors found that I had something new and definite to say, that I had solved the so-called problems of Shakespeare's biography and reduced the confusion to chronological commonsense, they were terrified. They paid me off quite handsomely and got one of their own Eng. Lit. Trade Union to write the Introduction on the old conventional, well-worn lines. I didn't much mind, but in fact a grand opportunity was lost. This edition comes out on much the same lines as any other complete Shakespeare, Peter Alexander's or C. J. Sisson's. What is the point of yet another, the mixture as before?

There is one improvement, which they owe originally to a suggestion of mine. There really had been no point in adhering to the First Folio order of the plays, which begins with *The Tempest*, one of the last of Shakespeare's works. If you want to understand an artist's work as a whole, you should begin at the beginning and go forward in chronological order — you cannot understand Beethoven by beginning with the last quartets.

This edition divides the plays into Comedies, Histories, Tragedies, Romances, followed by the poems, then within this arrangement attempts to follow chronological order. This is a sensible scheme, probably more practical and convenient; but it remains true that, if you wish to follow the

[1] *The Riverside Shakespeare*, ed. G. Blakemore Evans *et al.* (Houghton Mifflin Co., 1974).

development of Shakespeare's genius, you should read his work in order of composition. The problem is one of dating – and where is a historian more in order, indeed a necessity, than in helping to establish dates, from topical and other references, performances, etc.

Any reputable historian would make use of all the literary and textual aids he could gather: why are these Eng. Lit. people totally unaware of the aids made readily available to them by people who are much more *au fait* with chronology, topical references and dating, than they are? This edition makes not the slightest use of the relevant, and very revealing, findings of the historian.

This is only one aspect of a general defect. Hide-bound within their Eng. Lit. defences, blinkered to anything real in the real world outside, these commentators bury the plays under a load of sources – Italian comedy, medieval chronicles, Greek romances – and never mention the world in which Shakespeare lived and worked, the places he knew and which were part of his experience of life. In other words, there is little sense of *life*, only of academic literature.

Take *The Taming of the Shrew*. It has its author's recognisable Stratford and Cotswold background. Christopher Sly is of Barton-on-the-heath, Marion Hacket is the fat ale-wife of Wincot, and there's old John Naps of Greet – the conservative editor of the text absurdly keeps to the obvious misprint 'of Greece', putting the emendation in a footnote. But there is nothing of this in the Introduction, all in purely literary terms, missing out on the real environment.

Take *As You Like It*. The play has most revealing personal touches in it, quite apart from anything conjectural. For one thing, the Forest of Arden – from which both sides of Shakespeare's family came, his mother herself an Arden – is brought on the stage; for another, there are no less than three well-known references to Marlowe, including the one that corroborates the fact as to how he died: a quarrel over the reckoning in a little tavern room. No reference to this in the Introduction, though we are told that 'poetry is left in an uncertain position, partly redeemed from Plato's charge that it was an art of lies'. Can academicism go much further in irrelevance? Do you suppose that an Elizabethan working dramatist cared what Plato thought? He was thinking about his colleague and rival, Marlowe, whose poem *Hero and Leander* was at length published in 1598 and brought him vividly back to Shakespeare's mind.

Similarly with *Love's Labour's Lost* and *A Midsummer Night's Dream*. There is no sense of the environment in and for which these plays were written, and naturally they have got their dates wrong. We are told that *Love's Labour's Lost* is 'perhaps the most relentlessly Elizabethan of all Shakespeare's plays'. What is the point of this if you can't see the Elizabethan circumstances in and for which it was conceived? Commonsense as well as literary perception alike show that the play is closely related to the Sonnets about the Dark Lady — indeed the dark Rosaline in the play is described in precisely similar language. This is quite well known, as also that Berowne, who falls for the dark lady, expresses Shakespeare's viewpoint in the play. Both the play and those sonnets, and 'The Rape of Lucrece' which coheres with the sonnets, belong to the same period, 1593, when the theatres were closed: Shakespeare was free to write poems and sonnets for his patron Southampton, and the play was for private performance, a skit on the recurrent theme of Southampton's well-known reluctance to marry.

There is an historical mistake in the Introduction: the play was not produced again to celebrate Southampton's 'release from prison in 1604'. He was released in 1603; the play was revived to entertain King James at Southampton House in 1605. The play is obviously connected with the Southampton circle and is a fantasy upon the theme of the young patron's ambivalence about women.

The Introduction does see, however, that between *Love's Labour's Lost* and *A Midsummer Night's Dream* 'the connection is especially close', but without seeing why. The obvious fact is that both plays belong to the same period and to the Southampton ambiance. In the Sonnets of just this time we learn that Shakespeare was contemplating a midsummer's story; but when *A Midsummer Night's Dream* ends, with its stately elderly couple going to their marriage, the young people are coming back from celebrating Mayday. The play was evidently geared to the marriage of Southampton's mother to the elderly Privy Councillor, Sir Thomas Heneage, on 2 May 1594.

The Introduction comments sagely, 'unfortunately, neither a specific occasion nor the degree of Shakespeare's possible indebtedness to writers like Ficino and Pico della Mirandola has ever been satisfactorily established.' Both terms in this proposition are ludicrous; for the specific occasion is quite obvious – though Eng. Lit. commentators have been all over the place with their dating, as usual; while there is not the slightest likelihood that the busy actor-dramatist knew about Ficino or Pico della Mirandola. Pure professional bunk, showing no sense of the real environment or the life or how a real writer works.

Similarly with *Romeo and Juliet* and another professorial commentator. We are told that the use of a sleeping potion goes back to the *Ephesiaca* of the Greek novelist Xenophon in the fourth century A.D., that Masuccio of Salerno used it in 1476, and the feuding families in Italy from which Shakespeare may have got the names in the play. No idea that the action of the play was suggested by the happenings in the immediate circle of Shakespeare's patron, whose close friends the Danvers brothers were engaged in a bitter feud with the Longs on his threshold in Wiltshire. When one of them killed the son and heir of the Longs, Southampton helped them to get away to France, and his servant, John Florio, was involved in the business. Florio was Southampton's Italian tutor: one does not have to look far for the Italian colouring, names and phrases in these plays.

These points are comparatively obvious and I have brought them out in my work – though no notice has been taken of it: these people have nothing to learn. Naturally when it comes to more subtle matters like the background to *Hamlet* and *Troilus and Cressida* they fail to see the circumstances in the real environment, what was happening in the author's vicinity and in the theatre. Of *Troilus and Cressida* we are solemnly told that the motivation 'derives from a disabused pragmatism of the kind advocated by Thomas Hobbes' — i.e. fifty years on. What is the value of that? Mere academicism. It would have been more to the point to notice how that disillusioned play with its bitter reflections on politics itself reflected the atmosphere of 1600–3, the years of party-feuding, of Essex's dizzy fall, the sad expectations of the Queen's death, the sense of insecurity and nerves on edge. It is all in *Hamlet* and *Troilus and Cressida*; the commentator sees that they are 'closely associated', but not how close Shakespeare was to these events. We know how close he had been to Southampton, who was Essex's leading supporter, condemned to death with him, though the sentence was suspended in his case. Anyone at the time would recognise

What a noble mind is here o'erthrown:
The courtier's, soldier's, scholar's eye, tongue, sword,
The expectancy and rose of the fair state.

— Just what Essex had been to his hopeful followers and the public at large.

Or take the comment on *Lear*, which cites a Lord Mayor of London some forty years before who divided his estate among (not 'between') three daughters — and omits the immediate circumstance of the courtier Sir Brian Annesley, whose two elder daughters tried to get him certified as insane to get hold of his estate, while the youngest, Cordelia, tried to save him. This lady married the Countess of Southampton's young widower, Sir William Hervey. Again one does not have far to look — if one knows the age sufficiently well.

We are told, somewhat portentously, that *Lear* is 'in part a play about the end of the world'. One cannot too often insist

that *a play is a play is a play:* it is fundamentally a story of
which Shakespeare has seen the dramatic possibilities. This
leads me to a general point: not enough attention is paid to
dramatic criticism in this enormous tome, and far too much
to mere literary criticism, discussion of remote (sometimes
improbable) sources, etc. Again and again, however, the point
is made that *nowadays* some play, which a previous generation thought unsuitable for acting, in fact holds the stage.
This should give critics some pause, or at least a sense of
humour about themselves. The repeated phrase about the
'critical status' of a play of Shakespeare's is not only
impertinent but rather humourless – as if critics conferred
the value on the play.

The most enlightening criticism, and the most relevant to a
writer who was more a man of the theatre than any other
(except Molière), is that in terms of the theatre, above all the
conditions of the Elizabethan theatre, companies, acting,
personnel. These conditions were largely determining of
Shakespeare's dramaturgy – though in this book one misses
the proper appreciation of the work of our greatest authority
on the Jacobean drama, G. E. Bentley. His book, *The
Professional Dramatist in Shakespeare's Age*, is infinitely
more revealing than stuff about Xenophon's *Ephesiaca* or
Pico della Mirandola.

Nor does one want the whole plot of a play like *Lear*
repeated at far too great length by some professor, in much
less good language. My sympathies are with those of a real
poet, like my old friend Auden:

> Nor are those Ph.D's my kith
> Who dig the symbol and the myth . . .
>     I feel
> Most at home with what is Real.

Naturally the commentator on the history plays is closer to
the factual: he writes quite sensibly about Richard III, no
Ricardian nonsense – he has got that right. He is fairly good
on the difficult subject of the three *Henry VI* plays, though

here he too misses the actual environment that made for their success. They coincided with the Normandy campaign in France, led by Essex and in which young Southampton joined; this brought back memories of the French campaigns of the previous century to the popular mind.

There are not many historical mistakes. Cardinal Beaufort was not the brother but the uncle — as the table overpage shows — of Humphrey Duke of Gloucester, who was not Lord Protector of the realm, but merely protector or governor of the child Henry VI's person. The personality of Cardinal Morton is inadequately grasped, and Thomas More had more direct sources of information about Richard III than Morton — the Duke of Norfolk for one, who as Earl of Surrey had been in the room at the Tower when Richard made his *coup d'etat* and had Hastings summarily executed without trial. More's was not 'a Tudor party-line' about Richard — More was not a Tudor party-man — but just the general view of a king who had criminally murdered his brother's children.

The Introduction to Henry V is very poor. For one thing it is quite anachronistic, totally unable to grasp the Elizabethan conception of the king. To the Elizabethans and to Shakespeare he was a hero-king; to the professor he is 'that bloody monarch' and his heroic spell that 'short but flashy reign'. The professor simply doesn't know what he is talking about. He should have read the greatest authority on the fifteenth century, K. B. McFarlane, a singularly cool head, who says of Henry V: 'Take him all round and he was, I think, the greatest man that ever ruled England.'

This shows up the shocking limitations of the Eng. Lit. mind, not only the lack of historical perception and imagination, the meanness of judgement, but the smug complacency with which they think they have nothing to learn from the best authorities. In this case from McFarlane, who knew more about the fifteenth century than anyone has ever known — though in my own account of the play in *William Shakespeare* I make the situation quite clear. These second-rate people choose deliberately to ignore it: they think they have nothing to learn.

In consequence, the professor — even on his own Eng. Lit. ground — gets Shakespeare's play all wrong. It is, of course, different in kind from the other history plays — that is, in part, its interest. Shakespeare was attempting something new: an heroic play, with the Chorus an integral part of the scheme, plenty of pageantry in proper keeping with the hero of the play, who entirely dominates it, though at the same time the human side to the man is carefully presented. Fancy quoting the views of Hazlitt at length on the historical aspect, or the ignorant opinions of Chambers, or a Mark van Doren against Shakespeare's judgement of Henry V — he knew better!

The most unsatisfactory section is that devoted to the Poems and Sonnets. There is no conception of the relation of *Venus and Adonis* to Southampton's personality and situation at the time, quite well known and easily recognisable. 'Read as a mythological-erotic poem, *Venus and Adonis* is a vivid and fluent example of the type, not as successful as Marlowe's *Hero and Leander*', etc. — no idea that it was written in competition with Marlowe's poem for Southampton's patronage. Tucker Brooke rightly saw that there was no other Elizabethan dedication like that of *The Rape of Lucrece* to Southampton — E. K. Chambers, imperceptive as ever, couldn't see it.

The ineffable Professor Wilson Knight, who saw homosexuality in everything, couldn't see the obvious personality of Shakespeare's young patron in the Sonnets, ambivalent, feminine in looks, refusing to marry. E. K. Chambers and Dover Wilson tossed up and came down for Pembroke, always a roaring hetero and, at the time the Sonnets were being written, aged twelve to fourteen. Really, one doesn't urge a boy at that age to get married right quick and carry on the family! They got that hopelessly wrong by failing to notice that Mr W. H. was Thorp's dedicatee, not Shakespeare's man at all. Even this commentator is confused in saying that 'the initials, if they are Southampton's, are transposed.' This is silly: they are not Southampton's and they are not transposed. They are those of a person very close to Southampton from whom Thorp got the manuscript. People have been misled by 'Mr', i.e. Elizabethan for Master, and not knowing that it was regular social usage to address a knight as Master. If they do not know this simple piece of Elizabethan social etiquette, they should ask an Elizabethan social historian who does — not ignore what he is telling them for their benefit.

Southampton's mother died in 1607, leaving all her household goods and chattels to Sir William Hervey. In 1608 Hervey married Cordelia Annesley. This is why in 1609 Thorp wishes him 'all happiness', and 'that eternity promised by our ever-living poet' means the eternity of having progeny to carry on the family, as Shakespeare had promised Southampton in the Sonnets if he would marry and so continue to posterity. Q.E.D.

There is no point in quoting E. K. Chambers or Dover Wilson on the Sonnets, both of whom created unnecessary confusion, one of them characteristically imperceptive, the other notoriously erratic. The editor here sees sense in saying that 'an agnostic position with respect to the biographical significance of Shakespeare's Sonnets may not be one which is permanently satisfying to hold'. Well, of course. In that case, why say nothing whatever about the Rival Poet, clearly Marlowe? And what was the Rival Poet rivalling Shakespeare for but the patronage of the Patron? That is, the Sonnets were written for the patron. Q.E.D.

Many people have noticed the close verbal associations between *Venus and Adonis* and *Hero and Leander*. Indeed the verbal echoes from Marlowe are in evidence all through Shakespeare's writing; but this is a literary indebtedness not realised in an academic work whose contributors do not realise how real writers write. No conception, for example, that *A Lover's Complaint* is a prentice-piece reflecting the youthful Southampton's personality again. We are told that 'the poem is never referred to by a contemporary' – well, of course, it was privately presented to Southampton and was got hold of by Thorp in the same *cache* with the Sonnets: he printed them together, they belonged together.

Again and again in this edition the professors pursue the will-o'-the-wisps of pedantry, while failing to notice the real facts and conditions of Elizabethan life and theatre out of which the plays and poems arose. The editor himself, Professor Blakemore Evans, writes an Introduction on the transmission of the text. This struck me, though I am not a textual scholar, as excellent; then he goes wrong on the chronology of the Sonnets, where an historian is most needed. The bulk of literary scholars have sensibly seen that the Sonnets belong with *Venus and Adonis* and *The Rape of Lucrece*. An Elizabethan historian can confirm this commonsense from the topical references which follow, consistently and intelligibly, the sequence 1592, 1593, 1594-5. Q.E.D.

After ploughing through this enormous Biblical tome (or tomb) of 1902 India-paper pages, more suitable for a lectern than to hold, one is bound to ask the question: to what point all this effort, all the years of preparation, if only to produce yet one more Complete Shakespeare on conventional academic lines, the mixture as before, when it is all available already in other editions?

My own overriding principle is that nothing should be done to obstruct the reader from Shakespeare, that everything should be done to make Shakespeare clear to the reader, to help him, provide the necessary aids, and not clutter up the book with what is unnecessary – answering the 'critical' rubbish written by other professors, for example.

This purpose would be best served by modernising both spelling and punctuation, while keeping conservatively to the wording of the text. I have tried to provide a model of this kind in my modern edition of the Sonnets, adhering conscientiously to the text, the actual words, but with modern spelling and punctuation to help the reader to understand what is said. A number of intelligent people have told me that this is precisely what my modest edition helped them to do, that for the first time they understood what the Sonnets were saying.

But these people did not belong to the Trade Union, which chooses to ignore totally the work of the historian of Shakespeare's Age. That is very much in accordance with the inferior trade union principles of our time: the electrician must not touch anything belonging to the gas-man's job.

Perhaps, in return, the electrician may conclude that, after all the years this edition has been germinating, it has missed the bus in more senses than one.

# Shakespeare Trade Unionists and Others

A close season should be imposed on writing about Shakespeare: most people have nothing new or of any value to say about the subject. And when something new and valuable turns up, conventional academics or members of the Shakespeare Trade Union can't recognise it when they see it. It reminds me of Winston Churchill's *mot* about Abraham Lincoln: people couldn't see moral courage when it stared them in the face. Apart from that, these people after all have no *vocation* for writing, no call to write. Kindly disposed, I propose to arrange them in order of merit, down to downright demerit.

Miss Garber has a good subject and writes pleasantly; within the terms of her academicism of approach she has

written a good book.[1] Its only fault is its academicism, in the
pejorative sense. She begins: 'It is difficult to say that
Shakespeare made use of the work of any particular author
or school' – which immediately puts out of court any
pedantic approach. The next paragraph begins: 'Dreams in
the works of early classical authors tended to be either
objective and monitory or symbolic and allegorical . .
Homeric dreams . . .' As if going back to Homer, a completely different, immensely earlier civilisation, had any
relevance to Shakespeare.

We are introduced to the *Oneirocritica* of Artemidorus of
Daldis, and then to Macrobius. Do you suppose, dear reader,
that the busy actor-playwright had so much as heard of their
names? Anybody would think that he was a university
professor – the last thing he was like in real life. What
matters is what Shakespeare's contemporaries thought about
dreams. Here the evidence of Simon Forman is of the greatest
value – though none of these people, wasting their time on
writing redundant books, thought of exploring his manuscripts to find out. It is to be hoped that now that the job has
been done for them, they will take the trouble to instruct
themselves from a contemporary source.

When Miss Garber points out the great popularity of
dreams in the Elizabethan drama, and says 'both structurally
and psychologically the prophetic dream was useful to the
playwright', she is on the right tack and should have begun at
that point. It is indeed only part of the immense importance
Elizabethans attached to dreams in real life. Something of
this may be glimpsed in Holinshed, whom she quotes –
Shakespeare would be at one with his Warwickshire contemporary, his chief source for the history plays.

There are good observations in this book, like that on
*Julius Caesar* as revealing 'the strange blindness of the
rational mind – in politics and elsewhere – to the great

---

[1] Marjorie B. Garber, *Dream in Shakespeare. From Metaphor to Metamorphosis*
(Yale University Press, 1974).

irrational powers which flow through life and control it.' That is utterly characteristic of Shakespeare's cast of mind – though 'control' is hardly the right word: 'carry us away' would be truer to his view. Again, 'the fundamental reversal or inversion of conventional categories which is a structuring principle' of *A Midsummer Night's Dream* is a clumsy way of putting a simple point, which is yet important: the chief advantage of the dream to the dramatist is that anything can happen in it. Or, 'change itself is essentially an aspect of creativity in the realm of time' – people ought not to write about Shakespeare's plays like that, let alone the ineffable Professor Wilson Knight's 'the triumphant mysticism of the dream of love's perfected fruit in eternity stilling the tumultuous waves of time.' Pretentious stuff and nonsense – 'pseudo' writing.

'*The Winter's Tale* centres much of its attention on problems of timelessness and time.' Problems! To Shakespeare (as to Ben Jonson) it was a *tale*, which could be turned into a play. I am coming to think that the only Shakespeare criticism which tells us anything is dramatic criticism.

The academic dose is increased in Professor Leggatt's book,[2] and it is the less good for it. He begins, 'the complaint that there is not enough criticism of Shakespeare's comedies is now heard less often than it used to be. We have come to take these plays quite seriously . . .' Comedies depend for their appreciation on a sense of humour; not much evidence of it in that portentous remark – as if Shakespeare wrote his comedies in the hope that professors might take them 'quite seriously'. They certainly do. And 'predictably', if one may use a word on which a close season should also be imposed: 'so much of their fascination [the comedies', not the professors'] stems from their unpredictability . . . much of the dramatic life of a play, as I will try to show in a later chapter, depends on swift, unpredictable shifts in idiom', etc.

[2] Alexander Leggatt, *Shakespeare's Comedy of Love* (Methuen, 1974).

The fungus of academicism appears above ground early on, with 'perhaps Shakespeare, before he could use mistaken identity as an instrument, had to give it a thorough examination'. Do you suppose he gave such a process a thought? – more suitable to an examination paper. All the figures in the Shakespeare Industry – Trade Unionists, every man – appear and are cited. 'In the words of A.C. Hamilton', 'as E. M. W. Tillyard puts it', as 'summarized by Marion Bodewell Smith'. 'The contrast between lover-and-mistress and wife-and-husband is reviewed by Charles Brooks ... He takes a more sanguine view of Adriana's marriage than I have' (*sic*). Who cares? 'Here I take issue with the frequently expressed view that Aegeon's account of his misfortunes carries a nearly tragic emotional impact' – references to T.U. colleagues Charlton and Traversi. But who cares? 'Stanley Wells has pointed out the importance of non-sexual love as "a driving force" ': this throws more light on Dr Wells than on *The Comedy of Errors*. 'According to Gates K. Agnew, "through Berowne the fame-seeker's mentality comes to pervade the wooing game".' What pretentious rubbish!

The sad thing is that, like a good man struggling with sin, the professor, well-nigh strangled by scholastic commentary, occasionally has glimpses of the real world in which the plays were written, or at any rate suspicions that it exists. 'We may wonder at times if the characters are simply creatures of literary artifice, or creatures of a more real or normal world who consciously adopt literary artifice.' Well, well! He should read my account of *Love's Labour's Lost,* and that would tell him. Several sensible commentators have seen that Berowne is a projection of Shakespeare himself and expresses his point of view. Professor Leggatt struggles towards commonsense with 'if Berowne seems the most fully realised figure of the play, this may be because he embodies many of the play's processes in his own nature'; i.e. an academic half-perception that he embodies the play's creator. There follows a revealing comment, though the professor is unaware of its significance, when he says, 'there is something sadistic in Rosaline's attitude to Berowne'. Everybody knows that Rosaline is described in practically the same language as Shakespeare describes his real mistress, the Dark Lady. And Rosaline ends up with the declared intention to

> o'ersway his state
That he should be my fool, and I his fate.

Real writers write out of their experience of life, and some of them write it into their plays. Here it is not the play that counts, but the *idea* of the play, 'See Anne Righter (Barton), *Shakespeare and the Idea of the Play*.' Of *A Midsummer Night's Dream* we are told, 'much of its power to haunt the imagination comes from its suggestion of the ultimate unity of the various worlds it depicts'. What rubbish! It is the characters of the play and its poetry that haunt the imagination; Bottom warns us, 'Man is but an ass if he go about to expound this dream'. And Portia has the last word on the professors:

> O, these deliberate fools! When they do choose,
> They have the wisdom by their wit to lose.

In Elizabethan English wit meant intellect; exactly, intellectualising – particularly inferior intellectualising – gets in the way of any sharpness of perception or response.

Mr Colman is a virtuous member of the Trade Union, and carries his card; so, though assailing the bawdy in Shakespeare,[3] he has not been permitted to come upon my wicked explanation of the double meaning of Hamlet's description of the boy-actors as 'little eyases'. Elizabethans were much bawdier than we are, and Shakespeare was the bawdiest of their writers. It is a testimony to his heterosexual normality, for naturally homosexuals do not go in for promiscuous bawdiness. There is immensely less bawdy in Marlowe for the obvious reason: he was a homosexual, Shakespeare very much the opposite. (This is very important

---

[3] E. A. Colman, *The Dramatic Use of Bawdy in Shakespeare* (Longman, 1974).

for the correct reading of the Sonnets; though the fact is
perfectly obvious.)

The function of bawdy in Elizabethan plays was simply to
amuse the audience — that is the simple truth of the matter. Mr
Colman glimpses this, only to set it gravely aside: 'eroticism
is illustrative and auxiliary rather than fundamental to any
play's structure; and the dramatist often appears to be
deploying indecent humour simply for its immediate appeal
to a theatre audience.' For heaven's sake, what successful
dramatist would forego an immediate appeal to his audience?
This is a very nice example of academics seeing things, and
presenting them, arsy-versy. But the poor fellow has glimpsed
the possibility of a thesis and padding it out into a book: he
labours the idea that the function of Shakespeare's bawdy is
to delineate the characters for us. As if Shakespeare is not
perfectly capable of conveying character by any and every
means! Indecency, we are told without a grain of humour,
'forms what might be thought of as fields of magnetic force,
not simply round particular characters, but in relation to
points of thematic energy.' Well, now we know what
indecency is.

The result of the inquiry has been the author's 'own
growing conviction that the golden rule is to be slow in
assuming ribald significance anywhere in Shakespeare —
above all when reading or directing the plays in the
sex-conscious and irony-loving atmosphere of the later
twentieth century.' This pronouncement is innocently
unaware of the fact that the Elizabethans were more
free-and-easy about sex than we are; the golden rule,
therefore, is to find out where Shakespeare stood in relation
to the sex-life of the age. Commonsense would indicate that
the ubiquitous saltiness of his plays was one factor in his
success with his audience — the normality of his nature was
geared to theirs.

Knowledge is the first rule, commonsense is the second.
The author is right to point out that there was no
commonsense whatever in Dover Wilson's 'explaining'

Hamlet's recommendation of chastity to Ophelia, 'Get thee to a nunnery', as meaning Get thee to a brothel. How foolish can professors be! Professor Virgil Whitaker is also taken to task, rightly, for interpreting Cleopatra's lament, 'The soldier's pole is fallen', as a reference to a detumescent penis. Really! and in the context,

> The odds is gone,
> And there is nothing left remarkable
> Beneath the visiting moon.

To understand Shakespeare there is no substitute for perception, sensitiveness and sense.

Instead of that we detect a note of insensitive patronage: 'it is perhǎps a measure of Shakespeare's relative inexperience at the time of writing *Romeo and Juliet* that his contrasting of the old and the young gives rise to some blurred emotional focus in the third act.' Or the downright silly: 'far from its being the case that, as some critics have maintained, Mercutio has to be killed off because he threatens our confidence in the hero, it would be truer to say that if Mercutio did not exist it would be necessary for Shakespeare to invent him'. What becomes clear is that these people are not so much concerned with Shakespeare as with each other: one professor suggests nonsense for another to answer it with hardly less nonsense.

However, it is nice to know that Helge Kökeritz is a member: he 'draws special attention to the qui's-quae's-quod's speech. He claims *qui's* as a pun on *keys,* but I am unconvinced that *key* as a slang term for *penis* was ever as common as this assumes.' Both are shown to be asses, for in the Elizabethan pronunciation of Latin English-wise, *qui* would rhyme with 'I' or 'die' anyway. A Kökeritz wouldn't know, and a Colman wouldn't see the point.

However, I am grateful to him for one small fact. He tells us that in 1608 a man called Stafford was indicted 'for committing buggery with a boy, for which he was attainted and hanged.' This must be the Humphry Stafford in Simon Forman's Case-Books, whose identification gave me the

greatest difficulty. In the end I ran him down as Humphry
Stafford of Blatherwick in Northants. Wherever one tests
Forman's information from external sources one finds him
nearly always corroborated.

Professor Vickers' volume[4] is the harbinger of six whole
volumes devoted to 'The Critical Heritage' of Shakespeare,
themselves but a small section of a vast series of more than
fifty writers — the critical heritage of such writers as Gissing
and Forster, Rochester and Pound. Think of it! it is enough
to make one dizzy. Is it fair on a bankrupt country to waste so
much paper and print on such a project, when what these
writers wrote about each other is in print already, even
assuming that it is worth reading? (Most of it is not.)
Especially is this the case with Shakespeare, when we have
several volumes of Allusion Books in print already, and
numberless collections of Shakespeare criticism easily
accessible.

The editor is a product of the Cambridge Eng. Lit. school,
as one might guess from the key-word 'evaluation' and his
insensitiveness to the language. I have always been surprised
by the deference accorded to the Master in the field of
literature when he had no sense of the language. The editor
does not know the correct use of 'shall' and 'will', 'should'
and 'would', on which he should read Fowler, *The King's
English*. 'The demands on space were strong, and although I
would [sc. should] have liked to include' . . . 'In 1623 we
will [sc. shall] find him praised . . .' Naturally there is no
sense of the use of the monosyllabic preposition 'to' to break
up clumsy aggregations of words, like 'Chettle regretted
having helped publish Greene's work', for 'helped to publish.'
It is always a wonder to me why people who have no
sensibility for words choose to write about literature — they
would be more at home with computers. And naturally a
product of this school, which disclaimed any truck with the
historical or biographical, does not get right the Elizabethan

[4] Brian Vickers (ed.), *Shakespeare. The Critical Heritage*, vol. 1, 1623–1692
(Routledge and Kegan Paul, 1974).

meaning of the word 'gentle': 'Gentle' Shakespeare did not mean soft, it meant gentlemanly. Of course, it always was ignorant nonsense on the part of this school to think that you could understand a man's work without knowing about the man, his time or even the meaning of his words.

And who wants acres of print containing adaptations of Shakespeare by inferior writers, containing such things as an operatic rendering by Elkanah Settle, with the wise rubric 'the ascription to Settle, made by F. C. Brown (*Elkanah Settle,* Chicago 1910) is not certain.' I am reminded of the note put up in the porch of a Cornish church by a dotty parson – 'The time of Evensong is uncertain': it had been uncertain for years.

One consequence of the professionals' leaving open questions which can, and have been, definitely answered – constituting bogus problems which they can go on discussing *ad infinitum* – is to confuse the minds of the unprofessionals, the non-unionists, who produce books like Mr Green's.[5] It does not have to be taken seriously, and yet he has got the point right that Mr W. H. was not Shakespeare's young Lord, but the publisher's, and the young Lord of the Sonnets was the obvious person, Southampton. E. K. Chambers, massively imperceptive, and Dover Wilson, enthusiastically wrong-headed, both got it wrong.

The textual scholar, Professor Charlton Hinman, said to me on this point: 'I am more in agreement with you than you are yourself.' And he gave me as the reason the argument that the reference to 'rose' and 'roses' in the Sonnets refer to Southampton's name, Wriothesley. That is a typical example of the way Eng. Lit. people think, even the best of them. It is, of course, completely wrong: the Elizabethan historian can tell them that the name was pronounced, and sometimes spelt phonetically, Risley. It came from the name Writh – nothing to do with roses. The quite unquestionable identification of Southampton in the Sonnets rests on far

[5] Martin Green, *The Labyrinth of Shakespeare's Sonnets* (Charles Shilton, 1974).

solider grounds – in fact, on every ground: it does not need the support of this nonsense.

Yet there is the effect of these confused professionals on an innocent amateur. Poor Mr Green says, 'both Professor Shackford and Professon Hinman surmised that Wriothesley, the family name of the Earl of Southampton, was probably pronounced "Rose-ly". I have no doubt as to the correctness of their surmise.' Well, their surmise was wrong: that is all.

With the silly habit of spelling everybody's names out in full – maximising the chances of mistakes for innocents – I am quoted as Arthur Leslie Rowse several times over. I should rather like to have been called Arthur, a good Celtic name anyway; but in fact, I was not. Another such innocent in America, unnecessarily spelling everything out in this fatuous fashion, lost the first syllable in his files, so that I found a book of mine cited, to my surprise, as by Fred L. Rowse.

What asses these people are, and what mingled fun and irritation their stupidity gives one!

# A Master on Marlowe

Professor Fredson Bowers is acknowledged the greatest textual scholar in the field of English literature today. A generation ago it was the redoubtable Sir Walter Greg. It is nice to think that, upon the summit of this rarified Olympus, Bowers can sometimes catch out Greg – a tribute to progress in scholarship. But, in addition to the masterly technique commanded by both – the expertise, the knowledge of printing processes, the sheer power of logical argumentation — Bowers is a more sympathetic figure: some-what unexpectedly in this frightening territory, he has the advantage of being an altogether more human person, and he writes better. So he appeals much more to me.

He now presents us with the finest text of Christopher Marlowe we are ever likely to get, beautifully presented by the Cambridge University Press.[1] What a difficult job it is, and how much light it throws all round the margins of that dark subject! No textual scholar myself, I can at any rate prcfit from inferences for the work in general, draw some conclusions about the most exciting of all Elizabethan poets, that elemental spirit, 'all air and fire', as Drayton called him: the Dylan Thomas of his time, and more.

It is clear that, after his death in May 1593, the publishers were keen to get hold of his manuscripts for publication. They intended to publish his uncompleted *Hero and Leander* — which he was writing in rivalry with Shakespeare's *Venus and Adonis* for the patronage of the patron (i.e. the Sonnets were written for the patron, and Marlowe was the Rival Poet) — as also his translation of Lucan.

Actually Marlowe's friend, Edward Blount, did not publish *Hero and Leander* until 1598, when it gave rise to Shakespeare's three most illuminating references to Marlowe in *As You Like It*. The translation of Lucan was taken over for publication in 1600 by Blount's friend, Thomas Thorp, who got Shakespeare's Sonnets for publication nine years later. Thorp's dedication to *his* Mr W. H. (not Shakespeare's) is responsible for all the rubbish written about Mr W. H., under the misapprehension that he was the young Lord of the Sonnets.

Thorp was in the habit of writing flowery dedications — like that here to Blount (the name was pronounced Blunt).

Blount, I purpose to be blunt with you, and out of my dulness to encounter you with a dedication in the memory

---

[1] *The Complete Works of Christopher Marlowe,* ed. Fredson Bowers, 2 vols (Cambridge University Press, 1973).

of that pure, elemental wit, Christopher Marlowe, whose
ghost or genius is to be seen walking the Churchyard [i.e.
St Paul's, where the bookshops were] in at the least three
or four sheets ... This spirit was sometime a familiar of
your own, Lucan's First Book Translated; which, in regard
of your old right in it, I have raised in the circle of your
patronage.

Thorp's metaphor is that of spirit-raising in a circle.

We see the kind of publisher, with literary pretentions,
Thorp was, and should be able to appreciate the trouble he
gave with his similarly flowery dedication of the Sonnets, 'to
the only begetter of these ensuing Sonnets': he merely meant
the one and only person from whom he got the manuscript.
And that would be somebody very close to Southampton: we
know now very well who, Southampton's young stepfather,
Sir William Hervey.

The different status of the texts of Marlowe's various
works — some reliable and close to his manuscripts, others
unsatisfactory, merely a remembered reconstruction of a play
by a couple of actors — is fascinating, exciting, maddening.
Only a Master like Bowers can hope to get it right; sometimes
he disagrees with Greg, as over *Dr. Faustus*, and he carries
conviction with me as the better detective, who seizes on the
simpler explanation and never overlooks the significance of
the obvious.

Look at the complexity of these questions. Bowers shows
convincingly, with regard to Marlowe's most famous play, *Dr.
Faustus,* that he wrote only the grand scenes, while a
collaborator wrote the comic ones. (I welcome his judgement
that they are not so debased as formerly supposed.) The play
was one of the most popular of Elizabethan dramas, and in
1602 it was given a new lease of life with additions by
Rowley and Birde. So what we have in the fullest text is
something of a tesselated pavement. But the original play
could well have been printed from the papers fair or foul, of
Marlowe and his collaborator.

This is far from the case with *The Massacre at Paris,* of which only a single copy of an early edition remains. Apparently it was published out of the interest aroused by Marlowe's tragic death, but — alas! only from the memory of an actor or two. On the other hand, there has survived a single leaf of manuscript — now in the Folger Shakespeare Library — in Marlowe's own hand, all that we have of his. All that an editor can do here is to present this unsatisfactory version and correct the actors' mishearings. Like the master he is, Bowers realises the limitations of the bibliographical approach — see his authoritative *Bibliography and Textual Criticism*[2] — and that in this situation the way is open for the critical and historical judgement to take over.

Here, in spite of the unsatisfactoriness of the text, one is struck by what authentic Marlowe *The Massacre at Paris* is. So many touches, of matter and phrase, bring him vividly before us. Guise's speech:

> If ever Hymen lowered at marriage rites . . .
> If ever Sun stained heaven with bloody clouds . . .
> If ever day were turned to ugly night . . .

recalls the phrases of the marvellous invocation to the spirit of poetry in *Tamburlaine*:

> If all the pens that ever poets held . . .
> If all the quintessence they still . . .
> If these had made one poem's period . . .

Many of Guise's speeches recall Tamburlaine:

> What glory is there in a common good
> That hangs for every peasant to achieve?

(Christopher Marlowe would not have fitted into the Lowest-Common-Measure society of today!). There are the Catholic touches that reflect the knowledge he acquired in the seminary at Rheims. And there is a sinister reverberation

[2] (Oxford University Press, 1964.)

in the action at the murder of Henri III; the Friar 'stabs the King with a knife . . . and then the King getteth the knife and kills him.' This is like what happened in the tavern at Deptford on 30 May 1593, when Marlowe struck Ingram Freezer with his knife; Freezer wrested it from him and killed him.

We have good texts of *Tamburlaine* and *Edward II,* probably printed from Marlowe's own papers, though the large number of errors in the text of *Dido* may be due to difficulties with handwriting. Anyone who wants to savour sheer technical virtuosity should read the pages devoted to the textual problems raised by Marlowe's famous lyric, 'Come, live with me and be my love'. An occasional comparison throws light on problems in the transmission of Shakespeare's texts — how we long for a survey of the whole field by this Master! He mentions, in passing, that poor remembered versions of *Richard III, Henry V, King Lear* were replaced by good texts; but that of *The Merry Wives of Windsor* comes from Crane, the Company's scribe's transcript of the prompt-book; hence the version we have in the Folio is not the reliable original text.

How much difference does all this brilliant expertise, this absolute mastery of such difficult technical problems, make?

It is precisely here that a great scholar recognises the limitations — it provides the conditions *within which we* arrive at the work, as best we may. 'As with Shakespeare', he says, 'an editor can but re-order a few details in the presentation of the text and occasionally glean a new reading . . . or remove a persistent corruption or two in the several texts'.

The modesty of the Master puts lesser people in their place (odd that they shouldn't know it!)

From our present point of experience, for instance, it is genuinely sad to look back to the high confidence of a John Dover Wilson juggling the bolts of the New Bibliography like the hero of a Strauss tone-poem. In his own

day Wilson was read with genuine excitement, for he
offered the certainty that appeared to be in a new
evidential basis for criticism. Now that we have been
forced to recognise that his speculative textual insights will
not stand up to present-day rigorous inquiry . . .

It is a kinder way of saying that Dover Wilson had
enthusiasm, but a most erratic judgement: he was one of the
people who never spotted that Mr W. H. was Thorp's man,
not Shakespeare's, and settled without thought, absurdly, for
Pembroke as the young man of the Sonnets!

Or here is McManaway of the Folger, writing portentously:
'a Shakespeare drama is not one, but many plays: the ideal
play as the author conceived it; the text as written; the tidied
up fair copy . . . the imperfect rendition on the stage; and the
printed text or texts, that may represent one or more of
these versions', etc. This sounds very impressive, until one
reads the incisive comment of a Master: 'some of these
neither bibliography, nor any other form of criticism can
recover'. McManaway is dismissed with the brisk remark,
'certainly we have no means of knowing what ideal form a
play took in Shakespeare's mind before he wrote it down'.

So much for the old buffer who said to me, 'Still I shall
always believe that we shall never know who the young man
of the Sonnets was or who was the Rival Poet.' People have
to earn their living, I suppose, but it need not be by making
the problems of Shakespeare – or Marlowe – more complicated than they are. A first-rate mind, like Bowers, pierces
through the complexities to make them simpler.

# II
# The Popularity of
# History

## 1

I have been asked to write about 'the interaction between historical scholarship and the creative spark — how to make the dry bones come alive', and also how history may be best taught in schools. The two subjects are related, but, since the first is much more difficult to write about, perhaps I may begin with the second.

I am a great believer in the visual approach to history. Here schools today have a tremendous advantage, in every way, over the days when I went to school. I am sure that fuller and richer use can be made of these advantages. There is not only the direct use of television and films, to bring home to schoolboys and girls historic events and happenings, historic artifacts — pictures, portraits, utensils of metal, glass, earthenware, furniture, equipment, armour, weapons — the widest net possible is bound to catch somebody's interest, suggest a line of exploration.

Then there are history plays, films of Shakespeare, to take one example. Shakespeare was deeply interested in history and had a remarkable grasp of it. It has often been noticed that, on the whole he gives you a fairly reliable depiction of English history, from Richard II to Henry VIII. The great Duke of Marlborough said that the only English history he knew came from Shakespeare. Well, he didn't do badly on it.

But not only Shakespeare. Take such a fine historic film as *Queen Christina,* produced by a director of genius, Rouben Mamoulian, who gave Greta Garbo her first great part in it.

(Curiously enough, this was Stalin's favourite film.) It evokes most vividly the Sweden of the seventeenth century. Then follow it up in class with Michael Roberts' *Gustavus Adolphus*.

Or Mamoulian's first film in colour, *Becky Sharp,* based on *Vanity Fair* — all about Waterloo days. Then carry on with Arthur Bryant's books about Wellington and the Peninsular war.

Nowadays schools can carry forward by going to Spain, or France, or Belgium and Holland.

If they can't, they can visit the historic towns, cathedrals, churches, castles, great houses, primitive encampments, stone circles, archaeological finds in their neighbourhood. Everybody is interested in archaeology nowadays.

Here is the overwhelming advantage of living in an old historic country, feet-deep in relics and associations of the past. Teachers should make the utmost use of this great asset, both to appeal to young people's imagination and add to their knowledge.

Transport is easy today. Not so when I was a boy — anyway I hadn't got sixpence to take me anywhere (how I resented it! Young people have got nothing to resent today — everything is done for them.) However, I did the best I could to explore everything I could within walking distance — an historic town like Fowey or Lostwithiel, a romantic castle like Restormel of the Black Prince and the Civil War, all the parish churches. In those days the historic country houses, with their portraits and books, evidences of a higher culture, were not open to me. Now what is left of them are open through the National Trust, which — under the inspiration of an eminent historian, G. M. Trevelyan — has done such incomparable work.

How, then, to follow up this kind of approach in class?

Here is one suggestion only. There is a good series, *A Visual History of Modern Britain,* edited by Professor Jack Simmons of Leicester University. The inflexion of this series is mainly modern, with the emphasis, reasonably enough, on the nineteenth and twentieth centuries.

It covers, in the most revealing visual way, such subjects as the history of transport, industry and technology, government, the land, the town, recreation, the arts, education itself, finally Britain in relation to the outside world.

I haven't now space to deal properly with the theme how to make the dry bones live; it is a whole subject in itself and has been the inspiration of all my work. I have always wanted to get as close as possible to the *life* of the past, through all its evidences — perhaps above all its music in which we can *hear* its living voices, hear the dead people breathe and listen to the beating of their hearts. Here, again, what advantages we have today! — with the musical resources of the Third Programme, of which we should make the fullest use; or with all the music available in records or on tape; besides concerts, choirs, school-orchestras, church-services. (Only the last was available to me as a boy.)

Not many historians are musicians, and few are aesthetes or have much sense of beauty, which they should cultivate. But quite a number have a fair acquaintance with architecture. (I have done my best to open up these approaches in the chapter on 'The Pleasures of History' in my little book *The Use of History.*)

All the great historians have had a visual sense — Gibbon, Macaulay, Froude; even the nasty Regius Professor Freeman, who was so jealous of the genius of Froude, was quite good on the look of Norman towns and castles. The best historians of our time have all had it — Trevelyan, Powicke, David Knowles, Arthur Bryant. That is one of the gifts that mark these men off from the ordinary academic historian.

To be able to make the dry bones live is a gift, and a rare one; it means that one must have a sense of the poetry and pathos of the past, some living inner spring of inspiration and intuitive insight.

I can hand on one tip which I learned from Macaulay: always to carry a notebook with one, so that one can describe everything one needs — ramparts of Berwick, the castle of Ludlow, the High Street of Edinburgh, the rose-red of Lanercost — exactly as it looks while under one's eye.

That is, at any rate, one help, if one has the art to communicate it. And that takes us back where we began — with the visual sense.

2

Why is history so excessively popular today? Almost too much so; for I do not think it altogether a good sign for contemporary society — rather a reflection on it. History seems almost to have ousted the novel as popular reading matter. There are not only the professionals pouring out more books than ever before, but all the amateurs, the journalists, even the novelists, taking to writing history.

It must represent some deeper trend in society than people are altogether conscious of. I suspect that it is partly nostalgia; partly that people are far more fed up and weary with contemporary society than the trendy spokesmen of the new social order would have us believe. The attitude of the public at large, with which I am much more in sympathy than they are, has this justification — *the past of this country is far more interesting than its future is likely to be.*

I have been asked to say something about my own attitude to the writing of history, but of course such a subject would require a whole book. Here I can only explain a few points that seem to be much misunderstood.

I have been hauled over the coals for my attitude to the Puritans, by two great historians, friends and mentors of mine, G. M. Trevelyan and Samuel Eliot Morison. But they mistake my viewpoint. It is the extremes on *both* sides that I disapprove of, the extremes on both left and right in my period, who were engaged in making life intolerable for sensible people in the middle.

And this for a profound reason, obviously related to the anguish we have gone through in our own time. In history, I isolate the element of dogmatic ideological certainty — particularly with regard to matters essentially uncertain in themselves — as responsible for untold human suffering. One side will burn the other for some highly disputable propositions, the other will hang, draw and quarter the first for similar reasons.

Each of them will do it in the name of their exclusive possession of truth — though a little later in history they find that these are no longer truths for which they killed, and are engaged in getting together ecumenically. I sympathise with the sceptical Samuel Butler's summing up of the ideological conflicts that led to the disaster of the Civil War:

To fight for Truth is but the sole dominion
Of every idiot's humour or opinion.

There is nothing out of the way in this point of view of mine — it is that held by the most intelligent and humane minds during the atrocious conflicts of Reformation and Counter-Reformation, by such as Erasmus, or Montaigne, or, for that matter, by Elizabeth I, Shakespeare or Bacon. I detest a Calvin as I detest a Loyola or an Inquisitor-General. I describe the Presbyterian leader Cartwright as 'odious', because he advocated that a Catholic priest should be executed simply for the fact of his priesthood. Well, wasn't that odious? But the opposite extreme was just as bad.

The plain fact is that I am a sceptic, and don't have much respect for what humans in general suppose themselves to think. (Politicians, priests, lawyers, doctors know well that most of what people think is nonsense; a lot of women know this instinctively too, and on this I am in sympathy with the woman's point of view.)

The difference is that I am an aggressive sceptic: I am not willing to let the matter pass. I am bent, in writing history, on pointing out their foolery — like a Swift or a Voltaire (who described Calvin as *cet âme atroce*) — partly for didactic reasons. How otherwise are they to learn?

It would be perfectly easy for me to go through my books and cut out the provocations, the asides that dullards take exception to. But I would not dream of making such concessions to them: such remarks are deliberately put in — not so much to provoke fools, but that they should learn from them. As Flannery O'Connor, an American writer of genius, says: *the first-rate should never make it their aim to satisfy the standards of the third-rate.*

What these people are not intelligent enough to spot is that, with regard to the matter in hand, I am a middle-of-the-road man, a moderate, a Laodicean. It is only the manner that is sharp-edged, immoderate – partly a question of temperament, partly for aesthetic reasons: one always wishes to express the point as incisively, as arrestingly as possible, and to keep the reader on his toes.

If you look, you will find that my sympathies – unlike those of most intellectuals – are usually with government, not the opposition; with the leading figures in an age, not the simpletons. The problems of government are always more complex and difficult, more worthy of an adult mind, than mere opposition, mere criticism. *Anyone* can criticise, anybody can oppose – but can he do the job?

An old friend of mine has had the kindness to say that he would not come to me for a 'balanced view' of an age. Himself of a dissenting background, with a heavy list towards Cromwellians and Levellers – a tiny minority of the nation – a sense of humour, if nothing else, should tell him that I am much more likely to exemplify a balanced view as an historian. And, actually, one more in keeping with the feelings of the great majority, the public. Hence the public's response, whatever the minority-minded think or say.

# McFarlane on the
# Fifteenth Century

## 1

After an example in Kamen's *The Iron Century*[1] how history should *not* be written, here is an example of how it might and should be.[2] K. B. McFarlane probably knew more about fifteenth-century England than anybody else; at Oxford he was treated with bated breath, not only by his pupils, as the 'Master'. The paradoxical thing is that, if he hadn't died, we should not have had the works that his enviably devoted pupils are bringing out.

I am the only person to have succeeded in getting a book out of him, the *Wyclif* he wrote for my series *Men and Their Times*. For the rest he published only learned articles. This admirable and very readable work was not written as a book; it consists of two series of lectures, written out in full, now produced by his pupils.

Yet it is obvious that he *was* a master, indeed *the* Master of his subject; for these lucid, well-written lectures, which can be read by any layman, rest upon an enormous amount of detailed research. They represent his conclusions, and it would be very hard to gainsay them. Even the asides, characteristic of him, are masterly; he *knew*. It is 'unreasonable' to call Henry IV's usurpation of Richard II's throne a 'revolution'. There was no constitutional principle about it: the great Stubbs was 'wholly wrong'. It was simply 'a personal drama', not a constitutional conflict. Richard was too sensitive to be 'sensible' — a characteristic touchstone in

[1] See below, p. 201.
[2] K. B. McFarlane, *Lancastrian Kings and Lollard Knights,* ed. J. R. L. Highfield and G. L. Harriss (Oxford University Press, 1972).

McFarlane's deflationary values. Much of what the Lollards taught was 'dreary cant' – but then what else would one expect? And so on. Though I knew him intimately longer than anyone, I was as surprised, as much as amused, by some of these flouts. Above all, I enjoyed the book, and read it avidly – such a relief to read something by a master.

His whole account of Henry IV, and the relations between him and Richard II, is obviously right and convincing. There was never any cordiality between the two. Richard, sensitive, effeminate, an aesthete, must have been envious of Boling-broke, handsome, male, able, a first-class man of action as well as an intellectual, always popular. He had all the qualities for kingship which Richard lacked.

Richard alienated the ruling class, was quite unreliable and partial, with no sense of justice, vindictive, self-pitying – and so followed the tragedy. Henry tricked him into surrender, by promises which he didn't mean to keep; but neither did Richard. 'This does not excuse Henry's treachery, but it makes it difficult to feel much sympathy for his victim. Like Charles I, Richard thought that his divine authority justified any duplicity.' When Richard's adherents attempted a *coup*, intending to scupper the new king and his family at Windsor, Richard's murder 'followed as a matter of course'.

What McFarlane's indefeasible commonsense saw was that it was all a matter of self-preservation: Henry could never have trusted such a man as Richard. What is of more general importance, this first-class historical mind saw that constitu-tional historians, especially if they are Victorian Liberals, attribute far too much logic to human events. McFarlane could cast a very cold eye upon humbug, pretentiousness, theoretical constructions, nonsense, as upon undergraduate impertinence.

But he had a warm side to him, and he does not fail to notice the loyalty and love that Henry's son – Shakespeare's 'Prince Hal' – felt for King Richard rather than for his father. Richard must have had personal charm for the boy.

All this is in keeping with traditional views, and it is obvious what respect this master-technician had for Shakespeare as a historian – whether of Richard II or Henry V or Richard III – with his marvellous understanding of human motives, as against third-rate popularisers who don't know what they are talking about.

The second half of the book rests on very specialist knowledge and techniques. McFarlane had found that Lollard sympathies were more widespread than anyone realised; that it represented increasing moral fervour of the laity as against the sacramental system of the Church – which could be dispensed with – a kind of Bible Christianity. Here he uncovers a group of knights, prominent at Court, several of them known to Chaucer, who were persecuted neither by Richard nor by Henry. Nor were the bishops anxious to persecute their fellows of the landowning class. It was only the 'lunatic fringe' who asked for trouble, and even they did not always get it.

There are two points on which I dare to confront the Master. The widespread underground existence of anti-Church feeling, anti-sacramental convictions, Bible reading, objection to image-worship, cults, pilgrimages, etc, went right up to and fused with the Reformation. Though this ultimately came about as the result of state-action, by Henry VIII in Parliament, nevertheless Lollardy was continuous with the Protestantism of the Reformation. McFarlane would not have this to be, refused to call his book 'Wyclif and the Reformation', and insisted on the title *Wyclif and the Beginnings of English Nonconformity*. Rather pedantic – like pronouncing all the places Henry V captured in France in the English way, in his lectures.

He has a wholly favourable summing up on Henry V, 'Take him all round and he was, I think, the greatest man that ever ruled England.' That could be: Henry was a wonderful man. But there is no mention of the horrible consequences of his conquest of France. It kept England entangled for a couple of decades, to be humiliatingly extruded in the end, after frightful depredations upon the French, and was a considerable factor in bringing on the Wars of the Roses.

Henry V was a great conqueror; but conquests in later history are apt to be temporary affairs, as with Louis XIV, Napoleon, and Hitler, made when other peoples are weak, to vanish when they recover. A sceptic of human action, like myself, wonders why they do it.

2

The most remarkable and unexpected work to come out of McFarlane's *Nachlass* is this book on the painter Memling.[3] We all knew that McFarlane was a great authority on fifteenth-century England, but this masterly fragment on the fifteenth-century Bruges painter is an extraordinary bonus. The editors tell us that it is 'only a shadow of the book he would have published'. Knowing him, this I take leave to doubt: he would have gone on accumulating more and more material and putting off the date of publication.

What we have is vintage McFarlane, absolutely first-class and fascinating to read; filled out with admirable notes by the editors and 153 illustrations, it makes a beautiful book. They have certainly done him proud. It contains all that McFarlane had to contribute to the subject.

That is sufficiently important in itself, for it is quite new and startling, and overturned the applecart for the art-authorities. What McFarlane discovered was that the famous Donne altar-piece in the National Gallery had been wrongly dated. That sounds simple enough, but it is the consequences that matter — for the interpretation and criticism of Memling's work, and even the implications for our conception of the late Middle Ages.

It had been assumed that Sir John Donne had been killed at Edgecote in 1469. McFarlane found out that it was his brother who was killed and that Sir John lived on until 1503;

[3] K. B. McFarlane, *Hans Memling*, ed. Edgar Wind and G. L. Harriss (Oxford University Press, 1972).

other circumstances too showed that the picture could not
have been painted before 1480. All this was mother's milk to
McFarlane, who knew more about fifteenth-century families
than anyone has ever done since.

But the consequences for the poor art-historians! ...

For they had erected whole constructions of art 'criticism'
upon a mistake, and stuck their necks out, for the McFarlane
guillotine to descend on them. I can imagine the pleasure it
gave him, from the sharp edge on the writing, for he really
detested, as I do, pretentious theoretical constructions
instead of ascertainable facts and valid inferences.

He certainly caught these large Teutonic authorities out,
without any clothes on. Based on the assumption that this
was an early work of Memling, they erected a baseless fabric
of 'criticism' about Memling's incapacity to develop, the
'static' quality of his work, etc. The pundit Friedländer was
able to discern, in his heavy German way, that the triptych's
'early style is betrayed mainly by the thin, anaemic and dry
treatment'. What a joke on him, when McFarlane discovered
that the work was an example of Memling's full maturity.

The sainted, and duly venerated, pontiff Panofsky made
even more of an ass of himself by depreciation of Memling
erected into a system, all based on a mistake. After a brilliant
detective investigation of facts and dates McFarlane – who
himself had a clear, cold eye for a picture, unclouded by
theory – concludes: 'that Memling should have produced an
isolated example of his maturest style of portraiture as early
as 1467–8, three or four years before the Portinari portraits,
ought never to have been entertained.'

He proceeds to make fools of these portentous 'critics' by
quoting their crushing condemnations of Memling, without
getting the facts right; for more is involved. He realised that
they had a Teutonic prejudice in favour of the tortured,
agonising, or extreme in late medieval art, for Grünewald,
Patinir, or Bosch, and a prejudice against the quiet perfec-
tionism, the classic balance and proportion, the controlled
feeling, the *still* beauty of Memling.

Here McFarlane's masterly taking these art-authorities down a peg or two, his merciless exposure of their pretentiousness, remind me of A. E. Housman, who had a similar dislike for the blown-up, the inflated, in German scholarship. (One commentator in *The Times* has already noticed the comparison with my attitude to the nonsense I have to put up with in making clear the chronology and commonsense of Shakespeare's Sonnets. But McFarlane and I, of exactly the same generation and outlook at Oxford, shared the historian's view of the primacy of fact over theory, and a real detestation of people having no conception of truth.) To the art-critic, as to the historian, McFarlane addresses a salutary word in his usual magisterial manner:

> To equate novelty with life is to adopt a needlessly philistine solution to every historian's inescapable problem: how to distinguish the significant from the trivial. No mere rule of thumb can relieve him from the need to exercise his own judgement and consider pictures, like other historical 'facts', on their merits.

The trouble here is that the ordinary historian has even less visual sense, or appreciation of art, than the art or literary critic has of historical fact. McFarlane, a first-rate historian, had both: this is what makes him so icily dismissive (and me so hotly contemptuous) of people with neither.

McFarlane's detective work led him to an even larger, and more important, general conclusion – against the current view of the later Middle Ages.

> We have been told to associate the waning of the Middle Ages with an hysterical fear of the Day of Judgement, a morbid pre-occupation with such themes as the Dance of Death and the eternal pains of hell, fascinated and realistically expressed disgust with the corruptions of the world of the flesh.

He then scores another bull's eye: 'it would be difficult to argue that Memling was out of tune with his times. Yet there is hardly a trace of such morbidity in his work.'

There you are: a true view of the later Middle Ages would need to include both. It is far better not to go in for these generalisations but to stick to fact, and on that basis, getting the facts right, to interpret rather than go in for theorising and 'criticism'.

How fortunate McFarlane has been in his editors, and how paradoxical to think that if he hadn't died we should probably not have had the book!

### 3

How lucky McFarlane was in his pupils! — there they all are working away like beavers at his papers, and producing the books he could never bring himself to finish. Here is another fine monument to the man who knew more about late medieval English society than anyone — a masterly book;[4] and there is to be yet a fourth from his *Nachlass*.

This volume deals chiefly with the nobility, the governing class who ran England in the later Middle Ages, people vastly more important and more interesting than the peasants so beloved of 'bourgeois historians' (his phrase, not mine). Characteristically enough, this governing class — presenting far more in the way of intellectual interest — had been much less treated, less *tackled*, perhaps because it presented greater technical difficulties. McFarlane was above all a technician, and did not burke tackling the problems again and again, from different angles and at various times. No one was more honest, and he was not afraid to confess when he changed his mind on some questions. This was one reason why he rarely brought his work to the point of publication. All the same, this book is as masterly as its predecessors, edited with like devotion and skill by his pupil, Mr J. P. Cooper.

As McFarlane's close friend over a longer period of time than anyone, I have my own evidence to offer, though not called upon to give it. With regard to his thesis on Cardinal

---

[4] K. B. McFarlane, *The Nobility of Later Medieval England* (Oxford University Press, 1973).

Beaufort's Finances, from which all his work exfoliated, he told me: 'They didn't work out.' Earlier statistics rarely do – a good reason for not placing so much reliance upon them as more naif historians do. Of his chapter on 'The Lancastrian Kings' in the *Cambridge Medieval History*, he said to me briefly, 'It is all wrong.'

His *Wyclif*, for my *Teach Yourself History* series (now *Men and their Times*), is certainly the volume that contains the most original research – so like him. All the same it is a curious production. Mr Cooper speaks, rightly, of its 'excessive indulgence' towards Archbishop Courtenay. There is no sympathy in it whatever for Wyclif – which surprised me, for after all Wyclif was struggling away from nonsense propositions towards a glimmer of rational sense. And from a Labour man – as McFarlane had become, following my lead in such matters – the book was surprisingly authoritarian.

The reason was partly that, while writing it, he had had to exercise authority himself as Vice-President at Magdalen. He portrayed Wyclif as a tiresome, querulous, eccentric don, always in a minority of one on the governing body, and told me that a colleague – very recognisable as such – had sat for the portrait.

Mr Cooper has unearthed the fact, which I did not know that anyone realised, that in those early formative years McFarlane got a great deal of his general intellectual position from my obsession with Marxism. Few would know that now – and what does it matter? – but mine was the dominating influence. Mr Cooper has been discerning enough to discover it, and honest enough to state it.

I was obsessively concerned with the Marxist approach to politics and history in the later 1920s and early 1930s, and this deeply influenced the work we were both to do. It might be described as sociological history, trying to treat history down through all the strata of society. Naturally our work diverged in accordance with temperament, interests, and gifts. My approach was descriptive, aesthetic, personal, I hope poetic; McFarlane's was analytical, administrative, technical.

(He was the son of a civil servant.) I have always wanted to probe into the innermost recesses of the life of the past; he wanted to find out how things worked. But we both believed in the supremacy of concrete fact, as against theorising, in commonsense as against conjecture, in absolute fidelity to truth.

McFarlane was a man of rigorous intellectual rectitude; his dominant quality an inspired commonsense; with the highest standards, he had no illusions whatever – he was above everything a no-nonsense man. He took a malicious pleasure in pricking the bubble of the inflated and the pretentious, in showing up when the emperors among his fellow-historians hadn't any clothes on. One after the other, they go over like ninepins. Here is Christopher Hill, writing that Henry VIII's Duke of Buckingham was powerful 'because he had many feudal dependants who would fight for him'. The opposite was the truth: 'they would not fight and he knew it. He himself chose death with dignity rather than a show of resistance.'

Here is G. R. Elton knocked out for saying, 'the treasurership became a magnate office, held for prestige reasons rather than for the purpose of doing the work, *as any list of Treasurers will show*'. McFarlane proceeds to show him, with dry irony: 'The argument, which appears to be circular, will not commend itself to those who have had cause to study the official (and unofficial) activities of such baronial Treasurers as Lords Roos, Furnival, Hungerford, and Cromwell.' McFarlane simply could not bear people laying down the law without knowing the facts. Professor Postan was a favourite whipping-boy for thesis-mongering – and then getting the facts wrong. Why theorise if you don't know? There is a crisp and stylish remark in McFarlane's first Ford lecture I remember hearing: 'We historians have been very free with our views; it would be nice for a change to know.'

Then there is the question of bias. The impeccable Powicke – who wanted McFarlane to succeed him as Regius Professor, and how much better things would have been at Oxford if he had! – is given a prim rebuke for skating over Edward I's shocking treatment of no less than six noble families to scupper their inheritances for his own kith and kin. The English Justinian indeed! – 'Powicke has allowed himself to play down the unscrupulousness with which Edward pursued his dynastic aims – and still more the justice of the resentment aroused by some of the uglier strokes by which he gained his ends.' Mr Cooper says well that McFarlane 'did not lose his eye for injustice'; he says nothing about the undoubted pleasure he took in catching people out. Was there not something psychotic about that? In his inability to finish his own books, and in his envious attitude towards those who could?

He was anxious that justice should at least be done to people in the past, in particular to the medieval nobility, the governing class – the main theme of this book. He saw how silly, how irresponsible, it was of Galbraith to say that 'in the Middle Ages the members of the ruling class were in general men of arrested intellectual development, who looked to those below them in the social scale for the intelligence necessary to order and govern society.'

That may be a Balliol view, but it is nonsense nevertheless. Throughout this book McFarlane is at pains to explore the facts and expose the truth that the magnates who ran society were there because of their capacity to do so. Grandees who could not run their own affairs soon lost out in the race. They were no less able, on average, than the kings: primogeniture turned up nitwits and misfits among the monarchs (witness Edward II or Richard II) no less than among their nobles. This led him to make a general point of some importance for historiography – that most historians have a bias in their work in favour of the Crown. We may all be a bit guilty, but I suspect that medievalists may be rather more royalist than modernists are.

What emerges at every point from this master-technician's survey of late medieval society is the reduction of it all – constitutional vapourising, theoretical fantasying – to the commonsense facts of life. The nobility earned its keep, and its privileges, by a life of service, civil and military. They did not seek to be at cross-purposes with monarchs always in the right: some monarchs were difficult, or impossible, to work with. The nobility naturally preferred to co-operate in the work (and the gains) of government. But it was for the monarch to provide the driving force of government – if he couldn't, the machine faltered along for a bit, then broke down.

In one of his last papers McFarlane was not afraid to show that he had changed his mind about the cause of the Wars of the Roses. Earlier he had put them down to some fashionable secondary consideration: 'it was war finance that caused the Wars of the Roses, if any one factor is sufficient to explain them.' In his last years the simple fact stood out clear: if it had not been for the imbecility of the monarch, Henry VI, the breakdown of order in society need not have occurred. The old-fashioned explanation in terms of the personality of the monarch was quite sufficient (as it is with Edward II, or Charles I; James II or Edward VIII). Yet, when I made this simple point in my *Bosworth Field* I was reproved by some ass of a young historian for writing my book 'as if McFarlane had never existed' – with whom I had discussed history constantly over thiry years!

The general point is familiar enough to modern historians. Then what was so original about McFarlane in making the obvious commonsense of it clear? Well, in the first place academics, unlike detectives, often miss the significance of the obvious (as I have found in explaining the commonsense facts behind Shakespeare's Sonnets). Secondly, there is the sheer difficulty of interpreting medieval evidence, often so fragmentary and inconclusive. Here he was the supreme technician among later medievalists.

If I may dare to query the master on his own ground, I do not think he need have been at such pains to prove the literacy of the late medieval nobility. A little more imagination, a little less of the academic, and he would have realised that men do not have to be literate to be intelligent. Henry VIII's Earl of Pembroke could not write – but he was a very able servant of the Crown. It was Renaissance humanism that placed such a high value on education for courtiers. In the next generation the Elizabethans sent young peers to the university. And this was a new emphasis, a difference marking it off from McFarlane's medieval nobility.

But why was it that such a master – who wrote so well when he put pencil (not pen) to paper – could not finish his own work? Mr Cooper tells us that 'this turning away from earlier projects was partly a matter of temperament, of an inability to bring long-term projects to what he regarded as a worthwhile conclusion'. But there seems to have been something psychotic about it. Mr Cooper knows that he was 'seriously ill' in the summer before tackling the chapter in the *Cambridge Medieval History*. Does he know that it was a nervous breakdown? From which McFarlane was rescued by the distinguished practitioner, Helena Wright, wife of a surgeon whom McFarlane later brought in to rescue me when at death's door.

In reading this remarkable book, so skilfully put together by a pupil, I cannot but be touched to be once more in company with, hear the recognisable voice of, my dead friend.

# Private Lives of Tudor Monarchs[1]

The Renaissance saw a remarkable development in the art of portraiture – we are reminded of that by Holbein's achieve-

[1] Foreword to Christopher Falkus, *The Private Lives of the Tudor Monarchs* (Folio Society, 1974).

ment in depicting the denizens of Henry VIII's Court. There had been nothing like it before in England. The same increased awareness of men's individual personalities and characteristics is witnessed in historical writing and literature. Before this, even with those much exposed figures, monarchs and royal persons, it is often hard to come at what they were like as human beings, their private lives.

The point is borne home by the contrast between the first Tudor sovereign, Henry VII and his son, Henry VIII. The first Tudor was not only reserved and secretive, giving nothing away though under constant observation from his position, but there is little enough of a personal character reported on him, still less by himself. We have to construct our picture of him from the traces left of him in the documents, from his politic actions and his day-to-day activities.

These last are more personally revealing, and somewhat surprising. They show Henry VII as rather more extrovert than people conceived, in lighter mood than the severe and cunning statesman, playing at tennis, practising archery, hunting — more of an out-of-doors man than we had imagined; and the miserly king seems to have lost a good deal at cards.

Then there was music. We must never forget how large a part music played in their lives, instruments, singing, dancing. There are constant payments in Henry's accounts for lute, harp, recorders, to minstrels, pipers, tumblers, jesters, players. I am intrigued by the considerable reward to 'one Cornish for a prophecy': I suspect that that was to William Cornish, of the family of leading musicians and makers of pageants and interludes at Henry and his son's Court. But what did the prophecy say? — how much one would like to know. Only once is the veil drawn fully aside, and we see Henry and his wife, Elizabeth of York, prostrated by grief at the death of their son, Prince Arthur, and sending for each other for consolation.

In the next generation, with Henry VIII, we mark the change from medieval to modern. For all his political secrecy — 'If I thought my cap knew my secrets I would throw it into the fire' — he stands fully revealed to us as a man. We come upon him maying in the woods in the glad Maytime of his youth, or coming in from tennis, the fringe of red-gold hair showing above his cambric shirt. A healthy sportsman, he took women in his stride, like Bess Blount here — he was not besotted on them like his Yorkist grandfather, Edward IV, after whom Henry chiefly took, or his rival Francis I, of whom he was jealous, monarch of a bigger realm.

It is good to have the most intimate records Henry left of himself, his love letters to Anne Boleyn — totally omitted in his latest 'biography'. We see that he was passionately in love with her, her French elegance — compared with the dowdiness of the Queen, her spiritedness and intelligence: all the more because she kept him at bay so long and was never in love with *him,* merely with his crown. Poor Queen Catherine took the point when she said, 'My Lady Anne, you have good hap to stop at a king; but you are not like others: you will have all or nothing'.

Henry took an almighty revenge when his love turned to hatred, for the frightful dance she had led him and the inextricable knot of trouble in which it involved him. The clue to dealing with him was always to give way, as Cranmer did, and as Anne of Cleves very sensibly did — 'the great Flanders mare' as he ungallantly called the German *hausfrau* that she was. Having submitted, she was then treated very generously: she did well out of it.

For this book points up a theme one must remember in considering these royal persons — the inhuman pressures to which they were subjected, the frequent crises political, dynastic and personal, the constant demands of everybody upon them all the time. In quite recent history George V once said to Queen Mary, 'we are not supposed to be human.' Queen Mary accepted the position: 'we are set apart'. This was what Edward VIII could not stand; but after all it was his *raison d'être*: so he became Duke of Windsor. Elizabeth I once alluded to the burden, in approaching age: 'to be a king and wear a crown is a thing more glorious to them that see it than it is pleasant to them that bear it'. One can sympathise, in more senses than one, with Henry VIII, writing in the midst of the daily business of kingship to Anne Boleyn: 'I would we were together of an evening.'

The boy-king Edward VI had boyish spirits enough until his final illness came upon him. A contemporary poem describes him playing hide-and-seek with his companion, Nicholas Throckmorton and, catching sight of him lying behind a great chest, Edward suddenly dubbed him knight. Or one sympathises with him in the political crisis of his uncle, Protector Somerset's fall, being dragged out of bed at Hampton Court in the middle of the night to be carried off to Windsor Castle: 'Methinks I am in prison: here be no galleries nor gardens to walk in.'

Mary Tudor's personality comes across to us clearly enough: the dinky little woman with her deep voice (unlike her father's and sister's), her stubborn opposition to him until forced to obey, her Spanish pride, her royal snub to Protector Somerset's brother who sought her advocacy in his suit to marry Henry VIII's widow, the Queen Dowager: 'If the remembrance of the King's Majesty my father (whose soul God pardon) will not suffer her to grant your suit, I am nothing able to persuade her to forget the loss of him who is as yet very ripe in mine own remembrance.' What reason she had indeed to remember him!

Best known of them all is Elizabeth I, with the progress of time and its greater expressiveness and from the span of years in which the dazzling light of the sun beat upon her – even so there remain some secrets. It is good to have her education described, for she was a precociously intelligent child and grew up to be something of a blue-stocking. She was particularly gifted at languages, as her monument in Westminster Abbey records. She found great pleasure in reading, her godson Sir John Harington tells us, often taking to a book to quieten her mind after passions were roused and tempers ruffled in council (I find reading a useful remedy too: people might try it more).

What a complex personality hers was! – many facets of it are revealed in these documents. There is the royal impinging upon the personal, the leading theme of this book. We observe her exhibitionism – playing to the gallery is a necessary art for public persons; we see her performing on the virginals to impress the Scottish ambassador, comparing her charms and aptitudes with those of the younger Mary Queen of Scots. (Elizabeth was rather less royal than the latter – and the better for it).

We can appreciate the majestic consolation offered to her old friend, Lady Norris – 'Mine own Crow' (who was very dark) – on the death of yet another soldier-son in her service. A humorous letter about Leicester's diet is a joke on his appetite: he was a big eater, where Elizabeth was very sparing in her diet. A good deal of comedy may be extracted from all the sparring about marrying Catherine de Medici's son, Anjou, who was years younger: offsetting her admission of 'excess of years' with 'such kingdoms as we have' and the unspoken confidence that he would not find her person too old for him if he came to see for himself! (Walsingham said that she was 'still the best match in her parish'.)

We are in luck to have so close-up a portrayal of her as we get from her godson: the alternations of temper by which she kept everybody on his toes, an essential kindness of disposition when people were reasonable, a royal wrath when obedience was lacking, to remind people 'whose daughter she was'. She could never be taken for granted – indeed she could not afford to be – so that it was not easy 'to find her right humour'.

Harington describes for us the sadness of the woman in her last days, after Essex's execution who should have been a son to her, and cruel necessity forced her to execute him. Her godson's presence reminded her of Essex, and she broke down in tears. 'When thou dost feel creeping time at thy gate . . .' The mask is dropped; the woman contemplating her end comes through.

# Henry VIII

1

It has been amusing to observe the reception of this book by the Sunday reviewers.[1] Awe-struck perhaps by its length and breadth and scholarship, they have settled for it as 'the standard' biography of Henry. This it is not, and anyway they would not know. Mr Scarisbrick offers it, more modestly, as 'neither a private life of Henry VIII, nor a comprehensive study of his life and times. Rather, it is something in between'. Actually, it is a little difficult to say what it is; good in some respects, especially in matters of detail, unsatisfactory in others. Its main defect seems to be inadequate intellectual grasp of the whole; from this arises the uncertainty in intention and execution.

Let us say, first, what is good about it. Mr Scarisbrick, thank heaven, has no thesis to urge. Thesis-pushing is the bane of contemporary historical writing: it distorts (and spoils) some of the good work done by Trevor-Roper, Elton, Stone and Hill. Pushing some thesis or other is contrary to the nature of history; Mr Scarisbrick is content to follow where the evidence leads him, and so does better and is more reliable. He even faults A. F. Pollard for urging the thesis that Wolsey's combination of spiritual and temporal authority paved the way for the Royal Supremacy — and Mr Scarisbrick is right. He is just and even generous in his estimate of Wolsey, and that too is a correct emphasis. Wolsey has been a much maligned man, unpopular with historians incapable of seeing much below the surface, of appreciating the immense ability, the political penetration, the organising capacity, the grasp. Wolsey carried the burden for the first half of Henry's reign. All the same, Mr Scarisbrick is insufficiently critical: there were contemporaries of good will who wanted Wolsey

[1] J. J. Scarisbrick, *Henry VIII* (Eyre and Spottiswoode, 1968).

to address his immense powers and capacities to reforms in Church and State, instead of wasting so much time and energy on cutting continental capers really beyond the strength and resources of the little country that England was: she could not much affect the issues in the grand Habsburg-Valois struggle, let alone decide them. Granted that all this appealed to Henry's colossal exhibitionism and egoism, for which Wolsey had to provide some outlet: it was a prime condition of his own exercise of power.

In matters of detail Mr Scarisbrick gives us several new insights. The Field of Cloth of Gold was, of course, exorbitantly wasteful; but he points out that it was something that the two chivalries of France and England were meeting to joust and dance and feast, not to fight. He tells us that it was Henry, not Wolsey, who urged on his candidature for the Papacy; and, more important, he argues that Wolsey's line about the divorce from Catherine offered at least a better prospect of success than Henry's obstinate, blundering fixation on the Levitical line, the sin of marrying his brother's wife. The whole business of the divorce was bungled from beginning to end; Mr Scarisbrick gives us a convincing account of the inextricable tangle. But there is no need for a whole chapter on the Canon Law of the matter — a brief summary would have been enough. For a less naif view of history brings home the fact that human beings can always think up arguments to justify what they want: a clear realisation of this obviates the necessity of a lot of historical argumentation (about the Intellectual Origins of the Civil War, for example). One just does not have to take all that seriously the smoke-screen that people put up: one sees through it. So that one does not need again a whole chapter on the Theology of the Royal Supremacy. It is true that Henry fancied himself on his theology, and just enough to illustrate that would have been enough. In history it is the facts and what happened that matter.

Now, in justice, for some of the defects. It is extraordinary, in a biography of Henry, not to realise where so many of his characteristics, physical and mental, came from. He was hardly at all like his Tudor father, Henry VII, introvert, cautious, prudent, financially and in every way. The son turned after his Yorkist grandfather, Edward IV, in bulk, physical characteristics, an extrovert nature given to sports, taking women in his stride, impulsive and dynamic, the Yorkist strain of cruelty. Not to see this shows lack of imagination; it is far more obvious than the crude psychologising, 'possibly he had an Oedipus complex: and possibly from this derived a desire for, yet horror of, incest, which may have shaped some of his sexual life.' Apart from this, Mr Scarisbrick's estimate of Henry's sex-life is quite sensible.

Mr Scarisbrick emphasises the splendour of Henry's frame and physique; but there was obviously something wrong with him, with all that swollen obesity, some glandular complaint, in addition to the varicose ulcers on his leg. It seems simply commonsense to suppose that the pain he suffered at times contributed to the spasms of cruelty – from which Mr Scarisbrick lets Henry off too lightly. There is no letting him off the deaths of More and Cromwell, on one side or the other. On the other hand, Mr Scarisbrick thinks that Anne Boleyn was not guilty of adultery. 'Is it credible that, as has been suggested, adultery was the last throw of a woman who despaired of conceiving a son and took to this extreme in order to disguise her failure (which was probably not hers anyway)?' Mr Scarisbrick asks 'would she have been so extravagantly indiscreet as her accusers alleged?' Though this was precisely what her cousin, Catherine Howard, was and did, by everyone's admission. I do not feel that Mr Scarisbrick has much grasp of the modes and morals of a Renaissance Court. When he comes to the misconduct of Catherine Howard, he misses the crucial point of the necessity to have the succession certain and unquestionable. It is not just simply that 'Catherine was a woman, and a masculine world required that she must overlook in him what he must denounce in her'. In all aristocratic societies in history, but especially in royal families, a stricter rule has always applied to the females, for obvious biological reasons.

Again, fancy in a study of Henry VIII omitting his love-letters to Anne Boleyn, the most intimate and revealing things he ever wrote! And crucial to the understanding of the complex story — mostly omitted, by the way — of his relations with the woman he passionately loved and his revenge upon her for her coldness to him, her arrogance, the wound she inflicted upon his sensitive self-esteem. Again and again opportunities are missed of bringing Henry before us as contemporaries saw him; such as, for instance, the characteristic glimpses of him in Puttenham's *Art of English Poesy* (from someone who clearly knew Henry's Court well), or strewn across the *Letters and Papers*.

Professor David Knowles, who wrote the one qualified review the book has so far received, considered that there was far too much about foreign policy, the sterile exchanges of diplomacy, in the book. I agree, and there is far too much of the dead argumentation beloved of academics. The aim of historical writing, particularly in a biography, should be to recapture the life of the subject. There are a few perfunctory paragraphs on Henry's interest in music and his building: no real perception that, after Charles I, he was the greatest patron of the arts of all English monarchs. Yet a good deal about all this has been uncovered in recent books by Miss Auerbach, Dr Roy Strong, Sir John Summerson, and Mr Shelby who has written of Henry's passionate interest in military engineering, besides that in naval shipbuilding, we may add. But, then, few historians have much aesthetic perception.

T. S. Eliot once called attention to the 'fundamental brain work' necessary to the writing of poetry; it is still more necessary to the historian, and no amount of detailed scholastic research can dispense with it. In spite of having read the book with some profit and more pleasure — though it is not written with much literary sensibility, let alone subtlety — it cannot be regarded as wholly satisfactory, certainly not a 'standard' biography: it remains, as the author saw better than his reviewers, 'something in between'.

2

With this book[2] Baldwin Smith succeeds to the place of
Garrett Mattingly as our best Tudor historian in America.
Mattingly wrote the standard biography of Catherine of
Aragon, cause of Henry VIII's matrimonial troubles. Now
Baldwin Smith has written the most illuminating book about
the old tyrant — and one of England's ablest kings — that has
appeared. Baldwin Smith really has the clue to Henry and in
this portrait has *got* him as no one has ever quite captured
him before.

The fascinating thing is to observe how different Henry
really was from the popular idea of him. Or, rather, the
psychological truth is more subtle; for he was what he
appears on the surface, 'Bluff King Hal' — in spite of
everything he always had the gift of popularity — and yet,
underneath, there was a terrifying man, with the pounce of a
tiger, as cruel and almost as capricious.

He is rather like Stalin — and at one point Baldwin Smith
suggests the comparison. How those two cousins, Anne
Boleyn and Catherine Howard, could have taken such risks
with such a man astonishes one. But here, too, the public
doesn't know the truth. It never has known what Anne
Boleyn told the French ambassador — that Henry wasn't a
good performer in bed. Baldwin Smith tells us that Anne and
her brother laughed at Henry's 'lack of potency and
staying-power'. Hence he struck down both when the time
came. Anne and her brother paid for it with their lives,
charged with incest.

In spite of all his marriages, Henry was rather prudish,
'uncomfortable with smut and easily embarrassed by sex.'
This is true. There is a vast contrast between Henry's Court
and the French Court (in which Anne Boleyn had graduated)
where Francis I was riddled with syphilis, which brought the
Valois dynasty to its end.

Henry was, of course, a *faux-bonhomme*, as Sir Thomas
More well knew. When More was in favour and the King

[2] Lacey Baldwin Smith, *Henry VII* (Cape, 1971).

needed him politically, he would visit More at Chelsea and walk in his garden with great condescension with his arm round More's neck. It was an ominous gesture. 'For, if my head could purchase him a castle in France', said More, 'it should not fail to fall.' And it did, along with many other eminent heads.

For Henry believed, like Stalin, in ruling by fear; 'for it is the nature of the many to be amenable to fear', he said, 'but not to the sense of honour'. Each of them would have said that it was only thus that a country could be held together through a revolution. And, in fact, when the hand of 'the old man' — as the Henry of this book came to call himself — was removed the country fell apart.

The subject here is the Henry of the last decade of his rule, and this makes a more original book. For one thing, we have had enough of the Divorce and the breach with the Papacy; for another, the author thinks that, as with Churchill, age stripped away the earlier integuments and revealed the essential man. Here he is as the French ambassador saw him: 'He is a man to be marvelled at and has wonderful people about him. He is an old fox, proud as the devil and accustomed to ruling.'

He was more like a great cat, playing cat and mouse with the very able people who served him. He knew how to make use of them. He kept out of his will the ambitious Bishop Gardiner — through his illegitimate mother, a cousin of the King, and grandson of old Jasper Tudor, Henry VII's uncle. Henry said of Gardiner, characteristically: 'Marry, I myself could use him, and rule him to all manner of purposes as seemed good unto me; but so shall you never do.'

We are given penetrating character-sketches of these remarkable men around the death-bed, and a most revealing discussion of Henry's will. 'All the facets of Henry Tudor were focused on those twenty-eight pages of parchment: his love of pedantry and detail; his concern for conscience and his self-confident alliance with God; his ritualistic approach to religion; his emotional precipitousness; his innate caution and deep insecurity; his discomfort with final decisions; above all, his need to "show his absolute power".'

One criticism of importance, and a marked contrast with the philistine Stalin, typical of our time. Few historians are aesthetes, and we must not forget that this terrifying ruler was an accomplished musician and composer, the builder of Hampton Court, Whitehall and fantastic Nonsuch, a royal patron of the arts and of Holbein, in whose portraits Henry VIII's Court lives for ever.

# Cardinal Wolsey

Cardinal Wolsey (1471–1530) governed England for the first half of Henry VIII's reign, and was the most spectacular statesman the English have produced. In addition to wielding secular power, he possessed the advantage of being a Roman Cardinal who got the Pope to make him legate for life. This concentration of secular and spiritual power was unprecedented: it enabled Wolsey to move on the European stage the apparent equal of kings and emperors. By his diplomatic ability he raised his small country to an eminence that her intrinsic resources did not justify. His possession of power in State and Church could not stave off the Reformation; indeed, his fall precipitated the collapse of the Church's power. The whole fabric of his policy, international as well as national, crashed in ruins around him.

This makes for one of the most dramatic careers in history, and it is probable that most of us know Wolsey best from Shakespeare's dramatic portrait of him in *Henry VIII*. This is no bad source, for with his justice of mind Shakespeare gives us the essence of the man and his tragic fall. Professor

Ferguson's title[1] comes from Wolsey's last words as phrased by Shakespeare:

> Had I but served my God with half the zeal
> I served my king, He would not in mine age
> Have left me naked to mine enemies.

Yet why has Wolsey come down in our historical tradition as so unpopular a figure? It must be that we are allergic to the grand in our public men; we do not like arrogant, masterful types. The French do not seem to have borne so hardly on Cardinal Richelieu — perhaps the closest parallel to Wolsey in career and type. And we seem to have forgiven William Pitt, Earl of Chatham, than whom no one was more haughty and masterful. Both Protestants and Catholics were hostile to Wolsey, for different reasons, in their respective traditions. But is Wolsey's unpopularity in history altogether justified? I think not. In the first place, we must remember that his arrogance was chiefly directed against the Tudor grandees of Henry VIII's court, the Dukes of Norfolk and Suffolk — a most insufferable lot. The Cardinal was more considerate and charitable, especially where poor folk were concerned. As Lord Chancellor he consistently aimed at protecting little people from the depredations of the great. He earned the hatred of the latter, nobles and gentry alike, by his endeavors to hold up the process of enclosure that was forcing the peasantry off the land.

Then, too, Wolsey was a tolerant man. During the period when he wielded supreme power, no one was burnt for heresy — in itself a remarkable record. Under his successor as Lord Chancellor, the saintly Thomas More, burnings were hotted up. Wolsey, who was essentially an administrator, a politician, did not attach so much importance to people's opinions. He let off the brilliant musician John Taverner — composer of the exquisite 'O Western Wynde' Mass — who was tinged with Lutheranism, on the ground that he was only

[1] C. W. Ferguson, *Naked to Mine Enemies: The Life of Cardinal Wolsey* (Longman, 1958; Little, 1973).

a music-man. If there had only been more of this spirit, the sixteenth century would have been an altogether happier epoch.

Lastly, there was his passionate concern for education, particularly that poor men's sons should get a chance. When the town of Tonbridge objected to his dissolving a small friary in order to found a school, the Cardinal asked them whether it would be better to have 'forty children of that country [that is, county] educated and after sent to Oxford' than to have six or seven canons living among them.

On Wolsey's fall Henry VIII quashed the splendid school at Ipswich that Wolsey was building and took its property. With his noble foundation at Oxford it was a near thing, though ultimately the college emerged, somewhat shorn, as Christ Church, a living memento of Wolsey's magnificence and his belief in education. An old scholar of his college, I am grateful to his beneficence and glad that he should receive justice. It is the prime merit of Mr Ferguson's biography that he penetrates into Wolsey's personality with more sympathy and understanding than has any other biographer. Sympathy and insight, added to scholarliness and judgement, make this a good biography.

In recent years we have learned from local records in Suffolk more about Thomas Wolsey's origins: we know that they were as low as his enemies said they were:

Born by butcher, but by bishop bred,
How high his Highness heaves his haughty head.

His father was an unrespectable butcher at Ipswich who was early in trouble with the town authorities for giving short weight, selling bad meat and at one time keeping a disorderly house. The son emancipated himself the classic way, via Oxford and the Church. He was a precocious scholar, the 'boy bachelor', taking his degree very early, and then as bursar of his college, Magdalen, showing those administrative talents that made his career – the famous Magdalen tower was finished while he was bursar. (The tower is a Somerset tower in type, probably built by Somerset workmen, and Wolsey's first benefice was in Somerset.)

Wolsey was over thirty before he was taken up by Henry VII, and nearly forty before he became Henry VIII's chief Minister. That is to say, his life was more than half over: such frustration and long waiting are often a recipe for unrestrained ambition and arrogance when the chance comes — Sir Walter Ralegh is another case in point.

Mr Ferguson understands the psychological motivation of all the magnificence and the histrionic element in the Cardinal's make-up. 'He had the pride of a man who is afraid other men will forget his worth.' (Or is not 'vanity' the word rather than 'pride'? — a proud man would not bother.) 'It revealed the defiant insecurity of his nature and his need as an Ipswich yokel to be constantly reassured and propped.' ('Yokel' is not the right word, but the point is a valid one.)

In short, Wolsey's exhibitionism and ostentation were by way of over-compensating for the squalor of his origins. Inwardly there must have been a feeling of insecurity, which shored itself up and took shape in his mania for building. He simply could not stop building — in that, too, he was like Richelieu. There was the palace at Whitehall, besides many manors and houses — and we still have Hampton Court and Christ Church. We must remember, however, the impulse of the age — this was the Renaissance, and Wolsey was by nature and inspiration an artist.

And what a fabric of a career he proceeded to erect! Though it all crashed in resounding ruin at the end, for a decade and a half the butcher's son governed England and was a prime figure in the Europe of the Renaissance. We must never forget his inordinate ability — he was inordinate in everything, a glutton for power as for work. When the fabric of his international policy was falling to pieces after Pavia and the fall of France, Wolsey was at Arras trying to patch things together. His confidential servant, George Cavendish, who always loved him, tells us that the great man remained in his chamber one day, writing for sixteen hours, without a break. Wolsey was capable of eliciting affection and loyalty – Thomas Cromwell was loyal to him to the end; Henry VIII was more attached to him than to any other of his servants.

We must remember not only Wolsey's immense ability – and plausibility: he was a persuasive and artful orator – but the conditions within which he worked. Henry VIII was, above all things, wilful – and not necessarily wrong: Wolsey said that he had often knelt to the King for hours, and that with tears, trying to move him from his will. It seems that Wolsey had a simpler and more effective remedy for the imbroglio over Catherine of Aragon: if it was no marriage in the first place, then marry Anne and get on with it – i.e. the production of an heir. It seems to have been Henry's legalistic mind with its fixation on *Leviticus* that produced the inextricable complications and confusion.

No doubt, by then Wolsey had had his day – and rather missed his chance as a reformer: the Cardinal may be said to have set the model for the suppression of redundant monasteries, for the better purposes of education. And he had to go along with his monarch's rather adolescent desire to cut a figure in France – another condition of the retention of power. (What some statesmen have had to put up with from some monarchs!)

He was caught in the insoluble dilemmas of government and diplomacy, of the onset of the Reformation – between Henry VIII's need of an heir and the conservative forces of the old order, between the nationalism of the English and loyalty to the universal Church. It was his failure to obtain from the Pope an annulment of the King's marriage to Catherine of Aragon that chiefly led to his fall. There was his ultimate fidelity to the last: by throwing over the universal ideal could he have saved himself as King's minister? But that was unthinkable, and indeed impossible for him. A new deal was necessary – and a new man to carry it out: it is ironic, and yet in a way appropriate, that the man who ultimately took over and carried the necessary work forward had been

trained up by the Cardinal, the ablest and most faithful of his
agents: Thomas Cromwell. Under revolutionary appearances
there is often continuity.

# Thomas Cromwell as Reformer

An admirable blurb gives one – more completely and succinctly than most reviews – the purpose of this book.[1]

It is to discuss Thomas Cromwell's intentions and achievements as a reformer, particularly in the realm of economic
matters and in regard to the law. These lectures complete and
correct Professor Elton's earlier exaggerated emphasis on
what he called the Tudor 'Revolution' in government. He
now concludes that Cromwell's 'cast of mind was less
determinedly secular and less ruthlessly radical than I had
once supposed'.

This is an honest withdrawal, but it shows once more the
dangers of thesis-history, as I am always urging. Professor
Elton's mature view of Cromwell is more convincing, and I
am happy to be in agreement with him. He sees the great man as
not an Erasmian humanist, but a reformer with Protestant
inclinations. This, after all, is but a return to the traditional
English view. What is chiefly new is that it brings out the
intellectual interests of this largely self-educated man: fluent
in both French and Italian, able to read Latin, with the
statistical turn of mind that made him ordain the keeping of
parish registers. Then there was his interest in books and
writers, if with an eye on them for the uses of government;
and moreover in the scriptures – the ordering of the English

[1] G. R. Elton, *Reform and Renewal: Thomas Cromwell and the Commonwealth*
(Cambridge University Press, 1973).

Bible into the churches 'should after all be regarded as his monument'.

We are now presented with a Cromwell who was more of a middle-of-the-road man, leading – shall we say – from Left Centre, and more of a pragmatist. But then any practical politician has to be a pragmatist – as against the doctrinaires and intellectuals, a Stephen Vaughan and a Starkey, who urged him on the road of reform. Several of these elect, if self-elect, spirits looked to Cromwell to reform the common-weal. But so had some men, Richard Fox notably, looked to Wolsey. In the event, Cromwell was almost as much frustrated and defeated, by the facts of human nature, the power of vested interests, the sheer selfishness of men, the opposition of King or Parliament.

It is the usual story, the essence of politics – the inability to carry through what is obviously right and desirable in the common interest. Cromwell did what he could, as he pleaded in his call for mercy from a merciless master. 'And what does it all amount to? The large schemes of new institutions and organisations to find work for the unemployed, provide a proper enforcement of regulations, and convert the wealth of the Church to national purposes, all came to little or nothing.'

This book is not concerned with the great work Cromwell did achieve – the dissolution of the monasteries and the release of most of that wealth for secular purposes. Though some of the details offer rather small beer and 'a total tally fell well short of what had been intended', we need not doubt the conclusion: 'in Thomas Cromwell a sincere passion for reform combined with a singular ability to get things done'.

We could well have sacrificed some of the historiographical onslaughts for revealing insights into the man. No doubt Professor Elton is right against Pollard's view of the part played by Parliament and has 'laid the spectre of Henry VIII's subservient Parliaments, rubber-stamping all that was put before them' – we know that that was very far from the case: the governing class did not stand for anything that was not in their interest, defeating Cromwell, as they had done Wolsey, over enclosures and rural depopulation, for example. McConica's book is convicted of 'an excessive addiction to pattern-making', is 'misleading', and we are treated to a page of his 'factual errors'. Ferguson 'falls victim to it to a lesser extent'; excessive schematisation 'afflicts Jones'; even Zeefeld 'writes as though he was unaware of the profound transformation in historical thinking he was initiating'. As with Leavis in literary criticism, this is academicism, not artistry.

We could have dispensed with much of this for a missing shaft of light. In 1535 Cromwell thought Rastell 'a suitable man for the hopeless task of proselytising among the London Carthusians'. Next year Henry VIII commented to Sir Ralph Sadler that 'the Charterhouse in London is not ordered as I would have it', and that he had commanded Cromwell long ago to put the monks out of the house. Cromwell had been too lenient and written that they had submitted; but Henry would not now accept their obedience 'seeing they had been so long obstinate'.

This significant exchange has the advantage of showing up which was the moderate and which the brutal in the suppression of the monasteries. It is worth whole pages of argumentation about other professors' views on this and that.

# Utopia versus Realism

Professor J. H. Hexter is the most interesting historian writing in America. His achievement does not put him in the class of Samuel Eliot Morison; he is rather the successor of Carl Becker — an ideas-man, concerned to discuss historical ideas, rather than to write straight narrative history.

In these discursive essays[1] Hexter has a subject that appeals: they pivot upon Sir Thomas More's *Utopia*, about which far too much has been written, both by partisans and sectarians, neither class particularly intelligent. Not so with this book: I find it the most illuminating I have read on the subject (most books about *Utopia* can be disregarded). Hexter is right to underline the close sympathy between More and Erasmus in their view of society, their detestation of war and the military aristocracy whose vocational occupation it was; in their views on education, their Christian humanism, their dislike of scholasticism and propagation of the new Renaissance ideals of learning, attention to the text of Scripture no less than the classics, in place of mountains of medieval commentary; in their preference for Greek. And also in their view of Christianity as a way of life. Catholic commentators from the first underplayed More's close association with Erasmus – the Catholic martyr with the ambivalent intellectual who was half-way to Luther. It is true that, later, their paths somewhat diverged: the different circumstances in which More found himself with the progress of Lutheranism in England forced him into reaction and persecution.

Even Hexter, good as he is, does not bring out the contrast between the young More, idealistic and hopeful, and the older More, frightened of the future, savage defender of the past. Nor does he realise that *Utopia* is the work of a youngish man – it is possible to take the *jeu d'esprit* too seriously; the facts of life, politically and socially, were far harsher, as he learned on the way to the scaffold. Not that either More or Erasmus had illusions – but earlier they had hopes.

More's condemnation of the military aristocracy of the time was understandable in a middle-class intellectual; all the same, this governing class was the fundamental fact of social

[1] J. H. Hexter, *The Vision of Politics on the Eve of the Reformation: More, Machiavelli and Seyssel* (Allen Lane, 1973).

life. To be more exact – it was an aristocracy based on land, whose social function was to fight, to defend the country and maintain order within it. Hexter does not see far enough into the nature of society or the nature of human beings: they *are* fundamentally aggressive, the law of life is the struggle for survival, with human as with other animals. From this point of view, the man of ideas doesn't see what the practical politician in history does – that sometimes it is advisable to give the fighting fools their head in a foreign war, to deflect them from making trouble at home. This is the kind of thing that a realist like Machiavelli well understood.

But the Yale professor, with a recognisable brand of American naïveté – especially where monarchs are concerned – does not. 'Henry VIII was the very model of the predatory leader of a predatory semi-ruling class; he was magnificent, splendid, spendthrift, idle, envious, treacherous, rapacious, and stupidly and stupefyingly vain-glorious.' This is the less important part of the truth; the omission of what is more important makes it a superficial and stupid judgement. In fact, Henry was so able a political leader that he carried his country through a revolution, making it far stronger in the process. One of the conditions of the practical politician's success is that he should be sufficiently one with his governing class to be able to lead them. It is perfectly true that Henry liked his *Chevauchées* into France too much, but they do not seem to have damaged his own country (or France) much.

Poor Elizabeth I is derided for the opposite quality. 'Even when Elizabeth was dragged kicking, and screaming into Europe's religious wars . . .' Two comments on this: (1) Elizabeth was a woman of peace, and capitulated only to the absolute necessity of saving Dutch independence from Philip II. (2) In fact European Protestantism was saved – not by the Calvinists, as Hexter supposes, but by the power of England and English aid, as Philip realised. The professor doesn't see the significance of the circle of councillors around

Elizabeth, when he singles out those most sympathetic to Puritanism: Mildmay, Knollys, Walsingham. Except for the last, these were not really important, compared with the Queen and Burghley and Nicholas Bacon – the real rulers. The significance Hexter misses is that the Elizabethan governing circle really were Protestant humanism in power.

And, of course, he doesn't sympathise with, or even understand, what the Papacy had to contend with: it too was engaged in a struggle for survival, the acquisition of temporal power in Italy was the very condition of its independence. He probably does not know, what contemporaries knew, that Alexander VI and Julius II – those 'choice specimens' – were the two ablest men of the whole Curia; the first pushed forward the temporal power by diplomatic means, the second by warlike – but no one had any doubt of Julius II's greatness. Once the Renaissance Papacy had emerged from its struggle for survival, it embarked on the Reform of the Church.

Machiavelli understood the essential basis of politics, the exigencies and necessities in the struggle of the human grouping – whatever it is, state or church, monarch or president – to survive. The professor has a very academic essay, a study in semantics, on Machiavelli's *lo stato* and its different connotations; but the latter is absolutely clear that politics is about power, and when he praises *virtú* he means effectiveness in action. The struggle for survival is what all politics are about at bottom. Idealists like More learn the facts in the end by participating in them – and suffering from them; a highly intelligent observer like Erasmus learns – and is disillusioned. What Shakespeare said about it all in *Troilus and Cressida* is quite true: the natural aggressiveness of the human animal; the animality, the sordid brutishness; the necessity, the absolute necessity, of authority and order and discipline, if society is not to break up in dissolution.

The youthful More imagined that Communism was a

remedy for our wickedness; and Hexter seems to share his
dislike of Renaissance Europe's governing class. Would he say
that that of Communist Russia was any better? – or even
that of America?

# Erasmus – Great European

Erasmus is very much a Man for our Time, and it is good to
have a biography by a scholar who appreciates the intellectual issues involved.[1] I cannot quite see that Erasmus 'has
never had his due'. True, he never founded a church like
Luther or Calvin, but his influence on Europe has been
prodigious and pervasive; he has always been regarded as one
of the greatest of Europeans – not least by Voltaire, who
resembled him in some, not all, respects. At a time when
Europe is trying to forge a unity, what more symbolic a
figure? Born in Holland, Erasmus lived in France, England,
Italy, Germany, Switzerland, leaving his mark and a seminal
influence at work in all those countries, and others beyond.

Then, too, the story of his life, with all the morals to be
drawn from it, is very symptomatic, with its message for us.
Erasmus began as, and always remained at heart, a liberal and
a reformer, hating the abuses of Church and State in his day,
the corruptions of monasticism, the worldly secularism of the
Papacy, the inane wars between princes and peoples. He was
a passionate internationalist, a sensible pacifist, a progressive
pointing the way to a better future, not only a brilliant
humanist but a human man. He was sadly right in his views.

Then see what happens. The liberal reformers let loose an
avalanche of revolution. The Reformation – which Erasmus

[1] R. H. Bainton, *Erasmus of Christendom* (Collins, 1970).

hoped against hope to keep within bounds — destroyed the unity of Christendom. Reformation and Counter-Reformation fought each other in ulcerated religious wars; Catholics and Protestants burned or hanged each other in thousands. A number of Erasmus's friends perished on scaffolds — among them More and Fisher in England, his disciple Berquin burned in Paris. For all the high hopes with which Erasmus had begun, and which he had so largely shaped, at the end he looked out on a Europe and Christendom torn in two, a world of misery, as he now was forced to describe it, the 'worst century'.

How like the twentieth! It is a sad thing in history that people can hardly ever bring about a desirable measure of reform — political, religious, or social — without clumsily bringing the house down upon their heads, killing thousands or millions. As with the French Revolution, or the Russian in our time, the Civil Wars in Britain or America, the religious wars following the Reformation.

Now, four centuries later, the 'dialogue' between Catholics and Protestants is beginning again, and this is the perspective in which Professor Bainton has written his book. He tells us candidly how much he is drawn to Erasmus:

> I share his aversion to contention, his abhorrence of war, his wistful scepticism with respect to that which transcends the verifiable; at the same time I am warmed by the glow of his piety . . . I endorse his conviction that language is still the best medium for the transmission of thought.

There is one for MacLuhan and his like, with their pernicious inversion of sense — so characteristic of our time — that it is the media that determine the message.

Erasmus hated ideological strife — and this was the attitude not only of a sensible man but of the most brilliant scholar of his age. He might have said what Scaliger said, on being shown the hall at the Sorbonne 'where the theologians have disputed for three hundred years' — 'And, pray, what have they settled?'

Professor Bainton goes into all the issues: his is really an intellectual biography. It is not so much the human biography that Huizinga gave us; that is still the best, for Huizinga was a historian of genius, with a more subtle psychological understanding. He appreciated the complexity of another man of genius — Erasmus's extreme sensitiveness, the one skin too few, the homo-erotic element that comes out in his emotional friendships, that keeps the whole circle so tingling with life, where others are forgotten. The American professor is simpler and more naif.

Even on the intellectual side Professor Bainton is at pains to make Luther and Erasmus more alike than they were. There was a profound cleavage of type between them: Erasmus, the good European, who held by reason, moderation, freedom of the will; Luther, the characteristic German, who denied its freedom, asserted the subjection of the will, appealed to unreason, believed in thinking with the bowels. Can there by any doubt which course is the civilised one? — the German way has been a tragedy for Europe and themselves.

A good book deserves relevant criticism. Linacre was the founder of the Royal College of Physicians, not Surgeons: the distinction was very significant in the sixteenth century. Dean Colet, More and Erasmus's London friends were not members of the aristocracy: they were the cream of the middle class. It is funny that American scholars cannot get social classes right: after all, it is a part of knowledge like anything else.

# The Reformation Parliament

Professor Lehmberg has written a good book on a worth-while subject.[1] Not many history books deal with a subject so important as the long Parliament of Henry VIII that brought about an ecclesiastical revolution and opened the floodgates of the Reformation in England. That parliament was almost as epoch-making as the Long Parliament of Charles I, and its work — the reduction of the Church to size, and the beginnings of modernising the state — was more lasting. Henry VIII, by contrast with the Stuart king, was working with Parliament and the nation's will, not against it.

Bringing Henry's Parliament alive is a much more difficult job, because of the patchiness of the records. But Professor Lehmberg has made a success of it, with common-sense judgement, a sound perception of the personalities involved, and a proper sense of the process of politics. Instead of useless theorising about the theology of the royal supremacy, or a disproportionate concentration on minutiae of consti-tutional law and administration, he shows us how the Reformation Parliament worked and brought about its fateful legislation in terms of real politics. We are made to realise how, in its first two sessions, Henry was without a policy to deal with his urgent matrimonial problem, the need to provide for the succession, besides the pressing need for money — and so the Commons took the initiative in pressing forward with anti-clerical legislation. The unpopularity of an over-mighty Church, rich and overbearing, provided the leverage; the Commons' legislation pointed the way to the effective attack and started the avalanche. Neither Wolsey, nor Warham, nor More's policies — we must not forget that

[1] S. E. Lehmberg, *The Reformation Parliament, 1529-1536* (Cambridge University Press, 1970).

More as Chancellor took his part in forwarding the
Divorce — offered any solution to the king's difficulties: the
way was open for those who could. There is a most revealing
speech of Henry to a number of the Commons in 1532, when
he pointed out that he was now forty: it was high time he
provided a male heir to the throne. As a matter of fact the
fragile youth of Edward VI showed that Henry had already
left it perilously late. The minority of Edward as king showed
how bad this was for the country.

Professor Lehmberg insists that Parliament's social, economic and legal reforms were almost as important as its
ecclesiastical. (One hardly knows under which heading to
include its Act against Sodomy, hitherto an ecclesiastical
offence — in both applications of the word: the act was part
of the smear-campaign against the Church, it would seem.)
He makes it quite clear that Parliament was not subservient
and could on occasion oppose Henry's policies. This book
sees things in terms of real events — instead of academic
notions — the tug-of-war of conflicting interests and personalities, the fluid political situation, the changes from day to
day in accordance with public opinion or unexpected factors,
favourable or unfavourable. This is real history, like life not
theory. Henry had luck with him in the death of Archbishop
Warham, a doughty and respected opponent. Naturally Henry
appointed a successor who would promote his policies, and
the complexion of the bench of bishops changed markedly in
the course of this Parliament. But isn't that just like any
President of the United States gradually changing the
composition of the Supreme Court to taste?

Professor Lehmberg is convincing as to the composition of
this Parliament, and the character of its course. 'Nothing
could be more misleading than an attempt to determine the
views of the Commons at the opening of Parliament on the
basis of their later affiliations and actions.' He concludes
roundly that, in the end, 'they sought the general good of the
realm, the common weal of England.' (It is doubtful if that
can be said of the Parliaments of the 1930s, or today.) As to

its composition he shows that it effectively represented the
dominant interests in the country, from the forty-shilling
freeholders upwards – though we might ask whom the
mitred abbots in the Lords represented. The boroughs were
represented mostly by their own residents – middle-class
burgesses, in trade and the law. This is a marked contrast
with the later Parliaments of Elizabeth I, where the majority
of the boroughs were represented by country gentry. What
more significant evidence could there be as to the Rise of the
Gentry? But, indeed, there never was any sense in question-
ing it – *everything* in the age shows that the gentry just rose.
That controversy was as silly as it was superfluous.

Professor Lehmberg notes the neglect of the House of
Lords in recent parliamentary history, and has a valid
comment on the concentration upon the Commons among
historians – I suppose a lag-over from the mentality of
Victorian Liberalism. We have little excuse for that today: it
always rested upon an incorrect reading of human psychology. Admiration need not exclude one word of criticism.
The author is unfair to Wolsey in his opening pages: Henry,
rather than Wolsey, was responsible for the French war of
1523, and Henry's capricious will was a factor in aborting his
minister's policies. However, though Henry was a bully, he
was not a despot: this book makes clear that he worked in
and through and with Parliament, and kept on the whole on
the right side of public opinion. The professor concludes, 'on
balance there was surprisingly little evidence of serious
opposition to the king's new marriage or to the steps which
had been taken to validate it.' People probably understood
that Henry simply *had* to do something about it.

I have noticed a few misprints; but one is of interest:
James Trevyniarde, M.P. for Liskeard. This is an attempt to
anglicise a well-known Cornish name, Trewinnard, and an
amusing bit of folk-etymology. For it has nothing whatever
to do with 'vineyard'; 'winnard' in West Country dialect
means a redwing: so Trewinnard means 'the place of the
redwing'.

# Tudor Politics

Professor Elton is a Good Thing on the academic scene: with his combative energy, his aggressive scholarship inspired by secular commonsense, his sheer enthusiasm, he keeps us alert and on our toes, constantly reminding us of his presence. He has now brought together a mass of his serious studies, along with reviews.[1] Those modest men of genius, Gibbon and Maitland, had their miscellaneous papers collected for them after their deaths; not so the Professor.

I, for one, am glad that he did not wait; though I think it was a mistake, in these hard times, to produce two volumes where one would have done. Besides, it could have been better organised: two excellent papers in volume one on Thomas Cromwell, then one has to look in volume two for an illuminating third on his political creed. The proper thing would have been to concentrate, and omit the Forewords to paperbacks, like the not very good ones on Creighton's *Wolsey* and *Queen Elizabeth*.

The most original essays are the two on Sir Thomas More as Councillor and as involved in the opposition to Henry VIII. These present a rather different More – an altogether fuller and more comprehensible one – than that with which the general public is familiar. Even apart from the hagiographers, there is the sentimentalist like R. W. Chambers, no historian but an Eng. Lit. man, devoting most of their books to the last phase in the Tower.

Actually More spent twelve years, one-third of his adult life in Henry VIII's service, for the most as a kind of secretary and intellectual ornament, if not companion. He

---

[1] G. R. Elton, *Studies in Tudor and Stuart Politics and Government. Papers and Reviews 1946–1972*, 2 vols (Cambridge University Press, 1974).

was quite well rewarded, and 'there really is no evidence at all that he lived twelve years against the grain.' With the growth of Protestant opinions he found a vocation as controversialist and persecutor. Professor Elton tells us that in controversy he was 'petulant and fierce,' that he outdid Tyndale and others in offensiveness and 'at no time troubled himself about such things as scholarly caution, chivalrous moderation, or even elementary truthfulness.' Really! but I fear, sadly, that the Professor is right.

As a persecutor More was relentless, and regarded Wolsey's tolerance — one of his endearing qualities — as almost criminal. More had a sarcastic edge to his tongue — the Professor sympathises with poor Dame Alice, the mere woman's point of view, as I have always done. More was completely the Bishops' man in the gathering clerical Opposition to Henry, which Cromwell outmanoeuvred and defeated. It was Henry — who, though Catholic enough in his theology, was anti-clerical in action — that struck More down. It is ironical to think that, as with Anne Boleyn, Henry's affection turned to hatred: his ego had been wounded and he felt betrayed. Cromwell was more merciful, again ironically, to More than to poor Anne.

Until Professor Elton arrived on the scene to put us right, Thomas Cromwell was the most mis-estimated statesman in our history. *There* Elton effected a revolution — rather than with his over-enthusiastic views of an administrative 'revolution' — and I am in agreement with his view of Cromwell as a statesman, if not wholly as a man. (His behaviour about poor Anne Boleyn was not precisely *chic*, but neither was anybody else's, and he was utterly the King's servant, there to serve his purposes.)

We have heard more than enough now about Cromwell as administrator, the account of his Decline and Fall is far more riveting and, as with More, convincing: the Professor has got the dog by the tail. Striking down his ablest servant was one of the worst things Henry ever did — all the same it was popular. Elton says that Henry 'never, in fact, went counter to the inclinations of the people on whom his power rested.' In other words, Henry *was* an able politician; and this contradicts Professor Scarisbrick's rather silly view of Henry, as 'fundamentally not very competent,' which Elton agreed with earlier in his review of him.

Nor is his view of Wolsey – another much underrated man – any more compelling. It is surely rather humourless (not much evidence of a sense of humour anywhere) to treat Wolsey, in control of government for nearly twenty years, as an 'amateur'! Nor is there any imaginative perception – though we have evidence – of the difficulties the great Cardinal encountered in Henry's juvenile ambitions for caracolling in France. Elton sees that Wolsey managed to 'satisfy' Henry – an absolute condition of retaining power – till towards the end; when he failed, he was thrown to the wolves, like Anne and Cromwell. This is politics.

Apart from politics there is no appreciation of other aspects of these great men's lives. Both Wolsey and Henry were splendid builders: their works remain, Hampton Court and Christ Church and Trinity, when their politics are but dust. Wolsey was a collector, a cultural patron, Henry's Court depicted, immortally, by Holbein. The works of men's hands, the productions of artistic genius, remain when all their silly statutes are, or should be, forgotten.

I am always campaigning for historians to open their eyes, develop more visual sense, understand the past through the real relics of it that remain about us – not even much subtlety of sense of character here. By the same token I constantly urge more artistry in their books, less academicism, apparently in vain. A simple point to observe is that, when the building is up, the scaffolding should come down.

Here it gets continually in the way: the historiography is all mixed up with the history. The Professor cannot let a point go: it is like a dog with a bone. Professor Mackie 'could not free himself from an outdated framework'; 'Mr Cooper would have done well to heed a hint in my earlier article . . .'; 'if the point at issue were only Mr Cooper's view of my methods and scholarship – or, for that matter, my view of his . . .' This kind of thing becomes a nervous *tic*, one understands all too well its psychological origins; moreover, it is Germanic pedantry rather than necessary to scholarship. 'Dr Hurstfield's gloss on this passage really will not do.' 'Professor Hexter should know that even news of the products of American university presses,' and so on. 'The Abbé Constant, summarising (as was his wont) other people's views in language free from other people's reservations . . ..'. 'Mr Cooper's gibe convicts me of over-conciseness.' 'Mr Zeefeld is misled into supposing . . .' Even the great Maitland cops it: 'for the demolition of his argument, cf, my remarks above.' Mr Cooper again: 'the reader may judge whether a charge of making heavy weather applies more suitably to my six lines or to Mr Cooper's half-page . . .' Poor Mr Cooper!

Comic enough in its way – everybody out of step but our Johnny – it gives an unfortunate impression of the writer.

We all have the defects of our qualities. Though the professor has little perception of character and no sense of art or aesthetic taste, he is excellent about the germination of statutes, for people who like that sort of thing. They should have been left in the decent obscurity of the specialist periodicals in which they appeared, the arguings and academic quarrels left out. Then we should have had a viable one volume, which I should be the first to hail and appreciate.

# The Court of Henry VIII

One of the more agreeable pleasures of travelling about the Continent in the years before the war was to piece together in one's mind, from the Holbeins in various galleries, a picture of the court of Henry VIII. No English court has ever been rendered by a greater painter, or one that was more veracious and convincing. None of the facile romanticism of Van Dyck – which gave Charles I, with his diminutive stature and his red nose a romantic aura; or of the fleshy and coarse-grained glamour of a Lely. Never was the art of portraiture more authentic, more absolute, than with Holbein: one feels one knows those characteristic Tudor faces across the centuries, with their wakeful, watchful eyes always on guard – they had reason to be – and their double dose of life.

There they are rendered for us for ever. In Vienna the portrait of John Chambers, the King's physician, with his heavy jowl and shrewd old eyes – himself a strong recommendation of his expertise, for it was taken at the age of eighty-eight. In the Louvre Archbishop Warham, with the veiled expressive face of a great ecclesiastic, his jewelled mitre and cross on either side of him, his hands spread before him on the cloth-of-gold cushion. In Dresden, the double portrait of the Godsalves, father and son, the son slinking submissively in the background as a Tudor son should do, the father kindly enough, but authoritative, released. At the Hague, Robert Cheseman, the King's falconer, with his ringed fingers and gay-painted bird. And so on. Wasn't it a pity they had got so dispersed? – I used to think – I suppose when the Royal collections were sold by the Commonwealth. Was there no way of bringing them together again, except in the dreaming head of a young historical student who cared for such things?

But have we not an opportunity now such as will never occur again? Might we not bring back at least from Germany – as some recompense for the destruction they brought upon us – the portraits of these Tudor Englishmen that once were at Windsor and Whitehall? I suspect the Russians exacted some retribution for the deliberate destruction of cultural objects the barbaric Nazis unloosed.

Meanwhile, we are given a delightful volume to go on:[1] the

---

[1] K. T. Parker, *Holbein's Drawings at Windsor Castle* (Phaidon, 1964).

wonderful Holbein drawings at Windsor, many of them studies for paintings, though all of them portraits in their own right, are reproduced in this scholarly volume. Since one can no longer traipse round the galleries of Europe, one can get something of the same effect sitting in a comfortable chair by the fireside. The whole court of Henry VIII, or a good deal of it, files before one's eyes. It is an astonishing procession: there is all the greed for life and gain, the passion for place and power of the English Renaissance, the cultivation and cruelty, the hardness – the survival of the fittest, indeed – along with the more comfortable virtues, the buxom wives, the touch of other-wordliness in the More circle, in Bishop Fisher, the pathos of those other too secular, too intense lives.

One's pleasure is greatly enriched by knowing some history, one's feelings moved by knowing what went on behind these faces with their cunning or reserve, their slyness or pride, or their naïf charm. The women come off best: life was not quite such a *sauve qui peut* for them. Begin with the drawings of Sir Thomas More's family: it was to him that Holbein got his introduction from Erasmus, on his first visit to England. There is the famed charm of that family with the finger of fate upon it: the expressiveness of Cicely Heron's face, the plain parted hair under the wimple, her father's bright eyes that look upon another world. And then one remembers what happened to them all: the martyrdom, death, separation, exile – the circle broken for ever. There is Fisher, with the wizened, ascetic face, the knife-edged lips that would yet break into a smile; and Warham, the churchman, old and worn and creased with age. Go on to the courtiers, worldly, rapacious, all on the make, whom Holbein drew on his return to England to become the King's painter. Over all there is the presence of the figure who does not appear once among these drawings: that masterful personality with the aggressive stance, positive, powerful, the small calculating eyes, the puffy cheeks, sparse beard – as one sees him in the Walker Gallery at Liverpool. *There* he stands: *I am your master*, he seems to say, with every fibre of the heavy, unwieldy body.

# Anne Boleyn

This is the most sympathetic account of Henry VIII's second wife (to speak popularly) to appear:[1] it adheres scrupulously to the evidence and it convinces me that we have here the essence of the matter. A skilled writer, Miss Chapman dexterously makes the story as readable as it was dramatic. Even better, she brings out its inherent strangeness; the tale is so familiar that we omit to notice how very strange it was — one reason why it reached the proportions it did, a European scandal, and one that had decisive consequences in history.

What is astonishing is that Henry and Anne should have waited six years from the beginning of the affair before consummating it. The King had no difficulty in making Anne's sister, Mary, his mistress. Anne was a very different proposition. Hers was a striking personality, with her French elegance — she had received her training at the French Court — her dark looks, brilliant, magnetic eyes, her sharp tongue and defiance of conventions.

Then there were her vitality, her courage and daring. She was the outstanding personality around poor Queen Catherine, who one day said: 'My lady Anne, you have good hap to stop at a king; but you are not like others: you will have all or nothing.'

Earlier, she had been in love with the Percy heir, and

---

[1] Hester Chapman, *Anne Boleyn* (Cape, 1974).

hoped to marry him. Cardinal Wolsey stopped this, for the King had other plans for her. Anne vowed vengeance on the Cardinal, and his failure with the Papacy to get Henry's marriage with Catherine declared null brought about his ruin. When he was dead, his former servant Cromwell vamped up the 'evidence' that brought Anne to the scaffold. Such are the ironies of history – this book has several: Sir Thomas More warning Henry earlier not to overstate Papal supremacy, for one!

Henry also was caught in a cleft-stick: he *had* to produce a male heir to the throne, but indubitably legitimate. If Anne had produced it, all might have been well. But one never could tell with a man like Henry. Miss Chapman has grasped his terrifying personality very well: the *faux-bonhomme*, the self-deceiver, always in the right, with great charm – who would have your head off the next minute. (By all accounts Hitler and Stalin could exert charm too; Henry was more like the latter.)

His love for Anne was the great passion of his life – fortunate that we have his love-letters (in French). The patience with which this most wilful egoist waited and negotiated and argued to make the way clear for a legitimate heir is hardly credible. Miss Chapman has the advantage of her sex in making all clear to us: 'His and Anne Boleyn's excursions into the *pays du tendre*, while failing to reach a climax and thus avoiding the risk of pregnancy, seems to have become their practice up to the last months of 1532. She then conceived, and continued to do so until he discarded her.'

Before four years were up he had her decapitated on the scaffold. This also was unprecedented, a crowned and anointed Queen!

Was she guilty of the charges brought against her?

Most people believed she was, she had so many enemies – and people will believe anything. Henry certainly believed her guilty – but he always believed what suited him – like (a very unlike character) Mr Gladstone. But Anne, by this time

willing enough to die – after all the anguish and strain, the
hatred and hysteria released by those nine historic years –
never admitted that she was guilty. Archbishop Cranmer
heard her last confession, but could say nothing; there is a
strange story, from her daughter's reign, that he believed her
innocent.

Miss Chapman makes the good point that Wolsey's devoted
servant and biographer never censured Anne, even in the
reign of Catherine's daughter, Mary. Among many good
points she misses one: that Shakespeare's Dark Lady should
have been the official mistress of Anne Boleyn's nephew,
Elizabeth's Lord Chamberlain, patron of Shakespeare's
Company.

As for Anne herself, what a wonderful, tragic play it would
make.

# Katherine Parr: an Amateur View

It is a symptom of the time that reading – and writing –
history is so popular. And, indeed, what wonder? When
society is visibly breaking down all round us from the
intolerable strains we have placed upon it and the ludicrous
liberal expectations people have entertained of it, such as
that everybody can get a quart out of a pint pot. Liberal
illusions – whether Lord Robbins' about students or
Wedgwood Benn's about the trade unions – have been idiotic
all along, as everybody should be able to see now.

This is merely to suggest one reason, and a symptomatic
one, why people prefer to read about the past. As a practising
historian I am all in favour of it, especially if they have the
sense to learn from it.

But the popularity of writing history by amateurs raises problems. They are all engaged in doing it — disgusted journalists, tired novelists, poets without inspiration. One simple point: they have no idea that it is the more difficult the further one goes back into the past. It is not so difficult for such people to take a shot, for example, at writing about Queen Victoria as it is about Mary Queen of Scots or Shakespeare (most of the nonsense written about him is by people who know nothing about the Elizabethan Age).

Mr Martienssen, I see, has written two previous books about Hitler and his Admirals, and about Crime and the Police. This, I fear, does not qualify him to write about Katherine Parr;[1] with the best will in the world to be kind, this must — to be conscientious — be a cautionary tale.

What is known about Katherine Parr?

Not a great deal; perhaps that is why those who are qualified have not devoted a book to her — an essay would be enough. She was the last wife of Henry VIII, and she survived him, to marry her real love, Protector Somerset's brother, and die of it. She was an intelligent, kind, well-educated woman, whose role was like that of Madame de Maintenon with Louis XIV — to make a decent family-life for the old tyrant, bringing together his children by different women, treating them kindly and reconciling them to their difficult parent.

Katherine was also a patron of the new learning, and that brought her to an awkward pass with her spouse, in daring to argue with Henry who fancied himself as a theologian. However, she excused herself as merely trying to amuse him; he, of course, knew better. The old egoist was appeased by timely submission, and she survived — to die in childbirth from the more potent Lord Admiral.

How does Mr Martienssen tackle sixteenth-century history, a subject evidently unfamiliar to him? Let us look at one paragraph early on, on page three. Henry VII's mother, Lady

---

[1] Anthony Martienssen, *Queen Katherine Parr* (Secker and Warburg, 1973).

Margaret Beaufort, is described as the widow of Edmund Tudor, 'Duke' of Richmond. It should be Earl: unimportant, but one should get it right. She was not only a descendant of John of Gaunt, but his heiress-general: important, for it was this that made her the Lancastrian heir to the throne. 'She endowed new colleges at both Oxford and Cambridge'; it is a matter of common knowledge that she endowed two colleges at Cambridge, none at Oxford. 'She took up the role of patroness of the New Learning' — she did not: she was patroness of the old medieval piety, under the influence of her confessor, John Fisher. I am afraid that page three gives one no confidence for the 250 pages that follow.

On the other hand, Mr Martienssen knows what nobody else knows. About Henry VIII, for instance: 'he loved the swiftness of women's thought and its apparent inconsequence, pitting his own exceptionally agile mind and breadth of learning against theirs, goading them on to extravagant arguments, and shouting with delight if he succeeded in trapping them with their own words.' Of Katherine Parr, after her second husband's extrication from the Pilgrimage of Grace, 'she felt there was no crisis she could not overcome.' How *does* Mr Martienssen know?

It is all on a par — if the pun may be permitted — with the naif nonsense about Henry's father bringing the 'old feudal nobility to its knees at Bosworth': schoolboy stuff. Or *naivetés* about education: 'instead of having their lessons beaten into them by rod and birch, strong efforts were made to hold their interest by less drastic means.' Really! Mr Martienssen should read Ascham's *Schoolmaster*, or about the treatment meted out to Lady Jane Grey, or for that matter James I.

Among the things he does not know is that the letter, supposed by Anne Boleyn (quoted from Wood's *Illustrious Ladies!*), is an eighteenth-century fabrication — anyone with the slightest sense of the sixteenth century would know that it is not genuine. From a French ambassador's description of Mary Tudor we learn one little thing: she had 'a voice more manlike for a woman' than her father had 'for a man.' So Henry had a light, small, not very masculine voice – which would be appropriate with his small cruel mouth.

# Doctrinaire Academics

The Tudor period, and the Reformation in especial, brought about a decisive change in the universities and in education in general. It is interesting to compare it with today, where the contrasts have a salutary message for us. After the Reformation, the overriding idea was a more modern society, more efficient and better educated, after the waste and muddle of late medieval society, the idle unproductiveness, cutting out the dead wood.

In the Middle Ages, students had milled about in the streets and ill-kept hostels, with frequent disturbances and many of the phenomena – though not public exhibitions of nudity – with which we are so familiar. Tudor society was not standing for that. Hence students were brought into the colleges, expanded for the purpose, that they might be better disciplined and better educated: the two things go together.

Another feature was that the universities ceased to be exclusively clerical. There was a strong belief in education: the governing class – gentry, middle class, even the nobility – realised that they needed to be educated to cope with the needs of a more complex society. Instead of feudal fighting turkey-cocks who couldn't sign their names, you got educated persons, like Essex and Ralegh, Bacon and Southampton, patrons of the arts and sciences.

What was wrong with this? Most sensible people have always thought it a desirable, and necessary development. It would make a significant story to tell, though a difficult one, in the right hands and with the right approach. What is indispensible is a sense of the complexity of society, of the variety of its needs, its integrated structure — and also a sense of life.

Mr Kearney has little of this: he has a simple view which he enforces again and again.[1] 'By 1600, England was sharply divided into two nations, the "gentlemen" and the rest, the great majority. In creating this social division the universities were a major instrument.' This is absurd. We are told that 'this was a situation which was bound to create a combination of religious and social discontent.' This is so simple-minded as to be farcical.

'The object of the colleges was not freedom but control, and to lose sight of this fact amid the splendours of college architecture is to risk being blinded by sentimental nostalgia.' This attitude of sour suspicion blinds Mr Kearney to the fact that there was plenty of room for freedom — quite as much as was good for anybody. A little more sense of life, let alone humour, would have revealed to him that there was plenty of fun and frolics. A little more knowledge of the facts would have opened his eyes to the jolly life lived by such students as Robert Greene and Thomas Nashe at Cambridge, or John Lyly or George Peele at Oxford.

For the facts are no more to be relied on than the argument. William Carnsew was not a Puritan, any more than Christ Church was a Puritan College. It is ludicrous to say that 'Oxford adopted a distinctive form of country Puritanism from the mid-century onwards' — Puritans there were a small minority. Wrong about Oxford, it is also wrong about Cambridge: Christ's, which really had a strong Puritan element, is overlooked.

What accounts for this distortion?

The book is riddled with the contemporary Leftist clichés about a social élite and élitism.

---

[1] Hugh Kearney, *Scholars and Gentlemen: Universities and Society in Pre-Industrial Britain, 1500-1700* (Faber and Faber, 1970).

The words appear a score of times: we are even told that 'the Royal Society was an intellectual club for the social élite.' Most sensible people know that its purpose was to advance science. Mr Kearney lets the cat out of the bag when he tells us that 'tutorial supervision in the 20th century aims at creating a critical attitude of mind.' There you have it: criticism before you have anything to go on, before you know anything, before you bother to learn the facts.

This is an example of the way students are taught history in the universities: it is a direct consequence of the absurd rate of expansion, with the inevitable lowering of standards. Is it any wonder that students behave as they do? A considerable proportion of them show plainly enough that they don't want to be there – is there any reason why they should be?

Many of them emerge semi-educated. Is that any wonder either, when so much of the teaching of history, for example, aims at turning the concrete realities of history into the question-begging assumptions of half-baked sociology?

Academic 'historians' of the school of *Past and Present* have been partly to blame, though already it is more past than present – to judge from the younger (and better) historians of the Civil War, putting behind them the out-dated theses of Christopher Hill, Trevor-Roper, Lawrence Stone and company.

# Elizabethiana

It might be thought that, after so many years of research and writing and reading about Elizabeth I, the subject would have no allure for me. That would be so with any average, humdrum production; it is decidedly not the case with Paul Johnson's biography.[1] I have read it with refreshment, pleasure, even excitement; I have learned from it, it has so many fresh insights, a continuing understanding of the problems that confronted her and how she dealt with them. The book has already had a good reception; but only someone acquainted intimately with the subject can appreciate how good it is. It is indeed the best historical biography I have read for years.

The reason is not far to seek. Paul Johnson read history at Oxford under one of its best tutors, K. B. McFarlane; he is a practised and gifted writer. But the real value of this book lies in its *political* understanding. Elizabeth was first and last a political personage and a very clever one; to understand her at all one needs to be well up in politics. This is where Paul Johnson scores, at every point and all through. I have never read a better analysis of the crises that confronted the Queen over Mary Stuart and Norfolk during 1569-72, and again over Mary before she was ultimately brought to book. These matters are highly complicated; it takes a trained intelligence to penetrate into them, and this is the most *intelligent* biography of Elizabeth we are ever likely to have. We need no more.

The trouble with women-writers' books on their heroines is that they usually miss out the politics — a defect when one is dealing with a ruler. A really perceptive writer like Elizabeth Jenkins appreciated that and made the woman's personality the theme of her *Elizabeth the Great*. This was its valuable quality: after all, imperceptive males cannot tell from the inside what the strains feel like upon a highly strung woman. And imperceptive academics reviewing her book failed to appreciate, as usual, that they had anything to learn. I learned from her, as I now learn from Paul Johnson. He comprehends Elizabeth without any sentimentality; she was not a sentimentalist herself, he describes her politics as

[1] Paul Johnson, *Elizabeth I: A Study in Power and Intellect* (Weidenfeld and Nicolson, 1974).

'unsentimental realism' – though one should add that it was touched by the poetry of patriotism. (The third-rate today don't understand that.) On the other hand, there is no boringly subjective female sympathising with Mary Queen of Scots. If anybody ever dug her own grave, she did: Elizabeth did her best to keep her out of it as long as she possibly could (on her own terms, naturally. That is just politics). Paul Johnson's account of Elizabeth's virtual breakdown when the execution was forced upon her by combined government, Parliament and country, is astonishingly perceptive and brilliantly written. The practised writer knows infallibly what is significant to quote.

Mary was a Frenchwoman. I remember a Catholic prelate of my acquaintance commenting on her: 'no one brought up at the Valois Court would find the idea of assassination at all remote.' Her own ambassador, the Bishop of Ross, told the diplomat Dr Wilson that she was 'not fit for any husband: had poisoned her first, had been a party to the murder of her second, and would not have kept faith with Norfolk even if she had married him.' We must exonerate her from the first charge; even so, we appreciate Wilson's shocked comment, 'Lord! What people are these! What a Queen! What an ambassador!'

Paul Johnson's achievement is the more remarkable coming from someone with a Catholic background. When one considers the tedious sectarian bias of previous generations – with writers like Lingard, Belloc and Chesterton, let alone Evelyn Waugh and inferior Jesuits (simply because they were defeated) – it seems that the climate of today, in this respect at least, registers some progress. In addition, the man of the world recognises politician's humbug, ecclesiastical or secular, for what it is. On the hoary old issue of Elizabeth's legitimacy, he says crisply: 'it is true that the annulment that made Elizabeth illegitimate was based on the grounds that the marriage with Anne had been void from the start, since Henry had already committed adultery with Anne's sister Mary. But this was just clerical lawyers'

nonsense: it could be reversed, and was.' And he makes no
bones about Mary Tudor's personal responsibility for the
burnings that effectively ended Catholicism in England; she
was a fool, ruined by her convictions.

Mrs Luke ends her trilogistic love-affair with the Tudors
with a long book devoted to Gloriana.[2] Americans like
writing their books too long — they think it more impressive:
it is part of their naïve charm. And this book is too
wordy — better if it were half as long. However, the author
appreciates the look of the places where the things she writes
about happened, as few Americans do — at least not much
visual sense shows up in their history books.

Women writers understand Elizabeth's distaste for
marriage, which ultimately prevailed with her. (Her sister
Mary should not have married, and not overthrown the new
deal in religion but modified it in a conservative sense — as
Elizabeth all her life struggled to do.) The men all wanted
Elizabeth to marry, to end the insecurity and provide for the
succession. Her indiscreet exhibitionist flirting was characteristic of her mother too — probably as innocent in Anne's
case as in the daughter's. Mrs Luke's book, conscientiously
got up from secondary authorities, may have its appeal on a
rather lower level than Paul Johnson's. She has got the story
right in its main lines — though wrong about Bess of
Hardwick and her husband, the Earl of Shrewsbury: she
should not have relied here on her own unaided judgement,
but on better authorities.

Mrs Luke is at least readable; I do not find Miss Lloyd so.[3]
She has set herself an almost impossible task. I do not know
what led her to choose Captain Christopher Carleill for
subject. There is very little material about him, which makes
it still more difficult for an amateur. There are many more
interesting Elizabethan adventurers who would make rewarding subjects, in the proper hands. Carleill surfaces only

[2] Mary M. Luke, *Gloriana. The Years of Elizabeth I* (Gollancz, 1974).
[3] Rachel Lloyd, *Elizabethan Adventurer. Captain Christopher Carleill* (Hamish
Hamilton, 1974).

occasionally in the life of the age, comes into the light of day most clearly, if briefly, as commander of the land-forces in Drake's West Indies Expedition of 1585. An educated man, a good soldier, step-son of Walsingham, he was for some time bogged down in the dreary complications of Ulster, as bloody and inextricable under Elizabeth I as under Elizabeth II. Since there is little enough to go on, the book is padded out with background to all this: it does not make for interesting reading.

A professional historian prefers the raw material from records, so much more revealing of the social life of an age. The Essex Record Office, through the devoted work of Dr Emmison, has been a pioneer in their preservation and exhibition to the public in their beautiful Elizabethan mansion at Ingatestone Hall. He now gives us a second volume[4] on the social life, mainly from the archdeacons' courts. It may be surmised that in their splendid Record Office Essex has done more for scholarship than by their deplorable university, on which it must be considered that the county's money has been mostly wasted.

The records of these courts deal chiefly with lesser offences )— mainly sexual, bastardy, incontinence, libel, drunkenness, indiscipline in church and so on — graver offences were dealt with at grander courts with severer sentences. With these we are at the coal-face of local life, and are observing the misconduct of simple folk — the gentry and upper classes in general were not cited at this level: it was for them to maintain standards, exercise discipline. The charm of these documents is that here one listens to people's very words, as in a Shakespeare play. The more one reads of them the more one realises how true he is to the life of the time.

Here is a maidservant, whose master John Lawrence

desired her on a certain night to hold his back which did ache. Which she, refusing, was eftsoons required by her

[4] F. G. Emmison, *Elizabethan Life: Morals and the Church Courts* (Essex County Council, 1970).

dame, Joan Lawrence, so to do. Whereupon she, lying upon the bed in her clothes holding his back a good time until she was a-cold, was desired and enticed by him and his wife to come in naked bed with them too. At what time he had carnal knowledge from time to time, her said dame lying in bed with him and warranting her that she should have no harm and that the other maids had used to do the like before.

The result of that back-ache was a child; the girl had to stand in a white sheet in church 'from the ringing of the first peal until they ring all unto morning prayer.'

When several people slept in the same bed it must have been difficult to resist these cosy comforts. A manservant went to bed with Agnes Davy, 'her sister Alice Davy lying by them in the same bed'; another fellow went to bed with his girl, 'her mother lying in the same bed'. All the evidence here confirms Simon Forman's depiction of how much more free-and-easy Elizabethan sex-life was. And with regard to stimulating objects, phallic figurines and such also; a woman who kept a free-house at West Ham had 'a glass like unto a pintle [penis] and a pair of ballocks for guests to drink in'. We have seen such objects – did we recognise their folklore signification? Anyone who knows the ways of old provincial pub-life will recognise the half-drunk Elizabethan who challenged his companion that 'his privities or prick was longer by four inches' than his friend's. Such are the simple ways of the sovereign people.

Thames Television produced a series for their benefit devoted to historic places with their associations – much good, let us hope, it did them; and recruited Paul Johnson to write the script.[5] They could not have done better: his visual sense accompanies his sense of the past, each illuminates the other. Here we have the island's story displayed for us all the way from the shrine of Welsh St David to modern Whitehall. The selection would not always be mine, nor was it Mr

[5] Paul Johnson, *A Place in History* (Weidenfeld and Nicolson, 1974).

Johnson's; but it is comprehensive in taking in the Industrial Revolution with Ironbridge, modern science with the Royal Institution, and the English Channel from the Roman pharos at Dover to hovercraft. It is to be hoped that such talents as an historian will not be engulfed in the ephemeral journalism of our squalid demotic society.

# John Stow as an Historian[1]

We are gathered here to do honour to a modest and sober Elizabethan, a good historian, and a devoted citizen of London. It is good for us that we should do so — and pay tribute to real and permanent values in a shifting and shiftless age. Who now remembers most of the glittering and gilded figures who attracted so much attention in their time? — John Stow has lasted longer and garnered more enduring respect.

The Elizabethan age saw the beginning of the modern writing of history, as it saw the beginnings of the marvellous achievements of this small country in the four centuries to come — achievements is so many fields: at sea, in the oceanic voyages, colonisation, the creation of an empire; in literature, drama, the arts and sciences; commerce, industry. All the result of initiative and hard work — a splendid arc of achievement spanning modern history — of which we are now witnessing the end.

John Stow was one of the best historians of that age; indefatigable in the trouble he took, thorough and conscientious, accurate — above all things devoted to truth — unlike

---

[1] A Stow Commemoration Address at St Andrew Undershaft.

our television historians today. He said: 'in histories the chief
thing that is to be desired is the truth' — that indeed is the
whole point of history; these gentry today would do well to
fix this as a motto above their glib typewriters and try to
adhere to it.

John Stow did so throughout a lifetime of hard work. He
began, as perhaps a young man should, more interested in
poetry, and later made useful contributions to the study of
Chaucer, best of our medieval poets, also a citizen of
London. He admitted that then he hadn't 'esteemed history,
were it offered never so freely.' But as he grew older he
corrected that and graduated to our delightful science —
history is the proper interest of mature minds. That he
should *write* history was suggested to him by that cultivated
Renaissance prince, the Queen's favourite, Leicester —
though he collaborated more closely with good Archbishop
Parker, a more respectable figure.

Shortly on coming before the public as an author, there
followed a feud with another historian — not unknown in
the profession today for, as we know, *odium theologicum* is
nothing compared with *odium archaeologicum.* The
chronicler Grafton, also a citizen of London, jeered at Stow's
addiction to old ways and 'superstitious fables foolishly
Stowed together.' Stow replied, in Elizabethan fashion, by
deriding the empty, echoing *tuns* and fruitless *grafts* of his
adversary, Grafton. He has had the last word with posterity,
for he was a better historian, worked harder, and produced the
goods. His *Summary* of English Chronicles was a best-
seller — and this does not give unadulterated pleasure to one's
colleagues; edition after edition was called for, so that his
dedication of the book is to successive Lord Mayors, with
aldermen and commonalty, over the years.

But in the Elizabethan Age one did not make money by
writing books, and Stow was always poor. He earned his
living for thirty years as a tailor, and then the Merchant
Taylors gave him a diminutive pension — though, a mere
historian, he was never admitted to the Livery. He writes of

his popular book, the *Summary*: 'it hath cost me many a weary mile's travel, many a hard-earned penny and pound, and many a cold winter night's study.' But this was in no complaining spirit, for he was a merry old fellow, pleasant and cheerful; I'll bet he enjoyed those winter nights' study — it was all a labour of love — and his foot-slogging kept him healthy to the end, a ripe old age, working joyfully to the last. It is true that in his last years he had to appeal to charity, but that may be partly that he spent too much money on books. Once, when walking with Ben Jonson, they met two cripples begging; Stow asked them what they would take to admit him to their order.

Something very Elizabethan about him was the ambition, the sheer scale of his intended enterprise — it is so like the grandeur of their aims, the expanding horizons that led them on. How inspiring it must have been to live then! — everything bore one up, everything encouraged effort, instead of dragging one down, nothing to inspire one, nothing to encourage, nothing but what calls for contempt on every hand.

Edmund Spenser wrote six books of the *Faerie Queene*, the great poem of the age, but he intended twelve; he was only forty-six when he died. Sir Philip Sidney, who was only thirty-two, never finished the *Arcadia*. Sir Walter Ralegh's *History of the World* did not get much beyond the Roman Republic; Richard Hooker did not live to complete his *Laws of Ecclesiastical Polity*. Similarly, Stow never published his vast intended *History of this Island*, of which his fat volumes are in a sense parts:

Lie heavy on him, earth, for he
Laid many a heavy pile on thee.

But altogether, not a bad record for a working tailor! — of course, there were not wanting people to say that his volumes were '*stitched* together'.

Actually they were written in good straightforward prose, like the stout broadcloth of the garments he fashioned, and described by his later editor: 'Expect no filed phrases, inkhorn terms, uncouth words nor fantastic speeches, but good plain English without affection, rightly befitting chronology. If Cicero's eloquence, Plato's oratory, or Virgil's lofty verse be thy chief desire, Paul's churchyard is now plenteously furnished to satisfy thee.'

Stow's *Annals*, with the increments added for the years as they passed, constituted his weightiest contribution, and the age considered it his most important. No doubt Stow thought so himself. It would not be the only time an author has been mistaken about his own work, and a book he undertook just for pleasure – as it were with his left hand – turned out the best, the book by which he lives to posterity. If Renan's recommendation be true, that one should write only about what one loves, then Stow's *Survey of London* is the book by which he lives for us still. He was born to write *that* book – others could write chronicles and text-books; only Stow could have written the *Survey*; he was in love with the subject. He had the right temperament for writing it; every parish, every street, every church, house and object of any interest was alive to him, with its memories and associations. And he had a most observant eye – he missed nothing, except, alas, the theatres of which, as a sober citizen, he disapproved. (So did the Lord Mayor and Corporation; they were always trying to suppress the theatres, when nobody was looking. Think of it, if the Lord Mayor and aldermen had had their way, there would have been no Shakespearean drama! Only the personal protection of the Queen saved it – one of her many contributions to the age, so rightly called by *her* name.)

In dedicating his *Survey* to the Lord Mayor, Commonalty and Citizens, Stow described it as 'the discovery of London, my native soil and country.' It is as much a voyage of discovery, if by foot, as Francis Drake's or any other of the famous voyages of discovery by sea, setting sail from the port of London. (By the way, he tells us where Drake lived in the City: in the great house in Dowgate Street called the Arbour, 'lately builded by Sir Thomas Pullison, Mayor,' but this was after Drake made fortune and fame by his voyage round the world.) The book is wonderfully alive: this is Shakespeare's London brought before our eyes, with its gardens and green spaces filling up with tenements, with increased prosperity and population; with the water being brought into the city, the new conduits going up, the swift water-channels and runnels; the transformation of so many churches to secular uses; the different characters of the wards still marked, the noise and hammering of the brass-founders, candlestick-makers and copper-workers in Lothbury; the bustle of trades, the clatter of signs, the busy, mercurial life of citizens, so vividly evoked about the same time at the beginning of Shakespeare's *Julius Caesar*.

I cannot go in detail into the book here, though it is precisely in its authentic evocative detail that the value of the book consists – unlike the generalities of sociologists, or the theories of historians anxious to be 'with it'. That great physiologist, Sir Charles Sherrington, tells us that 'a fact does not decay'; theories do, and no one is so quickly out of date as those anxious to be 'with it'. John Stow, indeed, was very anxious *not* to be 'with it' – the phrase itself is already out of date – that is why he has lasted. And he was very independent-minded; he didn't mince his words about the great – he was positively rude about the Queen's father, Henry VIII, for example, whom he disliked and disapproved of.

London at that time was engulfed in the process of emerging from the Middle Ages. The Reformation meant a vast destruction of monasteries and churches, of which the city had had far too many. This went to Stow's heart, as it would have to mine, had I been living then. He bitterly deplored the destruction of monuments and brasses in the churches, as did another inhabitant at the time:

When I have seen by Time's fell hand defaced
The rich, proud cost of outworn buried age;
When sometime lofty towers I see down-razed,
And brass eternal slave to mortal rage . . .

Stow always lets us know about the towers down-razed, the monuments destroyed, the brasses ripped up. On the other hand, he does not fail to let us know the immense outpouring of charity on the part of London merchants, their works of philanthrophy, the almshouses founded in almost every parish, the hospitals put on a stronger footing, the schools started. To this day the general public is unaware of the astonishing achievement of the Elizabethan merchants of London in schools, almshouses, benefactions, not only or even mostly in London, but in practically every county, all over the country. It was, quite simply, one of the grandest achievements of the age, along with everything else; it was one of the biggest, most constant and determined efforts. You don't hear about it from ordinary historians; they haven't the imagination, or perhaps the magnanimity, to appreciate it. But Stow saw to it that, at least in London, their charities should not be forgotten.

Since we do not have time to perambulate about the city with him, let us recall briefly the places where we know Shakespeare was living at the time. In the earlier 1590s he was living in the parish of St Helen's, Bishopsgate, for he failed to pay his assessment of tax there — a congenial, not to say endearing, failing. Stow has a full description of these whereabouts, so familiar to the dramatist and so convenient for the earlier theatres beyond the gate in the  fields of Shoreditch, where the theatre-folk and writers for them hung out. Stow describes Crosby Place, where Richard III had resided at the time of his *coup d'état,* and of course it features in the play: a monument of the past familiar to everybody. In the church the great merchant Sir Thomas Gresham had been recently buried under his fine tomb; his house he bequeathed for his foundation of Gresham College. Several ranges of almshouses had recently been set up by the generosity of Gresham, Sir Andrew Judd and his daughter, the wife of Customer Smith.

At the time Shakespeare wrote the French scenes in *Henry V*, about 1600, he was lodging in Cripplegate ward in the household of the French Mountjoys, headdress-makers. With Stow, go down Wood Street, 'there lower down in Silver Street, till ye come to the east end of St. Olave's church on the south side, and so to Monkswell Street on the north.' The house stood at the corner of Silver Street and Monkswell Street; in fact we have a tiny manuscript drawing of it, with its shop's-pentice in front; the whole area obliterated by the barbarians in the blitz of 1941. Of Shakespeare's parish church here, St Olave's, Stow tells us that it was 'a small thing, and without any noteworthy monuments.' A few years later, in the summer of 1607, there was buried in St Giles' Cripplegate the base-born child of Shakespeare's youngest brother, Edmund, another actor. Edmund was himself buried the last day of that year in St Saviour's, now Southwark Cathedral, aged only twenty-six, 'with a forenoon knell of the great bell.'

A few years previously, about 1599, William had a spell on Bankside, about the time James Burbage was transferring his theatre from Shoreditch to build the new Globe on the South Bank. At the end of his life Shakespeare owned a half-share in the gate-house going into Blackfriars, very convenient for the theatre within, of which he was part-owner. Stow has a full description of the precinct, which, since the destruction of the monastery, had filled up with an interesting variety of inhabitants, from grandees like Robert Cecil's troublesome aunt, Lady Russell, to foreign craftsmen, jewellers, printers like Shakespeare's schoolfellow, Richard Field, who printed his *Venus and Adonis* there.

Our one regret, our one legitimate criticism of Stow, is that his mind was so set on relics of the past that he neglected some of the amenities of the present — one cannot see him attending the theatre, for example. Twice the Fishmongers get a wigging for being so ignorant of their antiquities as not to know why or when they were joined in amity with the Goldsmiths; and when they repaired the monument of Sir William Walworth, the Mayor who struck down Wat Tyler, 'for lack of knowledge they followed a

fabulous book' and inscribed Jack Straw. Evidently they
should have consulted John Stow.

Indeed, we should continue to consult him; with him to
guide us we can hardly go wrong about Shakespeare's
London. And beneath the facts and the sober prose of the
historian, we sense the life: the games between the scholars
of St Bartholomew's and St Anthony's, dancing for garlands
in the streets, running at the quintain on Cornhill, out into
the fields that lay all round for May morning, garnishing the
doors with boughs and flowers for Midsummer, decking the
churches with green at Christmas; we seem to hear the bells
of St Peter's Cornhill, that were the fairest ring of six bells in
all England.

And so we bring old John Stow home to his resting-place
here in St Andrew Undershaft. We are right not to forget
him, for, in the end as all the way along, he was a good man.

# Fulke Greville

*The Life of Fulke Greville*, by R. A. Rebholz[1] is about a man
whose career and work are of considerable significance, and
touched both Elizabethan and Jacobean life at many points;
as Sir Robert Naunton summed up, he had 'the longest lease
and the smoothest time without rub' of any courtiers of the
time. Forty years of royal service, a very long and successful
span: he was early provided for by a virtual monopoly of the
clerical offices of the Council of Wales, executed by deputy,
which brought in £1000 per annum. Under Elizabeth
Treasurer of the Navy, under James Chancellor of the ·

[1] (Oxford University Press, 1971.)

Exchequer, under Charles I a member of an inner Cabinet Council, he had a good run for his money. His building up of his fortune, from office, patrimony and investment, to £7000 per annum is a study in itself; so is his rebuilding of Warwick Castle and his establishment of the Grevilles there, his chief monument today. His literary work as poet and dramatist (with which we are not concerned here) has been dealt with recently in a subtler and better written study by Joan Rees.[2] With these two books it may be said that this remarkable figure has at last been covered.

Many years of work have gone into Professor Rebholz's laborious work: it might have claims to be the standard biography but for a fundamental fault: the naïvety of this literary scholar's judgement of politics, the lack of historical sense. He simply identifies himself with the partisan viewpoint of Essex, of Greville himself, of Sidney's left-wing Protestant views at home and abroad. Robert Cecil 'engineers' the succession of James I: no idea that Cecil deserved the highest credit for the skill with which the inevitable transition, which might have been rough, was smoothly effected. Cecil's was a 'tyrannical faction': no idea that he served the central interests of the state, which was why the Queen backed him. Actually, it was Essex who built up a faction and turned it to treasonable purposes, which was why the Queen rather than Cecil, destroyed him. The professor speaks of Cecil's short-sighted 'megalomania'; the leading characteristics of that statesman were far-sightedness and his sense of moderation. Greville hated (was envious of) Cecil; Greville's loss of office was no act of 'vengeance' on Cecil's part: there was just no reason why he should strive officiously to keep an opponent alive.

The portrait of Greville that emerges is more convincing, though the author does not fully grasp that Greville is only a secondary figure, not powerful enough to influence events. Nor does he see that Greville's opposition to peace with

---

[2] *Fulke Greville, Lord Brooke, 1554—1628* (Routledge and Kegan Paul, 1971).

Spain was mistaken – a good reason for dropping him. A disillusioned idealist, Greville was as uncandid as everybody else, meaner and more cautious than most. Too cautious to marry, he was certainly homo-erotic, as the professor suggests: no doubt in love with Philip Sidney. For all his lofty principles and meanness about Cecil, he had no objection to buying office as Chancellor of the Exchequer from the disgraceful Somersets and Howards, nor to sucking up to Buckingham in the end: such were the exigencies of politics.

The best of the book is the way it relates Greville's writings to his career and shows how autobiographical they are – the extrapolation of his frustrations and grievances, his total disillusionment. It is easy to overestimate Greville's verse: it rarely gets off the ground. Even here Professor Rebholz misses the perceptive comment of Sir William Davenant, reported by Aubrey, that Greville 'with too much judgment and refining spoiled it': the poetry never had much spontaneity.

The writing of this book is of an unwearied pedestrianism, ornamented occasionally by such a dreadful word as 'triggered' for 'started', or 'positioned' for 'placed'. It is odd that persons of no literary sensitivity should choose to write about literature. The ground-plan of Warwick Castle upon which Greville worked was made by 'an architect named Robert Smithson' – no idea that this was the greatest of Elizabethan architects, to whom Mark Girouard has devoted a masterly study, which has both scholarship and sensibility. Finally, two technical defects: it is a mistake to relegate to footnotes something really significant in Greville's correspondence with Baro and an example of his skill as conciliator at the Council Board – matters about which we should be told as against much we do not need to be. There is a confusion between George Carew and George Carey on p. 143; George Carew went to Ireland, Carey not.

# Ralegh as Writer

This is the most important book to have been devoted to Ralegh's writings and ideas.[1] Professor Lefranc has been engaged upon it for fifteen years, and brings to it the combined standards of meticulous scholarship and high intellectual ability of the *Ecole Normale*. These are more indispensable than most writers on Ralegh have appreciated, any more than they have the excruciating difficulty of the subject, with its peculiar pitfalls at so many points. There is, first the fundamental question of establishing the canon of Ralegh's works. So far as the poems are concerned, this has already been achieved by Miss A. M. C. Latham. Professor Lefranc also goes through the attributed prose works one by one, establishing what may now be regarded as the canon. This is an important service, even if it does not much affect our picture of Ralegh's mind to throw out 'the Sceptick' as the translation from Sextus Empiricus it is: Ralegh's intellectual characteristics remain the same, and Professor Lefranc is right to emphasise Ralegh's natural, as well as conscious, Machiavellianism.

These subtle and complex matters demand treatment from a superior intelligence; and Professor Lefranc's qualification is the ability to perceive that all Ralegh's writings have some ulterior object in view, that they are almost always intended to subserve some purpose, personal or political – usually, since he was an obsessed egoist, a combination of both. Professor Lefranc brings this out in the best analysis that the *History* has yet received. He shows how naïf Strathmann was to accept the orthodox religious framework of the book *au*

[1] P. Lefranc, *Sir Walter Ralegh Ecrivain: l'oeuvre et les idées* (Armand Colin, 1968).

*pied de la lettre:* that was intended for the public, and had a large part in the book's success and influence with the Puritans – whom for the rest Ralegh detested. What he thought for himself may be read more acutely in the digressions. At every point, save one, Professor Lefranc is acute and suggestive.

The tone of the book is not only magistral, but magisterial: from its lofty point of view Mr Walter Oakeshott's work is characterised by *'légèreté de jugement'*, as Miss Bradbrook's 'School of Night' is dismissed for the mare's nest it is. One detects a certain superciliousness in this literary scholar towards the study of history proper, in his reference to *'l'extrême flexibilité du genre jusqu'à une époque récente, et du peu d'interêt porté par les historiens de la littérature à un secteur généralement considéré comme marginal.'* This leads him to a mistaken focus in his treatment of the historiography that was the background of Ralegh's work. The chronicle genre is in some ways closer to moder historiography than the more literary works of More and Bacon. Hence it is significant that Ralegh ceased to be regarded as an historian after the seventeenth century, Camden not, whose conception of history was more strictly historical – and whom for the rest Professor Lefranc hardly appreciates.

He has, too, one or two things to learn about the period from historians. It is not for him to dismiss the opinion of those well qualified to judge as to Elizabeth's real interest in sea-power; of course she wanted peace, but there was her financial interest in a number of the voyages, besides her aggressive support of her seamen (in contrast to Burghley's caution, for example). *'La médiocrité des perspectives d'avenir ouvertes par le nouveau Roi'* hardly does justice to the perspectives opened up by the accession of Scotland and the union of Britain. It is quite mistaken of Professor Lefranc to adhere to the date 1588 for Ralegh's marriage, simply because he put it forward in an article years ago, and, a young man, was wrong. We can all make mistakes – the point is to correct them when pointed out. He rightly accepts the sequence of dates as given in the Throckmorton Diary at Canterbury – it was not necessary for him to consult the original apparently: from this we know that Arthur Throckmorton first heard of Ralegh's secret marriage with his sister on 17 November 1591, the child Damerei was born 29 March 1592. Now, (1) it is utterly out of the question in Elizabethan circumstances that that marriage could have been kept secret for four years; (2) commonsense, completely corroborated by all that we know of Ralegh's character, tells us that the reason for a speedy marriage – which he had not intended – was that the baby was on the way. The name it was given, Damerei (or D'Amory), by the way, has nothing to do with any 'Celtic' fantasy of Ralegh's: his D'Amory descent was a royal one – that was its point to Ralegh, and quite in accordance with his character to assert it at such a moment.

This last is a small point – and there are one or two others; what is to be regretted is that obstinacy should have left this blot on a long-pondered, too meticulously detailed book. It is hoped that Professor Lefranc will rectify it when he produces his study of Ralegh's life and career, which no one is more qualified to write, in some respects, if not in others.

# Computer's History

In *Enterprise and Empire. Merchant and Gentry Investment in the Expansion of England, 1575–1630,*[1] Professor Theodore K. Rabb applies computer-methods to the familiar story of England's maritime and commercial expansion from

[1] (Harvard University Press; Oxford University Press, 1968.)

the 1580s to 1630, thereby giving us, he tells us, 'the benefits of quantification'. His aim is to provide a statistical survey of the investment that went into the expansion, and for that purpose, he says, 'the division of the investors into social classes . . . was of fundamental importance. Without a valid, consistent, and easily applicable definition of the difference between a gentleman and a merchant, there was no point in trying to evaluate their relative roles in the expansion.' Professor Rabb regards a gentleman as 'anyone whose income originally came from land', and a merchant as 'anyone whose income originally came from commerce'. Although this is very crude – for people's incomes are liable to come from different sources – let us accept it, and see how he applies it.

Unfortunately a doubt assails one, from the beginning, at his reference to Sir John Hawkins as 'himself a member of a great Devon family'. He was not; he was merely of a Plymouth merchant family, and a new one at that, whose money had been made in trade there by his father. When one comes to the detailed analysis of investors, one finds the class of all three Penruddocks given as 'unknown': in fact, they belonged to the leading gentry of Wiltshire. Similarly, all three of the family of Treffry, and all three of the name Trefusis are given as 'unknown': they belonged to well-known families of country gentry in Cornwall. The familiar name of John Tradescant, Virginia traveller, gardener and botanist, also appears as 'unknown', though we know a great deal about him.

One's original doubt begins to extend to the value of the whole undertaking: the computer is no substitute for knowledge and judgement. When it comes to a matter that demands plain commonsense – Thomas Thorp's reference to himself, in the dedication of Shakespeare's Sonnets, as 'the well-wishing adventurer in setting forth' – Professor Rabb creates a perfect mare's nest. No one has ever supposed that the words refer to anyone but Thorp himself. No one could ever suppose it, until Professor Rabb appeared, and goes through the lists of the Companies looking for a Mr W. H. One would have thought that only a computer could come up with anything so absurd.

# Thomas Hariot: Elizabethan Scientist

Thomas Hariot is known to the wider public chiefly for his famous *Brief and True Report of the New Found Land of Virginia* (i.e. North America), which he wrote in Armada year, 1588. It is a classic of scientific and anthropological observation by the most original and wide-ranging of Elizabethan scientific intellects. Some idea of its importance may be gathered from the fact that seventeen editions of it appeared in Europe in the quarter of a century after its publication: no other English book arrested so much attention on the Continent – certainly not Shakespeare. It had been translated into Latin, and published by De Bry with illustrations – in those days it was not necessary for anyone abroad to know English.

The little book was based on the experience of American conditions of the first Roanoke colony of 1585–6, which Hariot saw was of decisive effect for the future. When permanent settlement was achieved at Jamestown twenty years later it was founded on the knowledge gained at Roanoke, and summed up with concise mastery by Hariot. There he had been specially engaged in dealing with the Indians, and so the anthropological aspect of his book is even more valuable than his account of flora and fauna, foods and fruits, the medical uses of tobacco and sassafras (which

Elizabethans fancied a specific for venereal disease), the controversial potato.

Hariot learned enough of their language to communicate with the Indians about their beliefs. He found that some of them prophesied that 'there were more of our generation yet to come to kill theirs and take their places' – as the unfortunate Moctezuma had believed in Mexico. It makes one wonder if the Indians of Virginia could possibly have known what had happened there.

Hariot astonished them by showing them new perspective glasses – embryo telescopes – with which to observe moon and stars, burning glasses, spring clocks, the magnetic properties of the loadstone. On all this he was an authority, the most brilliant scientist of the Elizabethan Age, along with William Gilbert, author of *De Magnete*, a founder of the science of electricity. Gilbert's chief lack was a knowledge of mathematics; whereas Hariot was the leading algebraist in Europe between Viète and Descartes.

Hariot's seminal book on algebra, *Artis Analyticae Praxis,* was published in 1631, ten years after his death, and had its influence on Descartes publishing a few years later. An historian of mathematics, Cajori, tells us that 'Hariot's algebra is less rhetorical and more symbolic than perhaps any other algebra that has ever been written ... Hariot's *Praxis* stands out as a remarkable treatise for the beginning of the 17th century ... It is a book which excels all others in the great emphasis placed on symbolic algebra.' Historians of mathematics go into his specific contributions to algebra, and mathematical notation, including the use of the familiar symbols, $>$ and $<$, for greater than and lesser than. 'Few algebraists before and during the Renaissance understood the significance even of negative quantities' – Hariot was one of the first to use them.

A historian of astronomy, W. W. Bryant, tells us that Hariot made observations of the moon about the same time as Galileo's and on 'the new-found planets about Jupiter' during 1610–12; 'between 8 December 1610 and 18 January

1613 Hariot made 199 observations of sunspots and determined thereby the period of the sun's axial rotation.' In
navigation a leading authority, Professor E. G. R. Taylor, says
that on his voyage to Virginia, Hariot had tested the
customary methods of observation and found that 'the
latitude obtained by observation of the star differed by
nearly as much as a degree from that found by the sun. This
he rightly put down to the faulty Regiment of the North
Star, and he made continuous observations on the true
position of the Pole Star with a 12-ft. instrument (probably
an Astronomer's Staff) which he set up on the roof of Sir
Walter Ralegh's mansion in the Strand.' He was thus helped
towards calculating the precession of the equinoxes, the
variation in position of the North Star over the centuries. He
made a practical table of corrections for every tenth degree
of latitude for use at sea, and a new table of solar declination
to serve the period of Ralegh's Guiana voyages. But his
teaching manual, the *Arcticon,* has been lost, and he did not
publish his *Canon,* which was for Ralegh's personal use.

Kepler wrote to consult Hariot for his views on the origin
and essential differences of colours, the refraction of rays of
light, the causes of the rainbow and haloes round the sun.
Hariot sent back a table of results of his experiments with
thirteen liquids and transparent solids, with their specific
gravities; he discussed the reasons for refraction and put forth
his theory of the rainbow. The scientifically-minded Sir
William Lower, Hariot's pupil, wrote to him: 'Do you not
startle to see every day some of your inventions taken from
you; for I remember long since you told me as much, that the
motions of the planets were not perfect circles.' Kepler's
deduction of the elliptical orbits of the planets and Galileo's
observation of the moons of Jupiter dealt resounding blows
to Aristotelian orthodox belief that the heavens were perfect
and immutable. Hariot knew as well as Galileo and Kepler
that this was not so, both of whom got into trouble for
announcing their new and challenging knowledge.

Hariot kept silent. So, Lower warned him,

you taught me the curious way to observe weight in water
[specific gravity], and within a while after Ghetaldi comes
out with it in print. A little while before, Viète prevented
you of the garland of the great invention of Algebra. All
these were your dues, and many others I could mention;
and yet too great reservedness has robbed you of these
glories.

Lower was sure that there was yet more in Hariot's
'storehouse of invention'.

Why is it that we do not know more of this brilliant
intellect who was pushing forward the frontiers of science at
so many points?

For one thing, Elizabethans were not much interested in
the biographies of scholars or writers — this is why we do not
know more about the lives of, say, Hariot or Shakespeare.
Nothing odd about that, and in fact we know more about
Hariot than any other Elizabethan scientist except Dr Dee, as
we know more about Shakespeare than any dramatist of the
time except Ben Jonson.

There were reasons for Hariot's keeping quiet — Galileo
couldn't keep quiet, until silenced by the Inquisition. Hariot
was known to hold heterodox views, for all that he took
trouble to assert his orthodoxy, and insisted, for example,
that he had taught the truths of the Bible to the Indians in
Virginia. There were rumours about him: he was thought to
hold that there had been men before Adam; he was thought
unreliable on the subject of the Old Testament, the necessary
foundation of the New; he was attacked abroad by the Jesuit
Father Parsons, who wrote that Marlowe was reported as
thinking Moses but a juggler and saying that Hariot, 'Sir
Walter Ralegh's man, can do more than he.'

There were dangers in being Ralegh's man, who was
himself held to be heterodox and was in trouble for years,
and this occasionally involved Hariot. At Oxford Ralegh had
been an Oriel man. Hariot was born there in 1560 in the
parish of St Mary's — upon which I look out as I write; he

entered St Mary Hall, which was a dependency of Oriel College, and graduated in 1580. Shortly after he entered Ralegh's service and was connected with his affairs for the rest of his life. He became his scientific adviser, working with him on problems of navigation, geography, colonial settlement; he made Ralegh's maps for him, and looked after his affairs at home while the great man was away on his voyages and when he was confined in the Tower.

There, after Gunpowder Plot in 1605, Ralegh was joined by the 'Wizard' Earl of Northumberland, who also helped to maintain the distinguished scientist. Quite an intellectual coterie they formed, with time on their hands for the Earl's speculations, Ralegh's chemical experiments and writing his *History of the World*. For this last Hariot assisted in working out the impossible ages of the Patriarchs necessitated by Ralegh's disingenuous acceptance of the literal interpretation of Scripture.

Hariot himself was imprisoned at the time of Gunpowder Plot, for Northumberland had called upon him to cast King James's horoscope, which was thought a suspicious act. Hariot's study at Sion House was thoroughly searched, his papers ransacked. We have the questions that the King ordered Cecil to put to Hariot. 'What purpose he hath heard his Lord use anent my nativity or fortune? If ever his Lord seemed discontented of the State? If ever he heard him talk or ask him of my children's fortune? If ever his Lord desired to know what should be his own fortune and end?' – i.e. whether Northumberland was aiming at the throne.

Hariot protested his innocence to the Council: he 'was always of honest conversation, never a meddler in matters of state, never ambitious for preferments but contented with a private life for the love of learning, wherein his labours have been painful and great.' He begged Cecil to release him out of the dungeon where he was already ill. During his last years he was suffering from cancer of the face. In the next generation John Aubrey already had difficulty in getting information about this reserved, secretive man. But an old acquaintance of Hariot told him that

> he did not like (or valued not) the old story of the
> Creation of the world . . . He would say *ex nihilo nihil fit*.
> But a *nihilum* killed him at last: for in the top of his nose
> came a little red speck, exceeding small, which grew bigger
> and bigger, and at last killed him. . . . The divines of those
> times looked on his manner of death as a judgment upon
> him for nullifying the Scripture.

Hariot left a mass of papers behind him, which became
scattered and some of them lost, for example, his Latin tract
on Motion and the Collision of Bodies. He was anxious that
his constructive work on algebra should be extracted from his
papers, and this was accomplished with the publication of his
*Praxis*. But no further editorial work was done, in spite of
attempts and promises over the centuries since; the story of
Hariot's papers is in itself an odd one in the history of science.
There are many hundreds, if not a few thousands, of pages
covered with his calculations, interspersed with other matter,
verses about algebra and navigation, jottings, diagrams,
star-maps, including a fascinating map of the moon – of
special interest to us in our day when the moon makes news.
On the scientific level we should observe that man's amazing
achievement in reaching the moon has come about by
Hariot's way of patient scientific observation, endeavour and
experiment, not the way of his conventional and orthodox
critics. Even his amanuensis Torporley, who was a clergyman,
wrote of him:

T. H.

As an excellent mathematician one who very seldom ⎫
As a bold philosopher one who occasionally           ⎬ erred
As a frail man one who notably                       ⎭

And Torporley wrote *A Compendious Warning* 'for the more
trustworthy refutation of the pseudo-philosophic atomic
theory revived by him and, outside his other strange notions,
deserving of reprehension and anathema.'

We see how many reasons there are for the neglect of this important and original Renaissance scientist; but now at last things are beginning to look up. Most of his manuscripts remain, whole volumes in the British Museum, at Petworth House and Alnwick Castle — these last descending from his patron, Northumberland. Those in the British Museum I have been through, but it is obvious that only a mathematician — and at that, a historical mathematician — can deal with them. Some years ago I suggested to G. M. Trevelyan that he might interest a Cambridge scholar in the subject. Since then an Oxford scholar, Miss E. Seaton, has cracked Hariot's cipher — probably what Aubrey was referring to as 'an alphabet that he had contrived for the American language, ˙like Devils': Hariot's figures certainly have long tails.

In the last generation Henry Stevens of Vermont became an authority on Hariot and published (London, 1900) what is still the best book on him; but less than two-hundred copies were issued, and the promise of further work was unfulfilled. It is obvious now that one person cannot satisfactorily deal with Hariot and the mass of his papers. Happily a group of British and American scholars have recently got together, under the lead of Dr A. C. Crombie at Oxford — the Thomas Hariot Seminar — which published its first report in October 1969.

Mrs Rukeyser's book is appropriately entitled *The Traces of Thomas Hariot.*[1] The author is a poetic lady, not a scientist, and the book is an eccentric work, written very oddly in a mixture of evocation, impressionism, and quotation. The quotations are best, for Mrs Rukeyser has taken the trouble to go to all the places where there is Hariot material, has put in a lot of work at it, and there are occasional flashes of poetic insight. I hope it may be taken as a compliment if I say that the book reminds me, in a way, of Edith Sitwell's *Fanfare for Elizabeth,* though she too did not really qualify to write about the subject.

[1] (Random House, 1971.)

The book pursues a number of will-o'-the-wisps, nonsense-questions, which a sense of humour would have refined or altogether abolished:

> What is a dot?
> Is a shipload of men a homosexual culture?
> Is the Bible an atheist book? If you rub yourself with it?
> How do you get from a prison to the moon?

Even worse are the conjectures, creating superfluous confusion. There is no evidence whatever connecting Ralegh and Hariot with Marlowe's death: an idiotic supposition. Nothing is needed to account for that beyond the quarrel over 'the reckoning', after drinking all day at the Deptford tavern. Marlow was of the sort, like Dylan Thomas, who would come to an early end anyhow.

The book is improved by its illustrations, including Hariot's fascinating map of the moon. Even here there are needless mistakes, reproducing an Oxford portrait as Hariot's when the dates are wrong, a Cambridge portrait as Shakespeare's when it has nothing whatever to do with him; while the supposed portrait of the Countess of Northumberland is of half a century later, a lady of the Restoration.

It is best to conclude on the solid ground of the Elizabethans, with Chapman's tribute to the mysterious scientist — mysterious because a rational inquiring mind:

> To you whose depth of soul measures the height
> And all dimensions of all works of weight,
> Reason being ground, structure and ornament,
> To all inventions, grave and permanent,
> And your clear eyes the Spheres where Reason moves.

# Elizabethan Magus: John Dee

Anyone who has worked at John Dee knows that it is extremely difficult to get him right. Two professors reviewing this book[1] — Professors Trevor-Roper and Hurstfield — have already perpetrated a number of journalistic errors about him. He was *not* the first of Elizabethan scientists; he did *not* introduce Euclid to the English; he was *not* the leading navigational adviser to the voyages; he made *no* contributions to science, and did not leave any worthwhile 'books' unpublished; nor was he even an effective propagandist of empire, as Hakluyt was.

The author of this modest introduction to Dee knows better, in spite of his uncertain grasp of the background. It is very naïf, for example, to think that Sir William Pickering was a serious suitor for Elizabeth I's hand. It is not merely a mistake to suppose that Sir John Hawkins was a companion on Drake's voyage round the world, but shows no comprehension of the nature and circumstances of that voyage, or of the relations between the two men. Nor does antiquarianism begin with the Italian Renaissance: what about William Worcester in the fifteenth century, or for that matter Gerald of Wales in the twelfth? The remarks on Sir John Cheke, a significant figure at Cambridge, and Ciceronianism, a not very significant matter at Oxford, reveal a quite uncertain grasp of what the universities were really like and what went on there.

However, one can sympathise with the author's *cri de coeur*, 'What *can* one make of a man like John Dee?' Exactly. He goes on to tell us, 'he was entirely within the Hermetic movement so prevalent during the 16th century, but he was

[1] P. J. French, *John Dee. The World of an Elizabethan Magus* (Routledge and Kegan Paul, 1972).

one of its most exteme adherents.' That is to say that most of his speculation and the great bulk of his writings, concerned with communication with spirits, the invocation of angels, his learning in astrology and alchemy, were just so much nonsense. Mr French tells us one thing new — that there is no evidence either of Dee possessing a doctorate; so the 'Dr' in Dr Dee is probably mystagoguery too.

Now for what remains of Dee that makes sense. He was undoubtedly a learned man, with a wide range of intellectual interests; his library was the largest in England and was generously available to fellow-scholars, and therefore had its influence. He made no contribution to mathematics; but his celebrated Preface to Billingsley's Euclid had considerable effect in propagating the case for the utility of mathematics: in a word, it was programmatic. No comparison with Hariot, who was, with Viète, the greatest algebraist of the age.

Dee also had a wide knowledge of cosmography and therefore was consulted by the navigators. But he was found impracticable — as anyone who tried to sail the route he thought to exist from Hudson's Bay across North America, to come out in the Gulf of California, would find! No, the practical adviser to the voyages, whose geographical knowledge was factual not notional, was again Hakluyt.

Dee was a megalomaniac Celt — the American author simply does not grasp the importance of this in Dee's make-up and propaganda, always for a *British,* not an English, empire and role in the world. With his disparate interests of mind, there was something cracked about him, as contemporaries realised. His interests were quite sufficiently dispersed, without our taking Miss Yates's views on his Vitruvianism and its importance for architecture and theatre in the least seriously. *All* serious Elizabethan architects knew about Vitruvius without any such nonsense.

It seems the habit in this circle to depreciate the earlier biography of Miss Charlotte Fell Smith: I find her work more informative, more factual, based on a more thorough knowledge of the manuscripts, and of sounder critical judgement than theirs.

# Elizabethan Song-Writer:
# John Dowland

Dowland is the greatest of English song-writers: here at last is the definitive study of his life and work on which Diana Poulton — herself a distinguished lutenist — has been working for thirty years.[1] It is not only a masterly work of research and musical understanding, but a sumptuous example of production of which English publishing — especially in the difficulties and frustrations of today — may be proud.

Though the technical side is rather beyond me, there is much of historical interest to engage one. Dowland was probably the best known of Elizabethan musicians abroad, both as a performer for his technical virtuosity and by the popularity of his compositions. His famous 'Lachrimae' had the astonishing fortune of being sung, imitated, praised all over the Continent; referred to in contemporary literature more than any other tune, it was still going as a song a century after it was composed. Dowland's genius was symptomatic of the age; his career has both social and cultural interest for us.

We know more about him than about most Elizabethan composers, for he was very personal and confiding about his troubles, exceedingly sensitive and given to melancholy — which he expressed with the utmost poignancy, and thus spoke directly to people's hearts. There was a crux at the heart of his experience which intensified the pathos: though the most celebrated lutenist in Europe, he never got a post, or proper recognition, at the English Court until it was too late and his inspiration was over.

The reason was that he became a Catholic convert while *abroad*, in France when young. An historian may come to the

---

[1] Diana Poulton, *John Dowland* (Faber and Faber, 1972).

help of the musical author in regard to this. William Byrd became an uncompromising Catholic, but retained Elizabeth's favour as a patriot who was not subverted abroad. This made the difference, an aroma of mistrust — as with Russians deviating abroad today. Twice Dowland was disappointed of his hopes at Court; he was forced to go abroad for a living, as lutenist at the Court of Denmark. After a number of years there he was dismissed, Mrs Poulton does not know why; I think it was on account of his temperamental irregularity and overstaying his leave twice in England.

It is disputed whether he was an English Dowland or an Irish Dolan. The only lead we have is a dedication of a song in *A Pilgrim's Solace* 'To my loving countryman Mr. John Forster the younger, merchant of Dublin in Ireland.' 'Countryman', in Elizabethan usage, refers to one's own county or locality. When Dowland describes himself as 'born under her Highness', I think that the phrase is more likely to imply birth in Ireland than in England. Mrs Poulton takes the view that he was English; I incline to think Irish.

A generation ago English authorities were apt to see the wonderful flowering of Elizabethan music in too national a perspective. Mrs Poulton corrects that emphasis, and Dowland provides special opportunities for doing so, he spent so many years abroad, in France, Germany, Italy, Denmark. He won international fame as a virtuoso performer on the lute, not — it now seems — as a singer himself. Whether owing to discouragement or not, he never collected his compositions for the lute: Mrs Poulton has done that for him four hundred years after. It is encouraging to researchers to learn that as recently as 1926 the widow of a descendant turned up with a precious manuscript partly in Dowland's hand. The publication of his first Book of Songs in 1597 established the format for the next twenty-five years; the 'Lachrimae' of 1604, for five viols and a lute, again produced something quite new. By the time of his death — born in 1563, he died in 1625 — the golden age of English lute-music was over.

Mrs Poulton goes through the whole of Dowland's *oeuvre*

in every form — solo lute-music, song-books, consort-music, psalms and spiritual songs. Dowland's dedications of his works and his commendatory verses to others reveal a very wide acquaintance, from the King of Denmark and his sister, James I's Queen, down to the young Cornish gentleman-pirate, Digory Piper, for whom Dowland named an exquisite pavan and galliard. Of great utility to the general historian is the amount of material assembled in the chapter on 'Patrons and Friends'.

I have learned much from this book — here are a few small contributions in return. There is nothing surprising in so many dedications of musical works to Robert Cecil, for the clever statesman was also a connoisseur of music, as students of the *Salisbury Papers* know. This cultural side to him should not be neglected in any adequate biography of him — though average historians are not endowed with much artistic sensibility. Mrs Poulton is certainly right in identifying Dowland's prisoner taken at 'Cales' (Cadiz) as the book he translated, the *Micrologus* of the German Vogelsang, who preferred to be known as Ornithoparcus. A reference to *Ralegh and the Throckmortons* would have shown many more books taken at Cadiz. It might also solve the identity of 'Lord Gray' for Mrs Poulton: almost certainly the fifteenth Lord Grey of Wilton, son of Spenser's admired Lord Deputy.

# Mediterranean Epic

The Mediterranean is the seed-bed of European civilisation, and a great deal of European history may be regarded, as Ranke saw it, as a dichotomy between the Southern and

Northern peoples, the conflicts and dynamic interchanges between the two. Braudel points out[1] that, in the decisive conflict (in Western and Central Europe) between the Reformation and the Counter-Reformation, or Catholic Revival, Protestantism never effectively crossed the frontiers of the Mediterranean states. There were other conflicts, such as that between Latin Catholicism and the Greek Church, in which the former behaved with self-frustrating arrogance. The main conflict this book deals with is that between the Catholic West, led by the Habsburgs, and Islam; its originality lies chiefly in the attention he gives to the Turkish Empire and the Balkans so important in the sixteenth century — which the British with their eyes on the Channel and the Atlantic, their insular perspective, have been apt to overlook.

Braudel's book has been out for some twenty years, and has been acclaimed by academic historians as a classic. It is indeed a very fine book, suggestive and imaginative, by a cultivated historian who knows how to quote Stendhal and Théophile Gautier. No one approves of that in an historian more than I. At the same time, Braudel is not beyond criticism — as one would think, to listen to the *claque*: for one thing, he apparently does not know English, and is practically unaware of English scholarship, even that bearing on his subject. The gap is not insuperable; all the same it is a surprising defect.

It matters the less in that his subject is so very much the Mediterranean. Even here a significant feature before the end of the century was the English penetration in force. There was the most favoured nation status won from the Porte, the formation of the Levant Company in London — out of which shortly came the East India Company; big armed merchantmen fought their way through Spanish galleys and Barbary pirates to capture the growing trade, for example, in currants from Xante in return for English cloth and hardware. (This is reflected in Simon Forman's consultations with Levant

[1] F. Braudel, *The Mediterranean and the Mediterranean World in the Age of Philip II,* vol. II (Collins, 1972).

merchants over the movements of their ships, as in Hakluyt.)
All this is dismissed by Braudel in one throw-away sentence:
'in 1586 five English merchant ships sent the Sicilian galley
squadron packing! Unrecognised at the time, this was a
foretaste of the career ahead for the ship-of-the-line.' It was
far more than that – it was a portent of a new sea-power in
the Mediterranean, the tipping of the balance to the Atlantic
and the North-West.

Most valuable is the treatment of the rhythm between the
expanding power of Spain, rendered possible by American
treasure, and the static Ottoman Empire. The latter, still
regarded as advancing, was actually declining, though it
managed to hold its own in the long war against German
power just before and after 1600. The Turks would never
have advanced so far and broken the kingdom of Hungary, if
it had not been for the idiotic divisions among Christians.
Indeed the way was made easy for them in the Balkans,
particularly in Bulgaria, by the social upheavals of peasants
against landlords, so that the Turks could move in. To begin
with, it may have made things easier for the peasantry; then
the Turks reconstituted the great estates – more efficient
anyway; thousands of Christians, Serbs especially, were sold
into slavery. The movement of our time has brought these
sub-peoples up again – as with Celts in the British Isles.

The Turkish Empire was more tolerant than the Christians
from a religious point of view; it is remarkable what a variety
of peoples contributed to ruling it – only one in ten of
Grand Viziers were pure Turks in nearly a century and a half;
while the running of economic affairs was enmeshed by
Greek and Jewish money-lenders. Turkish penetration was
thickest in the rich plains of the eastern Balkans, very thin in
the mountainous west. An essentially uncreative people, the
Turks did introduce rice, and the most heartening pages of
this book illustrate the rich intermingling of botanical and
plant contributions in the area – plane trees, coffee beans,
oranges, lemons, peaches, lilacs, cotton. Braudel would not
have known of the introduction of the yellow-damask rose

into England from Constantinople, by the Levant merchant, Nicholas Leate.

The Crisis-cliché, so beloved of this school and its followers in England, appears too frequently. The concept is fairly widely applicable at all times in history, since history is the record of ups and downs in the human struggle for survival. There was no greater a 'Crisis of the Aristocracy' from 1550 to 1640 than there had been before – indeed less of one than in the century before in the Wars of the Roses.

It is noticeable how few of Braudel's generalisations apply to England. He talks of the bankruptcy of the bourgeoisie: not so in England, where the middle elements of society in country and in towns were gathering strength. We are told of the increase of slavery: in England at this time serfdom was being ended. He notes a great increase in the number of the nobility: not so in England. 'The cultural waves which the Baroque unfurled upon Europe were possibly more deep, full and interrupted than those even of the Renaissance.' Once more, this was not true for England, nor did 'the harrowing scenes' he refers to in France and Germany apply here, as he says. Even the Civil War was nothing like so inhuman as the French Religious Wars, nor did it noticeably reduce the population – as the Thirty Years War reduced Germany by at least a third.

Mawlay Hasan, king of Tunis, 'left everyone who met him with the impression of a prince of great distinction, a lover of beauty, a connoisseur of perfumes and philosophy'. He was blinded by his son, and took refuge in Naples. Of course, *homo homini lupus* is true at all times, but it would be hard to parallel this in the reign of Elizabeth I. Braudel's ignorance of England leads to a few obvious mistakes. The port that profited by Atlantic enterprise in the later sixteenth century was not Bristol, but Plymouth. Surely Rome was not 'the most liberal of western societies' (with its Inquisition), nor was it the leading money-market: Antwerp was. Nor was Madrid ever the most 'dazzling' cultural centre – that was always Venice.

Some of the questions put are hardly worth putting, the answer is so obvious. Why did not Spain turn to the Atlantic? The answer is that she did, as far as she could — and remained the dominant power in Central and South America in consequence. She could not put the whole of herself into Atlantic enterprise because she was so much of an inland power, dominated essentially by Castile.

This leads one to a 'methodological' point — blessed word, beloved by technicians throwing no more light by it. Braudel confesses, 'no sooner does the historian think he has isolated the particular quality of a civilisation than it gives proof of the exact opposite'. Then what is the point of isolating it? This shows up the futility of trying to turn history into sociological analysis. It is more subtle and truer to the variety and diversity of historical phenomena to elicit the facts concretely and then to describe and relate them. Braudel's confession is an honest one, and his book is good precisely because he sticks to the concrete facts and sees their significant interrelations.

Braudel is a highly intelligent man, who tells us that his two-volumed book, in circulation now for twenty years, was an attempt to write *total history* on various levels. The quartet of volumes I have put forth covering the Elizabethan Age — from *The England of Elizabeth* to *The Cultural Renaissance* — have had precisely the same inspiration. My life's work in this field was described by a third-rate journalist as 'effrontery'; I suppose it will take them twenty years, too, to see the point of it, if then.

# III
# The Iron Century

This book provides an example of the kind of history that is the fashion with the current generation of academics – not with readers – at the universities.[1] The author tells us, 'I have chosen to concentrate on social change and the fate of the lower classes. This book is an essay in quantitative social history, in the material infrastructure of life rather than the cultural superstructure.'

Of course the lower classes – to which I myself belong – are always less interesting than the upper, intellectually and aesthetically, if not spiritually; and the surface of any work of art is more rewarding than its material infrastructure.

But that is not the point. The point is that these people want to quantify history, to subject it to technification like any mechanical or engineering subject – to equate it, for example, with their own 'social engineering' (silly phrase).

Of course it is not possible to reduce history to technics. History is an art, cognate with the art of life – and these people have very little sense of life, or perhaps sense.

But, to look into this example of current history in its own terms. It is full of figures, statistics and graphs. Very well: the whole point of such quantitative treatment is that it should be accurate. My suspicions were immediately aroused when I saw a summary of the population of the largest cities in Europe about 1600: London appears, along with nine other cities, in the class of 'over 100,000', while Naples and Paris appear alone as 'over 200,000'.

---

[1] H. Kamen, *The Iron Century: Social Change in Europe 1550–1660* (Weidenfeld and Nicolson, 1971).

Now it is fairly reliably known that London in 1600 had a population of some 220,000, and it was almost certainly the largest town in Europe.

This author's figures are apt to be unreliable, and so are a number of his facts. Other fellow-academics have pointed out some of the errors. Rouen is credited with 30,000 *compagnons* (organised industrial workers), when its adult male population as a whole did not reach half that size. We are told that 'nearly all' the first members of the Royal Society had been professors at Gresham College; in fact three were, out of fifty-two original members of the Society.

What is the importance of attaching so much importance to figures, if you can't get them right? In fact, earlier statistics are notoriously unreliable, and I attach more importance to good judgement.

The author has the sense to see that Trevor-Roper's equating of witchcraft with mountain-areas was nonsense, and he has a gleam of suspicion – as Trevor-Roper had not – that the figures of executions were ridiculously inflated. H. C. Lea – on whom Trevor-Roper naïvely based himself – thought that 90,000 people had been executed for witchcraft in England during the century when persecution was at its height. The true figure is known, and it was something less than one thousand.

Why are these people so keen on statistics, when they don't know what a statistic is?

The reason is partly fashion, but also, since they are incapable of art, they want to reduce history to technics.

Now, I am a moderate, and there *is* a place for statistics in history; but it is a subordinate one, as a useful 'tool' – to use their favourite word – and only when fairly reliable.

Judgement is more important in getting things right – in history as in life. Clerics were hot on witchcraft – naturally, because of their obsession with theological nonsense. And, by the way, Reginald Scot was *not* the most 'influential' writer on witchcraft; he was the best and most enlightened: he exerted no influence precisely because he was too intelligent and humane. And he did see that the brilliant Bodin was crazy on the subject, a case of 'great wit to madness near allied'.

Once again, law was *not* the leading study at the universities: theology was. And so far from its being true that 'neither Copernicus nor Brahe, neither Kepler nor Pereisc was a university man', it is well known that the first three were at universities for years.

However, I wish to be kinder to this young author than his colleagues in the rat-race. They have lately been engaged in chewing each other up about a 'General Crisis' in the middle of the seventeenth century. Another of these quasi-sociological 'problems' they like to distract each other with, instead of getting down to the facts — in some notorious cases, instead of writing their books.

Mr Kamen has the sense to see that 'virtually all periods in history can be described as periods of crisis'; and that historians 'readily find reason and order in events that appear not to possess any order'.

I give him full marks for these perceptive observations and wish him better luck next time, with a less ambitious and more concrete subject.

# The Protestant Mind

This is a vigorous and sensible book on a difficult subject upon which it is all too easy to be vague and diffuse.[1] Touched to good purpose by a perceptible, but not excessive, Marxist influence the authors have set themselves to elicit the positive content of the doctrine and practice of English Protestantism in its heyday from Elizabeth I to the Civil War. The portrait they give us is clear and just, free from so much claptrap and cottonwool. They characterise convincingly what Newman would have called the 'notes' of English Protestantism: the absolute rejection of transubstantiation and with it the magic or superhuman concept of the priesthood; the emphasis upon the spiritual state of the recipient of the eucharist that in turn goes along with the activising impulse of Protestantism in the world; in contrast with a certain passivity in Catholicism here, the impulse to withdraw into monasticism, the 'double standard' the Georges diagnose in Catholic morality as opposed to the Protestant effort to subject experience to one standard.

There follows a trenchant account of the too celebrated Weber hypothesis in an excellent section on 'Calling'. They indict Weber of constructing a concept of the 'spirit of capitalism', in the German manner, and finding its origin in a 'Protestant ethic' similarly arrived at: i.e. hardly more than a tautology, proving what he wanted to prove. In fact Protestant divines were severer than any on the taking of usury; and 'where is the "spirit of capitalism" in its Protestant guise? It simply does not exist before 1640.' The utmost that can be said is that the Protestant emphasis on work in the world aided the development of capitalist

[1] C. H. and K. George, *The Protestant Mind of the English Reformation, 1570–1640* (Princeton University Press; Oxford University Press, 1961).

economy. Here is the commonsense behind the welter of
sociological jargon in Weber and Troeltsch.

What is rather new in this study, and just, is its
appreciation of the coherence and strength of the English
Protestant position in this period, the agreement upon
fundamentals. The English church, they say, had reason to be
proud of its achievement by James's reign, while it showed
'surprising breadth and liberality in its willingness to recog-
nize the complete validity of other Protestant churches in
other nations'. Even Rome could be recognised as a 'true
church', though much needing reform of its corruptions and
excessive cults. One sees that the conversion of a Donne in
such circumstances was one of conviction.

Trenchancy has the defects of its qualities, and occasionally one is out of sympathy with too absolute judgements.
'Christian economic theory, even more than Christian political theory, was halting, contradictory and dishonest.' What
about the difficulties, the inevitable obstructions, the
obstinacy in things, which a Burke understood so well and
radicals never do? The Georges accept too one-sided a picture
of a 'deteriorating economic situation' for the Church in this
period. There always had been ills, and there were some
improvements, notably in the education of the clergy. And
many of the ills reflected the irremediable circumstances of
society as a whole, poverty of resources, sparse productivity,
periods of unavoidable dearth and want. 'It may well be that
the theology and psychology of English Protestantism were
too fundamentally at odds with the emerging modernism of
capitalist enterprise to allow ethical integration of the
Christian precepts of love, brotherhood, and charity with the
economics of capitalism.' But this is going too far the other
way: what about the astonishing effort in philanthropy,
charity, education brought home to us by Professor W. K.
Jordan, and of which these Protestants were properly proud
in their own day?

Like all works dealing in theory and opinion, the work is
occasionally too absolute in its terms and misses the subtlety,

and sometimes the truth, of fact. It is admirably fair-minded
however, and brings out the essential sensibleness of these
men — one even comes to appreciate the loud-mouthed
Perkins.


# Two Caroline Officials


## 1

Professor Havran has performed a useful service to studies of
the seventeenth century by this biography.[1] We hardly need
any more biographies of the primary figures, particularly of
kings and queens; we need more studies of the secondary
figures to fill out our knowledge of the age and time. This
young American scholar has devoted a number of years to
careful research among original documents and papers, and
he has come up with a convincing account of one of the most
important of Charles I's ministers. A difficult task, for,
significant figure as he was over a long career, the personality
and work of Cottington are by no means easy to make out, in
fact were traduced in the party conflict of his time and
mis-esteemed subsequently.

Professor Havran is right to point out that historians have
paid more attention — and perhaps too much respect — to
the opponents of the Crown than to its supporters. It is
certainly true that Victorian historians were far more
favourable to 'their ideological forefathers of the seventeenth
century', just as today Leftist historians attach more importance to Levellers and such than they had at the time, or than
the facts warrant. The problems of government, always more

[1] Martin Havran, *Caroline Courtier: the Life of Lord Cottington* (Macmillan,
1973).

complex and difficult than those of opposition, attract more adult minds and demand more sophisticated treatment. The best of judges, Clarendon, twice described Cottington as a wise man; but he was by no means an obvious one. He offers a challenging subject.

A West Countryman, of Somerset clothier stock, Francis Cottington came up through the ranks from modest beginnings. It is interesting that this devoted servant of the monarchy should have been a new man, while the Puritan Parliamentarian who displaced him as Master of the Court of Wards (with all its profits), Lord Saye and Sele, should have been descended from an ancient (and predatory) Treasurer way back in the Middle Ages.

An able career-diplomat, Cottington spent seventeen years in Spain in a crucial post; because he was reserved and reticent, people said he was Spaniolised. In fact, he was not popular in Spain, for he stood up manfully for his country's interests; and he had the courage to stand up to Buckingham over his absurd journey with Prince Charles to Madrid, and again over Buckingham's sudden reversal of the previous peace-policy. More than that could hardly be expected: Cottington jeopardised his career by his courage.

Recalled home, he became an able financial administrator, faithfully serving the interests of the Crown and effective in raising its revenues. Of course he feathered his nest and made his fortune; so did everybody else, except the excessively upright bishops, Juxon and Laud — though they fared no better at the hands of the fanatics when their time came.

Cottington was very unfanatical, cool and good-tempered, patient, persistent and hard-working, with a sly sense of humour — one sees the picture of the trained administrator, giving nothing away, rather uncandid, possibly disingenuous, when most politicians were all too angrily expressive. When faults on both sides brought about the disaster of the Civil War, Cottington lost not only his offices but his fortune, with his estates confiscated. The sainted Saye and Sele, 'Old Subtlety', got Cottington's Hanworth estate, worth £14,000 for £4000; Parliament, to reward its faithful, gave him another £10,000 compensation when the Court of Wards was abolished.

The observant Samuel Butler saw, without illusions, that 'as these Grandees, as they call them, are taken off with bribes or preferment, others start up in their rooms and keep the Party on it'. He concludes philosophically: 'Do what we can, that which is a free government to one Party will be tyranny to another; where every slight Faction and trivial Sect calls itself the Public . . . where every man can teach us how to govern, but nobody knows how to obey.'

And the upshot? — a ruinous, destructive Civil War, at the end of which a compromise was reached which should have been reached twenty years before, and saved all the trouble. By that time, Cottington, after a long and strenuous life, had died in exile. He had taken life in exile as calmly, and with his exceptional stamina as smoothly, as his days in power. His body was brought home at the Restoration to lie in Westminster Abbey in as resplendent a tomb as he would have had twenty years before, just as if nothing untoward had happened in the interval.


2

As with Martin Havran's study of Cottington, we are indebted to yet another young American scholar for this further venture into the tangled undergrowth of early Stuart administrative history. We have plenty of studies of medieval administration, often *pour faute de mieux,* but few for the Tudor and Stuart periods. Impossible as it is to make the subject of administration lively, it can at least be made human, and this Professor Alexander has done for us in this careful and exhaustive study of Charles I's able Lord Treasurer.[2]

The biographical is the best way to approach, and make clear to the intending reader, the functions and differences

[2] M. Alexander, *Charles I's Lord Treasurer* (Macmillan, 1975).

between these offices and officials, between Treasury and
Exchequer, Upper and Lower Exchequer, between Clerk of
the Nichills and Clerk of the Pells, endearing names – the
latter more familiar to us as a fat sinecure for eighteenth-
century politicians. Professor Alexander points out that the
conception of government of these administrators under
James I and Charles I, as of the Kings themselves, was
'basically Elizabethan'. Of course the creaking old system,
with its inefficiency and endless disputes and delays, gave
plenty of opportunity for corruption and politicians on the
make.

As if they are not always with us! But at least the country
was not over-governed, weighed down by bureaucracy at
every level, weakened by the insupportable burdens of social
parasitism. There remained plenty of room for individual
initiative and enterprise, of which able people like Weston
took full advantage. Of course they made money – but they
created a distinguished Caroline culture, built gracious
houses, the relics of which still illuminate a devastated
countryside. They patronised the arts; Weston himself was a
patron of Ben Jonson, and we owe to him the commissioning
of Le Sueur's equestrian statue of Charles I at Charing Cross,
celebrated by the poets and familiar to us all.

Weston was a man of sense and good judgement, maligned
as he has been in the history books. But they have mostly
been written under the influence of the Victorian cult of
Parliament and the Whig Interpretation of History, with
Puritan and Parliamentarian sympathies about which we need
have no illusions today. The great historian of the early
seventeenth century, Samuel Rawson Gardiner, not content
with being descended from Oliver Cromwell was also one of
the odd sect of Plymouth Brethren.

We can do better justice today to those who carried on,
and those who opposed, the King's government. Professor
Tawney, who embarked on the study of Weston's predecessor
and mentor, Cranfield, with the idea of catching him out, in
the end found that he was one of the ablest ministers of the

time with more sense of the country's best interest than most politicians. Professor Alexander gives us the evidence for a comparable view of Weston. On the other hand, he makes clear that an opponent of the Crown like the sainted Sir John Eliot was by no means the unselfseeking martyr depicted by the Parliamentary tradition.

It is not sufficiently grasped, or not at all imaginatively, that the appalling mistakes of Buckingham and Charles I were the mistakes of youth, rash irresponsibility and wilful inexperience, as so often in history. The consequences were with Charles right up to the Civil War and to the end of his life. It is indeed hard to understand the infatuation of Charles and his father for that *homme fatal,* Buckingham. The later mishaps and misunderstandings of the 1630s, the period of the so much abused personal rule, by no means merited the explosion, and the disaster, of the Civil War. Professor Alexander makes the interesting point that Weston probably conceived of the abstention from the amenities of Parliament as a temporary phase of cooling-off, neither meant to be permanent nor to introduce absolutism. Unfortunately the generation that went through the bitter experiences of the 1620s stored up their bitterness and preserved their heat. It was Parliament that drove forward the revolution in the 1640s, even if their motives were not revolutionary but those of fear and self-preservation, the igniter of most wars.

By then Weston was well out of it: originally a good Parliament man, popular enough in that querulous assembly, he had no real responsibility for the wrath to come, though greatly blamed. The consequences fell upon his family, as with so many others in that generation — there was no end to the tale of suffering and loss in the storm which Clarendon saw as a cloud no bigger than a man's hand approaching from the North.

# Durham in Transition

Professor James has added one more[1] to the admirable
regional studies which investigate in concrete detail what
happened in the transition from medieval to modern society,
which occupied, often painfully, much of the sixteenth and
seventeenth centuries – instead of putting forward theses
about some 'general crisis' or other. Not that he eschews
generalisation: his approach is a sociological one, but with an
historian's proper factuality and concreteness. Thus he gives
us not only a convincing picture of the Palatine Bishopric,
with its special institutions, the princely prerogatives of the
Bishop continued after the Reformation, the marked difference between upland and lowland society, the rapid growth
of the coal trade with its social and political consequences,
but something more original and suggestive. This is, in
essence, the development from an earlier society, feudal in
character, based on lineage and kinship, into modern
society – 'civil', he calls it – more individualistic, commercial
and bourgeois, describable in Hobbesian terms; its religion
symptomised by 'charismatic' preaching and the word,
instead of the visual appeal of medieval cult and ritual. By
the way, the author has many thoughtful and convincing
particular observations.

For example, the Pilgrimage of Grace only advanced the
destruction of the cult of St Cuthbert it thought to defend.
Catholic conversions, in the reign of Charles I, much
encouraged by the Blessed Dorothy Lawson, owed a good
deal to folklore belief in priestly exorcism (for this connexion, cf. the examples in my *Elizabethan Renaissance,* vol.
1, c. ix); but they served only to increase the anti-Catholic

[1] Mervyn James, *Family, Lineage and Civil Society ... in the Durham Region,
1500–1640* (Oxford University Press, 1974).

mania of the Puritans, which grew to the dimension of a
*Grande Peur* in 1641. The social transition was dramatically
pointed up by the pathetic Rising of 1569 and the collapse of
the Neville earldom of Westmorland – what an ass the
Elizabethan Earl was, driven on by a *dévote* wife! Professor
James tells us that money was more important than religion
in the affair, and when money dried up the Rising collapsed.

This, too, had the effect of leaving the Protestant Bishops
the prime potentates in the area – in human affairs things
usually work out contrary to popular expectation. It is an
indication of Elizabeth I's conservatism that she should have
left the Palatine Bishopric essentially as Mary restored it. No
one has ever said a word for Northumberland's division of the
Palatinate into two ordinary dioceses, Durham and
Newcastle; it has always been regarded as a piece of
self-seeking on his part. Actually it was a progressive step in
the right direction, and it is surprising that Elizabeth did not
return to it.

The Rise of the Gentry is very marked in this area,
probably more rapid and extensive than anywhere. There
were not only the usual new families raised on monastic
lands, but the new gentry arising from people doing well out
of the coal trade and shipping; in addition to these, 'perhaps
the most significant group of new recruits to the middle and
lesser gentry were the now married upper clergy . . . Bishops,
deans, and prebendaries were themselves founding landed
families.' We see how silly the whole controversy about the
Rise of the Gentry was, in general terms. Here is yet another
example of the right way to go about it; and we are told,
'what is particularly striking in the half-century after 1570 is
the increase in the number of families claiming gentry status.'
There were fifty-six armigerous families in 1575; by 1615 the
number was almost doubled.

The next step, of course, was the push for political power,
and the Durham gentry agitated again and again for representation in the House of Commons – their institution. We see
precisely how the government of Charles I and Laud

alienated the governing class; the latter's tactless High Church policy divided the Church interest in Durham and in effect aided its overthrow. It was not, however, only the Arminians who were out for preferment: Puritans were just as anxious, the usual envy of the *outs* against the *ins*. Professor James quotes the outburst of the Puritan aristocrat, Lord Brooke, against Charles I's 'low-born' clergy, such as Laud and Neile, Juxon or Sheldon: it was no defence that these commoners were incorrupt and beyond reproach. Aristocrats regarded it as a right to have their paws in the public till.

Professor James has his eyes open and observes the social transition in the houses and buildings of the area: from feudal castles with their community life to greater privacy, the dividing up of great halls into smaller chambers, the erection of small country houses for the increasing number of gentry. There goes with this the marked extension of grammar-school education, the decline of illiteracy, the new humanist outlook emphasising participation in politics and religion.

It is a pity that Professor James does not write so well as he perceives. He is rather dogged by the agglomerative jargon of the sociologist, e.g. 'there was the break with family background and setting in favour of the specialised environment and meritocratic hierarchy of the school, accompanied by the inculcation of the values and modes of expression of the system of humanist rhetoric.' He can never say 'crises' quite simply: it is always 'crisis situations', or 'appropriately sized' for 'appropriate'. I cannot accustom myself to the use of the noun 'gentry' as an adjective, to which this school is so much addicted: 'gentry families', 'gentry houses', 'gentry ways of life', 'gentry heads'! An insensitive way to write — professors of English history should write English, not sociological jargon.

# What Did the Civil War Settle?

The fashion among present-day academic historians is to go in
for discussing Problems. Usually not to much point — as with
the profitless controversy about the Rise of the Gentry, at
the end of which the professors were no wiser than they were
before. In recent years they have turned their darkened
spectacles — one can hardly say spotlight — on the Civil War;
it is scarcely surprising that clouds of smoke have appeared
before their eyes. (The image comes from Swift, who thought
about them much as I do.)

This book, however, is much better than most:[1] it is
edited by a dependable seventeenth-century historian,
Professor Aylmer, whose common-sense study of the concrete facts of society carries respect and is worth oceans of
vague theorising. Himself too respectful to the theorisers with
their transparent bias, a Christopher Hill or Trevor-Roper —
confuting each other, of course — Aylmer concludes, 'even
the most distinguished [!] historians have found it easier to
demolish the theses of others than to sustain a positive
interpretation of their own.' Q.E.D.

What this collective volume of essays sets out to explain,
or at least discuss, is why it was that, after all the effort and
bloodshed and waste and destruction of the Civil War, the
Commonwealth and Protectorate that won it achieved no
permanence, no settlement even. As Aylmer puts it succinctly, 'the King and his adherents had been well and truly
defeated by 1646.' Only thirteen years and 'the English
republic collapsed in 1659–60, when the monarchy returned
carrying back with it the House of Lords and the episcopal
Anglican Church.'

[1] *The Interregnum. The Quest for Settlement, 1646–1660,* ed. G. E. Aylmer
(Macmillan, 1972).

How to account for it?

The answer is comparatively simple to anyone who understands politics and the facts of society. Clarendon and Hobbes both understood what happened very well at the time. Not so the professors today – though some of the best contributions in this book come pretty close to it and give fairly clear pointers without bringing home the conclusion. These best pieces are by younger writers, David Underdown, Austin Woolrych, Valerie Pearl and Claire Cross – all good.

One of these showed up the silliness of putting forward theses – and, incidentally, a characteristically erratic judgement of Professor Trevor-Roper, who put forward the view that 'the enemies of centralisation were the radical parliamentarians, the Independents.' Contrary to commonsense, as usual: the exact opposite proved to be the case. The Independents in Parliament 'were in fact the centralisers, opposition coming mainly from the moderates, Presbyterians and non-party local gentry.' What this shows is the silliness of advancing theses. The proper way to advance historical knowledge is factual: to explore concretely what really was the situation in the actual counties, or cities, and this Messrs Underdown and Woolrych, Mrs Pearl and Miss Cross are prepared to do. They are not too proud to do their homework.

Professor Aylmer spends a little too much time politely discussing professorial theses apt to degenerate into argy-bargy about unreal issues – though his own approach is a common-sense one. He realises well enough that there were deep divisions within the Levellers – so much written up by the academic denizens of the Welfare State – as with any lunatic fringe. So too with the tiny minority of the Diggers: 'Cloud Cuckoo Land' is Professor Aylmer's phrase for them, (not mine – but that was certainly the land they inhabited). Neither of them are worth the time and scholarship expended upon them – when there are so many subjects from which one can learn so much more.

As a result of too much argy-bargy Professor Aylmer just misses the conclusion of the matter – which is implied not only in his essay but also in those of Underdown and Woolrych. The point is quite simple, and politicians understand it, when professors do not. What matters in society is power and where it lies, who possesses it and to what purposes they use it. It is not counting heads that counts, still less those of marginal minorities, and certainly not what crackpots think.

One reason why academics are led away into endless argy-bargy is because they read so much of what is in print – and there is an enormous pamphlet literature of the period, mostly written by the minority-minded and doctrinaires, even when doctrinaires of genius like Milton. (His only practical political importance was in so far as he attached himself to the holder of military power, who had won the war: Oliver Cromwell.)

The gist of the matter is this. The Civil War was the unintended result of the struggle for power between two sections of the governing class. The result they never intended – that power should fall into the hands of an Army dictatorship, enforced for a period by major-generals, and officered by a lot of lower-class people who had risen up through the ranks. Even Oliver Cromwell, who belonged to the governing class, never intended it: all along he wanted a limited monarchy ruling with Parliament. He tried again and again to find some settled basis for his temporary régime, bound to end with him; but no such basis could ever be found.

For both Commonwealth and, still more, Protectorate went clean contrary against the natural rulers in society, the governing class, the holders of the agglomerations of power in land and wealth, in every county and town throughout the country. Mr Underdown sees this concretely in the counties: 'the county communities, though politically submerged, did not lose their social cohesion; their gentry leaders suffered temporary eclipse, but they were not destroyed.' Indeed they never forgot their experience at the hand of Cromwellian colonels, risen cobblers, haberdashers and printers. 'The gentry never forgot the interruption of their accustomed authority, the imprisonment of friends and neighbours, the disruption of rural sports and freedom of movement.' We may add, the impertinence of upstart fanatics, the proliferation of sects, the threat to their society from the lower orders.

'Never again' must have been in the hearts and minds of the upper classes, who had been such fools as to drift into the Civil War and had to endure its aftermath. Whether Anglican or Puritan, Royalist or Parliamentarian, they came together in 1660 to restore their power in no uncertain fashion. They had learned their lesson.

And here I have a contribution to suggest. After their bitter lesson, after they got back in the saddle, got back the power that naturally went with the owners of property – nobility, gentry, commercial magnates – they put through a reaction that would hardly have been possible if it had not been for the Civil War. The rule of the squire and the parson was clamped down in every parish, that of the well-to-do in every town. At Westminster King, Lords and gentry ruled the nation through Parliament: they weren't going to make the mistake of letting things get into the hands of the people again. Nor did they – right up to the revolution of our own time.

One can see the Reaction in every field, in education as much as in politics and religion. Before the Civil War schools were being founded in every market-town all over the country. After the Civil War the schools – and the education of the people – went into a long decline. So too with the universities. The privileged position, the virtual monopoly, of the Anglican Church was restored; so were the large agglomerations of property of bishops and deans and chapters. No more encouragement to preaching cobblers and inspired tailors: all such were effectively put in their place, and on the whole kept in their place. Religious toleration was really marginal, enough to constitute a safety-valve for escaping gas.

That was what all the high-mindedness and effort and destruction of the Civil War achieved, the heavy burden of taxation it incurred and Pym's Excise to pay for it – which fell, of course, chiefly on the poor. No wonder somebody in London cried out that 'Money was the bottom of the business'; in the country in general, after the pointless struggle, Professor Aylmer concludes, 'nothing suggests that the masses would have fought, for the King any more than for the republic.'

It was just a struggle for power between two sections of the governing class – into which other folk naturally got drawn. But when the governing class saw the social chasm it opened beneath their feet, the threat of the breakdown of social order – for, of course, lunatic Levellers could never have carried through a real revolution – the natural rulers of society closed their ranks in 1660. Never again!

# Civil War Facts and Fantasies

Here are two good books relating to the Civil War – such a relief after so much piffle about history by amateurs. There is another dimension to good historical work on the English Revolution – for we are going through a social revolution and we have much to learn from the previous experience. One point that nobody brings out: a lot of the trouble was made by ignorant young people on both sides. They may have been idealists and thought they were fighting for something wonderful – the Liberties of the People, a Godly Reformation, the Kingdom of Christ on Earth (quite a number were fools enough to believe it); but they didn't know the facts of life, sociologically speaking, and were bitterly disillusioned by the upshot. Many good men lost their lives for nothing. The cynics, the compromisers, the sensible were proved to have been right all along. The great majority of the nation were neutral at heart – a pity they could not have had their way. As usual, it was an aggressive minority of militants who made life miserable for sensible people in the middle.

Brian Manning's book[1] seeks to rectify the concentration on the Gentry in this period by proper treatment of the Aristocracy and the Middle Class; his studies on these subjects are the best in the book. He notices how insufferably proud and arrogant seventeenth-century nobles were – infinitely more so than Charles I or Archbishop Laud, who wished to do their best for the country and for the people in general. Indeed, one of the chief objections to Laud, on the part of the grandees, was his 'mean extraction' (Mrs Hutchinson's[2] words): they were not going to take telling from *him*. Of course, what the aristocrats were out for was jobs, Court appointments, the profits of power. It is all very understandable – the struggle for survival is the driving force, self preservation the motive; and this is the rock-bottom of the matter at every level. The ultimate test is – whose interest is most in keeping with that of the bulk of people? The answer can only be the Monarchy; and this is what became clear after all the scuffling and killing, the propaganda and partisanship, the hypocrisy and humbug, the wanton damage and destruction.

On the threshold of the war, 'it became obvious to the whole of the aristocracy that the lords themselves would be endangered by the popular discontent if concessions to the peers were not accompanied by concessions to the people as

[1] B. Manning (ed.), *Politics, Religion and the English Civil War* (Edward Arnold, 1973).
[2] Lucy Hutchinson, *Memoirs of the Life of Colonel Hutchinson*, ed. J. Sutherland (Oxford University Press, 1973).

well'. How much the situation in 1641 reminds us of the French Revolution! Discontented aristocrats out for their own ends and bitter at power being in the hands of Laud and Juxon – who was made Lord Treasurer because he was an honest man – and such lower-class upstarts as Cottington and Weston, hating Strafford because he was guns for them; then in attacking King and Church they found that they were letting loose a social revolution. They had not intended that, and soon 'fell out among themselves, since there were not enough places to satisfy all of them, nor could they all take power'.

They had reduced the King to powerlessness in 1640. 'Then the threat of civil war and social disorder led a large part of the nobility to rediscover an identification between their interests and those of the crown, and so gave Charles a party with which to fight to recover his power.' They should have thought of that before. Some of the clever ones did think of it, but found – like the Earl of Holland – that they had embroiled themselves so far that they could not get out again. He ended on the scaffold, like a good many people who hadn't realised what they were letting themselves in for. Even those aristocrats who kept their heads didn't relish being pried into by Presbyterian discipline or ordered about by Cromwellian major-generals, let alone risen cobblers, hypocritical Saints who had been 'lawyers' clerks' (Mrs Hutchinson once more). Their motto with the Restoration in 1660 was 'Never again' – and this held good for them right up to the social revolution of our time.

Brian Manning's portraits of these aristocrats as they really were are far more convincing than the confused categories of so much academic theorising, by people who don't know what the world of social and political action is really like. His study of the Middle Class is no less excellent. He brings out well that their 'godliness' reflected their class-consciousness. They too were out for their own ends; in so far as they had ground for complaint that taxation pressed unfairly upon them (the aristocracy being let off lightly) we must sympathise with them. Though we could not stand their ghastly 'godliness', their all-night prayer meetings, their sermon-sessions lasting hours, their smashing of sculpture and stained glass windows, no doubt they were the sober, industrious, and saving citizens. In the result, by industry and trade they created an overseas empire – which their descendants in our time wrecked and lost.

A new consideration emerges. We all know how decisive the role of London was: it almost in itself won the war for Parliament, by its wealth and resources, its strategic grip on the nation via the seaways. But there was the sheer factor of numbers – they were able to turn back the King at Brentford. 'It was the apprentices of London who were most forward in the cause of Parliament, and it was claimed that 8,000 of them enlisted under the Earl of Essex. By origin and vocation they belonged to the middle rank of the population.'

One criticism here: Manning underplays the revolutionary implications of the militant Puritans. They were only a small minority, yet they meant to overturn and change the established religious order, which had been arrived at with such difficulty – and which, as events proved, best satisfied the majority of the nation – over the past century. As Archbishop Sandys, a moderate Protestant, wrote of a young Cambridge Puritan, Wigginton: 'he laboureth not to build, but to pull down.' Mr Collinson adjures us to make 'every allowance for the warped mind of this unbalanced and quarrelsome man.' I don't know why we should, or for such odious types as Prynne, Burton and Bastwick. They were unquenchable and unsilenceable; in England merely their ears were clipped: in Catholic Europe they would have been stifled. In Communist Russia even today they would be sent to lunatic asylums, and that was the right place for them.

A most useful study on the part played by the Catholics tells us something new – the great majority of them stayed neutral throughout the war. Christopher Hill described them as 'solidly Royalist' – as wrong about this as he was wrong

about science being the creation of Puritanism or the Civil
War being fought between Puritan heliocentrics against
old-fashioned Cavalier Ptolemaics. (What nonsense that was!)
We learn that Charles I's administration did not favour the
Catholics and that they actually were rather better off under
Cromwell; it is true that Charles I sent fewer of them to the
scaffold, but then his government was the most civilised and
humane in the century.

An essay on the Reactions of the Women is less interesting,
while that on the Levellers is positively boring. Why is it that
everything about the Levellers is so boring? I suppose it is
because the 'middle sort of people' were smug and self-
satisfied, yet they not only wanted a place in the sun but that
everybody should be like them. (The Puritans in New
England, having got their way, said as much: 'a city as it were
upon an hill', for everybody to imitate – and what a model
for cultivated people to follow!) This is why the average man,
*l'homme moyen sensuel*, detested them so much. Anyway, it
was a good thing that they were pushed out of the main
stream in 1660, to form their own dreary tradition of
Nonconformist minority-mindedness in holes and corners of
the land.

What the Puritan mentality was like at its best may be seen
in Mrs Hutchinson's Life of Colonel Hutchinson. It is a prime
document of the Civil War on that side, as Clarendon's
Autobiography is on the Royalist – and how much greater
charm, as well as poetry and colour, and magnanimity, he
has! Both Clarendon and Mrs Hutchinson have sharp eyes and
psychological insight; but the editor, James Sutherland,
concludes that she had 'very little Christian charity'. (What
Puritan had? Certainly not John Milton, greatest of them.)

Colonel Hutchinson and his lady, though undeniably
godly, did not belong to the middle sort of people but were
upper-class. With their cousin, Ireton, they were almost the
only Parliamentarians among the gentry in Royalist Notting-
hamshire. Her consciousness of class is frequently expressed
by Mrs Hutchinson (hardly at all by Clarendon). Cromwell's

Major-General Harrison was 'but a mean man's son and of a mean education, and no estate before the war.' Mr Lomax 'could not be reckoned among the gentry, though he were called by the name of Mr Lomax'. Alderman James was an honest Parliamentarian, 'but had no more but a Burger's discretion'. At Nottingham a beautiful girl, who was the granddaughter and heiress of a rich physician, fell for young Hutchinson, but 'his great heart could never stoop to think of marrying into so mean a stock'. She subsequently married the son of an Earl – a less snobbish Royalist, no doubt.

Colonel Hutchinson's minority-mindedness was the result of his education at Cambridge, his addiction to the Scriptures, and his own severe, stubborn character – one can see it in the long hammer-chin of his portrait. Actually he was at Laudian Peterhouse in its best days, but kept aloof from 'their stretching superstition to idolatry, though yet he considered not the emptiness and carnality, to say no more, of that public service which was then in use' (i.e. the poor Prayer Book!). 'He was enticed to bow to their great Idol – Learning, and had a higher veneration for it than can strictly be allowed.' But it was not until after his Cambridge days that he was smitten with the blinding truth of 'that great point of Predestination', which was not much appreciated by the bishops, 'but was generally embraced by all religious and holy persons in the land'. Humans are apt to fall under the influence of some particular formulation of nonsense in keeping with their time, but what so fascinated people, otherwise intelligent, in this special brand of nonsense boggles the imagination.

Mrs Hutchinson has a very disapproving page about the naughty goings-on at James I's Court, but allows that Charles I's was 'temperate and chaste and serious. Men of learning and ingenuity in all arts were in esteem and received encouragement from the King, who was a most excellent judge and a great lover of paintings, carvings, gravings'. This is high praise from such a quarter, for Courts as such were 'wicked'. We can regard it as a piece of carnality in young Mr

Hutchinson that he was ready to purchase a place in Star Chamber, and a providence that he was disappointed of it, for the court was shortly after abolished. But it was more than carnality on the part of Major Wildman the Leveller, 'a great manager of Papists' interests', who tried to do a dirty deal about a sequestrated estate Colonel Hutchinson had purchased and improved by a fourth, to get it back again for the family without allowing for its improved value. Even Saints are sometimes human – and Leveller Wildman piled himself up a very inegalitarian estate by taking advantage of other people's troubles.

Colonel Hutchinson's service to the cause was of historic importance: he held Nottingham for Parliament throughout the war, a strategic strongpoint. He took part in the operations against Royalist Newark, which have left their memento in the shell of the castle we see above the Trent. The Colonel went along with Cromwell and the Independents, when the split with Parliament came. Mrs Hutchinson observes truthfully, if sourly, 'the Presbyterians had long since espoused the Royal interest, and forsaken God and the People's cause, when they could not obtain the reins of government in their own hands'. Then Cromwell is disapproved of when he achieves supreme power. 'To speak the truth of himself, he had much natural greatness in him, and well became the place he usurped.' But 'his Court was full of sin and vanity, and the more abominable because they had yet not quite cast away the name of God, but profaned it by taking it in vain upon them. True religion was now almost lost, even among the religious party, and hypocrisy became an epidemical disease – to the sad grief of Colonel Hutchinson'.

To what point had been all the Colonel's efforts, when he thought the Protector's government 'greater usurpers on the people's liberties than the former kings' – as indeed they were. To what point the war, the enthusiasm, all the effort? The end of it was that he felt 'just cause to repent that ever he forsook his own blessed quiet to embark in such a troubled sea, where he had made shipwreck of all things but a good conscience'. For what that was worth! – he was lucky to have escaped the scaffold, for he had been a regicide. The Memoirs keep quiet about how he got off – chiefly by his wife's endeavours and the interest of her family, the Apsleys.

When the Civil War broke out Hutchinson was a young idealist of twenty-six, and didn't know what he was letting himself in for. John Milton was still more idealistic, and still more ignorant of the facts of life, political and social, even marital. Hutchinson died in prison, reading the Scriptures, which confirmed him in his illusions, and that he had been right. Reading the Scriptures has a lot to answer for in the troubles and sufferings it brought down upon men's heads in that century – reading Shakespeare, and reflecting on it, would have done them much more good.

# Civil War Cheshire

The subtitle gives us the subject of this good book: 'County government and society during the English Revolution.'[1] The conclusion tells us, 'the administrative, ecclesiastical, and social innovations (which by the 1650s made the rebellion worthy to be called a Revolution) largely vanished at the Restoration . . . the Revolution left few permanent traces on the institutions of church and state.' Well, exactly: then what had all the fuss and furore been about, not to mention the destruction?

Historians in their endeavour to make sense of the past impute a rationality to human behaviour which is not

[1] J. S. Morrill, *Cheshire 1630–1660* (Oxford University Press, 1974).

warranted by anthropology. They do not have the imagination of a Gibbon or a Swift, even a Namier, to penetrate the
nonsense by which men largely act. Professional politicians
are better informed — there was the disillusioned Liberal who
said, 'the longer I live the more I see that things really are as
silly as they seem.'

Mr Morrill's book is another example of the work of our
younger historians that is replacing the thesis-touting and
hairsplitting generalisations of the previous generation. There
was nothing 'remarkable' about their work except their
obtuse and obstinate argumentativeness. As if one ever learns
anything that way! I always held that the proper way to
investigate the Rise of the Gentry, or the causes of the Civil
War, was to explore the facts concretely county by county.
This is now being done; and what do we learn from this
book? Of the thirty-five chief gentry in Cheshire in 1540,
twenty-five families continued to rule up to 1642; there were
seven 'rising gentlemen', and two newcomers floating up on
monastic lands. So much for all the nonsense about the
Decline of the Gentry.

This investigation of the consequences of the Civil War in
the idiosyncratic country of Cheshire, for all its too great
detail about the functioning and finances of dreary committees, reinforces plain and simple conclusions as to the
eruption of 1640—60. The governing class of gentry were
virtually united in 1640 against the government of Charles
and Laud — Mr Morrill very properly says that Laud was
'misunderstood', and he was of course wickedly misrepre-
sented. The insane 'Catholic Fear which gripped much of
England in 1641' was paralleled by panic rumours of a
Quaker Rising in 1659 — such is the wisdom of the people.

The governing class of gentry backed Parliament, since it
was *their* institution: hence the absurd worship of the very
name of Parliament all through these alarms and disillusion-
ments. For, of course, the whole thing ended in utter
disillusionment and the Restoration of the old order.
Mr Morrill omits to notice the social reaction this brought

about: this might not have happened but for the idiocy of the Civil War. But they had allowed themselves to be divided and to fight; they lost out after 1653 to the Army, a military régime of 'low-born men'. Serve them right: 'Never again' became their motto, even in the tricky circumstances of 1688.

Mr Morrill says all this in rather less plain language. After the war 'the leading families were excluded by delinquency [i.e. as Royalists] or for openly opposing the execution of the King, while others refused to serve . . . Their places were taken by representatives of families with middling estates and less creditable genealogies.' The general pattern was for radical minorities to displace the ruling clique of moderates. The old governing gentry had unleashed 'a very real fear of social revolution' – there was the proliferation of lunatic sects: Mr Morrill agreeably refers to their 'poisonous social and political ideas'. There was also the increasing central-isation upon London taking away the gentry's local power – Cromwell nominated ministers to an extent Charles I never did; in addition to the far heavier taxation to support the military régime than ever Ship Money would have inflicted.

When Mr Morrill says 'the events of these years posed a dual threat to the power and continuity of the essentially conservative élite', he means the governing class. In 1660 'there was a return to consensus government by the old county élite', i.e. the leading gentry. When these younger historians talk about 'the fragmented community', the community of the county, all they mean is the county gentry. We are back once more with the dominant element in society, the factor of class – and there always was a significant element of class in the conflict for power that led to the eruption.

What the governing class found was that they could not keep order in the nursery – in other words, maintain their control of society – without monarchy and church, king and bishops. They were found to be indispensable.

That understood, we may pay tribute to yet one more study of how this worked out in a significant county during the eruption. One observes how much more efficient Parliamentary administration was than the King's, the greater resources and ability. No investigation has been made whether the wealth of the country was not increasing in those parts free from war, the South-East hinged upon London, to offset the burdens and damage inflicted elsewhere. Cheshire, like Cornwall, was impoverished by it.

Cheshire had a real natural leader in the Parliamentarian Sir William Brereton, almost a local Cromwell: a grasp of strategy, military as well as political, a man of conviction determined to end the power of King and Church, an incorrupt administrator who was awarded the Archbishop's palace at Croydon for his services to the good old cause. His wife was even more radical: this nasty creature had the stained glass windows of Neston church broken. We should like to know more about Brereton, his birth and family, appearance and characteristics. None of the characters is grasped or made real to the reader in this way; and though this is not an account of the fighting, some mention should have been made that at Brereton's siege of Chester there perished the most original genius among composers of the time, William Lawes, to the grief of the cultivated King.

The values of music and the arts are enduring; historians of average sensibilities find it easier to write about the functioning of committees. There are numerous misprints in this book published by the Oxford University Press, which used to be so good: one more sign of the decline of standards in our time. The author might have helped by refraining from absurd spellings like 'maltmakrs, breadmakrs', etc. In history books all quotations in antique spelling should be modernised, unless there is special reason to the contrary.

# Somerset Conflict

Mr Underdown's book on Somerset during the Civil War and its aftermath is quite first-class, a model of how these things should be done.[1] Half-a-dozen such books on representative areas – Yorkshire and Lancashire, the Severn country, the Midlands, Devon, above all London – and we could dispense with all the generalised argumentation and thesis-mongering that have largely confused people's vision as to the Civil War.

Somerset in itself was a most significant and representative county – one can practically see the whole Civil War conflict, its issues and upshot in that mirror alone. We begin with the alienation of the Country from the Court, the resentment against Charles I's personal rule and Laud's Church policy. Then as the conflict for power sharpens – for that essentially is what it came to – the governing class split: greater gentry with the Church, lesser gentry and middle folk, Puritan clothiers and such, with Parliament. Eastern Somerset was dominantly Parliamentarian, especially the Puritan triangle, Bridgwater – Frome – Taunton; Western Somerset more royalist.

The driving force of Puritan fanaticism expelled the Marquis of Hertford and for eight months, till April 1643, the county was under Parliamentarian rule. The choice consequences are to be seen in the destruction of altar rails, popish images, stained glass in the churches; the smashing of crucifixes in Wells Cathedral, vestments and linen sold, the bishop's palace looted, a painting of the Virgin Mary paraded round on a pike. Later, after the Parliamentary defeats at Lansdown and Roundway Down, their soldiery smashed up South Petherton church, organ, windows, monuments.

[1] David Underdown, *Somerset in the Civil War and Interregnum* (David and Charles, 1973).

For a couple of years the Royalist gentry governed the county in traditional fashion, but with the increasing burden of taxation for the war. In 1645 the superior strength of Parliament and the New Model overwhelmed the King's cause, but in the struggle Somerset suffered terribly. Taunton had held out against the Royalists — inspired by Puritan fanaticism and Blake's leadership — though in the end half-burned; a whole quarter of Bridgwater, held against Parliament, was fired; Bristol was grievously damaged in two sieges. By the end, there was a trail of gutted mansions and battered villages; it was 'a ruined and ravaged country' and after all the death and destruction, plague added its horrors.

Can anything have been worth it?

When academic historians argue the toss on the subject, they do not have the imagination or possibly the human sympathies, to envisage the consequences. The majority of the people at the time experienced them, and had little use for either side. Mr Underdown sees clearly that the war was 'fought between two minorities, struggling in a sea of neutralism and apathy'. Before the end masses of farmers and country folk — sick of the depredations, demands and impositions of both sides — began to organise themselves and there were outbreaks of the Clubmen in Somerset, Dorset, Hereford and elsewhere. 'A plague on both your houses' was their attitude. A lower-class man myself, my sympathies are with them — not with the missionary Puritanism of a Christopher Hill, descended from these middle-class Noncon-formists. And, of course, as an aesthete who sets far more store by the works of men's hands than the nonsense they mostly think, I detest Puritan iconoclasm.

After the war was over Taylor, the Water-Poet, reported the sad condition of Wells Cathedral, thieves stripping the lead from the roof — the Rump Parliament even considered demolishing all cathedrals. A leading Presbyterian divine from London, Cornelius Burgess, got the episcopal property and retired to Wells, where he proved an energetic exploiter of the estate and demolished much of the Palace, leaving the ruin we see today. Baptists prated on the tombs, while orthodox Puritans prated from the pulpits. Cromwell's régime was tolerant towards (Puritan) sects, while proscribing the Anglican Prayer Book, the accustomed religion of the great majority. Toleration is not necessarily a good thing in all circumstances. (I am not in favour of tolerating crackpots about Shakespeare for example.)

In any case the orthodox Presbyterians of Parliament were a small minority, who never rooted themselves even in Puritan Somerset. After the Civil War 'the lid was off', in Mr Underdown's phrase: Ranters ranted, Seekers sought, Quakers quaked. James Nayler entered Bristol, his disciples strewing garments before him, his hair-do made to look like a portrait of Christ. John Robins of Wells was 'proclaimed the great God, and came to a shameful end'; four of his disciples sold all they had, having heard 'a call to go and preach the gospel in Galilee'. They went to London to embark and were never heard of again. They were all drunk on the Bible, of course. Poor Archbishop Laud had been quite right not to encourage its reading. As for the Dean of Wells, Sir Walter Ralegh's nephew, he was murdered.

And what did they achieve by all their efforts?

A military dictatorship which nobody wanted, supported by a tiny minority, the burden of a standing army to keep the country down, the heavy expenditure on wars in pursuit of an aggressive foreign policy, a régime more oppressive than Charles I and Laud ever dreamed of. Even before the Restoration a younger generation turned cynical after the ardours and endurances, the consequences of so much high-mindedness. However, the upper classes learned their lesson – not only the aristocracy but the middle classes too – not to allow the lower orders to get out of hand again. The Puritans relapsed into the disconsidered minority of Dissent, put in its place, from which it should never have been allowed to emerge.

Sir Matthew Hale was a Puritan, but a sensible one, no fanatic.[2] He was an upright judge, charitable to the poor, a

[2] Edmund Heward, *Matthew Hale* (Hale, 1972).

would-be reformer of the law during the Commonwealth —
when a few small reforms were effected — highly moral. But
he was a Sabbatarian, who wrote reams of nonsense about
religion, a heavy smoker and he disliked music. Not my
type. The Commonwealth saw an outburst of persecution of
witches in Puritan East Anglia — nothing of that kind was
allowed under the civilised rule of Charles I and Laud. But
there was a further hysterical outbreak in that deplorable
area, in Suffolk in 1664, and the upright judge condemned
the poor creatures to death. Both Hale and his friend, the
Presbyterian divine, Richard Baxter, were strongly against
witches, being believers; both of them wrote books on God's
great mercy in preserving us from their malice — by con-
demning them to death. These eminent persons grounded
their certainty upon the Old and New Testaments — further
consequences of Bible-worship. Chief Justice Hale, who had
all the Puritan's conceit and self-esteem, took a gloomy view
of the state of morality after the Restoration. What else
could you expect after the rule of the canting hypocrites?

# Levellers' Nonsense

In the present log-jam in society, and the threat of
breakdown, the study of radical ideas during the Civil War to
which they led is fashionable among academics, and Christopher Hill is their leader.

We must pay tribute to his pertinacity: he is very prolific.
Recently he wrote an excellent book on Oliver Cromwell; but
it is a pity that he spends so much time in investigating
Levellers and Ranters, Antinomians and Grindletonians — for
what is the value of what such people thought?

What is the intellectual value, especially for students, of studying nonsense? It is far more important to expose them to commonsense and powerful minds, such as Hobbes and Milton. It would do them, and himself, a great deal of good if Mr Hill would next address himself to a penetrating thinker like John Selden, who saw through the delusions of both sides reducing their country to ruin in the Civil War.

And what good did it do? Or the radical ideas to 'turn the world upside down'?

I attach far more importance to people's happiness. Mr Hill might learn something from a pertinent observation of the Czech artist, Hollar, who told John Aubrey that:

> When he first came into England, which was a serene time of peace, the people, both poor and rich, did look cheerfully. But at his return, he found the countenances of the people all changed: melancholy, spiteful as if *bewitched*.

Well, of course, they all had been bewitched by these nonsensical ideas to which historians attach a quite adventitious importance today.

Their lunatic theories would never have worked, either economically or politically. No taxes, no laws, and 'all things to be governed by love', indeed! – no sense of humour, for they all fell out with each other like mad. The Diggers' attempt to dig up St George's Hill and hold the land in common melted away like snow in June. Their attempt to democratise the Army and run it from the bottom upwards lasted only a week or two.

What would Communist Russia say to such lunacy? Exactly what a practical man like Oliver Cromwell said and did – used them for a moment and then swept them aside with the remark, 'of whom there is no fear'. A whiff of grapeshot at Burford settled their hash.

We can sympathise, with these poor people's feelings about the hardness of life, poverty and injustice, without taking their 'thought' seriously. Three times Mr Hill uses the word 'solution' on the first page of *The World Turned Upside Down.* [1] These people had no practical 'solutions' to offer.

We see all round us in the crack-up today that these notions don't work: still more so in the more primitive society of the seventeenth century. Besides making men envious and miserable and bewitched, there was the sheer destruction of men's lives, of things of beauty, the works of men's hands, of far more value than the nonsense they think.

This school of historians never tells us about the terrible destruction of the Civil War: the wanton laying-waste of cathedrals and churches, the dispersal of the choirs, the ending of the wonderful school of English music from Elizabethan days. Destroy the 'monuments of idolatry', was one of these Radical ideas – that meant smashing the painted windows, the sculpture and woodwork, ripping up the brasses. Another Radical idea was to burn all books, except the Bible; i.e. the ignorant shall rule, for were they not God's Elect?

Their ideas were nonsense, hostile to all culture and civilisation – as the cult of them in the universities is today. Behind the quite disproportionate, and largely motivated, importance they are given, there is not only sentimentalism and exaggeration – evident in this book – but a real philistinism.

Though it is true that such people have not much artistic sense, or response to beauty, or much capacity for real thinking, it is better for them to be exposed to such influences than to studies which merely fortify the prejudices of the inferior.

---

[1] Christopher Hill, *The World Turned Upside Down: Radical Ideas during the English Revolution* (Temple Smith, 1972).

# The Fifth Monarchy Men

Who were the Fifth Monarchy Men?

They were those who, in the turmoil and disruption of the Civil War, expected to see, on the basis of the prophecies of Daniel and the Book of Revelation, a fifth kingdom after the four empires of Babylon, Persia, Greece and Rome. These empires were beasts; the last beast had ten horns or kings, and a little horn which would destroy several of these. After that the kingdom would be given to the Saints for ever — the Fifth Monarchy; themselves being the Saints, of course.

And what did they think?

They were against everybody else, even on the lunatic fringe, even against the harmless Quakers. Among the Fifth Monarchy Men were several Fifth Monarchy Women. Lady Eleanor Douglas was one, who identified James I as the little horn, and poor Archbishop Laud — who had tried to restore decency and order in the churches — as the Beast from the Bottomless Pit. To show what she thought she poured tar over the altar of Lichfield Cathedral; in the Civil War the Puritans completed the wreck. The lady very suitably enjoyed a spell in Bedlam.

But there was another prophetess, Anna Trapnel, whose trap should have been similarly shut. She went about identifying the mark of the Beast on everybody and considered human learning unnecessary: since, in the appalling doggerel which she was inspired to write in her visions:

Christ's Scholars are perfected
with learning from above —

i.e. herself, of course. A Warwickshire prophetess thought she was 'the Mother of God and all things living'. John Rogers, the Puritan minister at Thomas Apostle's in London, saw

King Charles as one of the toes of the image in the Book of
Daniel, destroyed by Christ. But there was disagreement
among the Saints about Christ, whether he intended to
appear and reign in person. Mary Cary and John Rogers
thought he would, others thought not; they almost fell to
blows about that. They were not even agreed that laughter
was a sin; some thought it was – I expect they were in a
majority.

Unlike the Quakers they had no objection to the use of
force; some of them thought it no murder to kill Cromwell
who – like the practical man he was – used their agitation
for his purposes then threw the lunatics over. Their only
practical importance was that at one point they had the
sympathies of one of Cromwell's Major-Generals, Harrison;
but Cromwell de-fused him and the Restoration executed
him as a regicide.

Dr Capp tells us,[1] 'up to 1653 [i.e. Cromwell's attainment
of personal power] several Saints saw Cromwell in the light
of an Old Testament Judge, and were ready to concede him
absolute power.' Exactly: they didn't care about liberty in
the least, as they pretended, only to inflict their lunacy on
others, i.e. the great majority. This corroborated the position
Charles I took up at his trial, as a *defender* of the liberties of
the nation – which he was, compared with the Puritans.

As for their 'thought', which Dr Capp takes seriously
without a spark of humour, they had 'a desire for liberty in
place of tyranny, and for godliness in place of idolatry.' It
does not require much knowledge of human motivation and
sectarian semantics to see that these people meant by
'liberty' to impose their nonsense on others and by 'tyranny'
any kind of government that prevented them from doing so.
By 'idolatry' they meant decency and order in church-
worship – any beauty or art such philistines would naturally
detest: nothing annoys the inferior more – it makes them
feel all the more inferior. As for Laud's 'Popery', he had

[1] B. S. Capp, *The Fifth Monarchy Men* (Faber and Faber, 1972).

personally converted a number of important personages away from Rome.

What is important is that the dominant Calvinism, with its idiotic doctrine of Predestination and the Elect Few, led precisely to this sort of thing in weaker heads. It is noticeable that it was a number of dreary Cambridge theologians who propagated these absurdities. One of them later declared that Charles II and James II had given the kingdom to the Beast, and that the Second Coming was at hand in 1691. He had been 'subject to depression and pains in the head for many years', and was vicar of Water Stratford, Bucks. I suspect he had water on the brain.

What nonsense sensible people in government had to contend with in the seventeenth century! The fact that they based their nonsense on the Old Testament didn't make it any the less lunatic, and the excruciating cult of the Bible – with its customs and values of a barbaric people two thousand years before – made them the more bloodthirsty. The Civil War gave them their chance – taking the lid off the top of society, one saw the scum on the boil. Or, to vary the image, it is like what you see when you turn up a stone in hot weather.

The freedom of the press in revolutionary circumstances enabled all these sects to publish their claptrap. And it provides material for modern academics in search of subjects for a thesis. It has been the fashion for academic historians, inspired by their revered Cromwellian captain, Christopher Hill, to rootle among this rubbish. It would be better for them to choose subjects from which they could learn something to their intellectual profit. Now that Dr Capp has rounded up the Fifth Monarchy Men – though bearing the marks not of the Beast but of a thesis upon it, his book is the more readable for being unintentionally comic – we really do not need to know any more about them.

# Oliver Cromwell

1

From Mary Queen of Scots to Oliver Cromwell, who killed her grandson, Charles I, it is a leap across a vertiginous chasm: one wondered how Antonia Fraser would manage it. She has accomplished it with unexpected ease.

*Cromwell: Our Chief of Men*[1] is a fine achievement, a more compelling and convincing work than her previous biography, where one expected her to be more at home. Cromwell's is a grander, more heroic subject: the author has responded to the greater challenge and produced an altogether maturer work.

She deftly turns the flank of academic criticism by saying that her aim has been to 'humanise' Cromwell. And this is precisely what she has achieved: she presents us with a more human and real portrait than do Victorian authorities, like Carlyle or Sir Charles Firth.

How has she managed it?

Well, in addition to four years of research, the patient industry, the skill in writing, the visual sense which academic historians lack (they should cultivate it), she has the feminine gift for perception of character.

Women have an enormous advantage here — one reason why they have made such good novelists; but no woman has tackled Cromwell on a large scale before, and sheer sympathy and patience have seen further into the nature of this extraordinary man, even if she has been a little too kind to the warts.

Oliver had greatness of soul, and was made on an epic scale, even if you don't like him and don't read epics. But

[1] (Weidenfeld and Nicolson, 1973.)

enemies as well as friends understood the scale on which he
was made. Before he was at all well known John Hampden
said of him, 'that slovenly fellow who hath no ornament in
his speech, if we should come to have a breach with the King
. . . will be one of the greatest men in England.'

The reason was what his enemy, Clarendon, saw: 'as he
grew to place and authority, his parts seemed to be renewed,
as if he had concealed faculties till he had the occasion to use
them.' That was it: he grew with every challenge and crisis
that confronted him, in a terrible time for the country.

Lady Antonia does not use the word 'dynamic' and does
not sufficiently stress the pragmatic in him, but these are
clues: he was a dynamo of energy, and a consummate
pragmatist, as a politician needs to be. She does not think
that he had much political foresight (who has?), and he let
the cat out of the bag (only once) when he said 'None rises so
high as he who knows not whither he is going.' This led many
observers to think of him as a sublime hypocrite — and there
was an element of that in him too.

During the Civil War he had the double advantage of being
both a General and a politician; he was a genius in both
fields, so it was the less surprising, in retrospect, that he came
out on top. (He also had the big battalions with him, the
money, and the faith; how could he lose?)

Lady Antonia sees, better than anyone has, the complexities of his character, the different strains in it; she makes a
good deal of the Welsh elements. His was a passionate nature,
though usually under strict discipline; when that snapped
there was a terrifying outburst, as in his rages against the
Rump Parliament, as well as at the Parliament he summoned
himself, and at the storming of Drogheda and Wexford. The
author puts forward a cool defence of Cromwell in Ireland,
which will be a surprise to Irish readers brought up on the
legend rather than the facts.

Like many men of genius, Cromwell was a manic-
depressive; bouts of cheerful optimism, often before battle,
alternated with black melancholy. When about thirty he had

a severe nervous breakdown, from which he was rescued by his 'conversion': henceforth he walked with the Lord, whatever he did.

Lady Antonia is very patient with him about all that — much more so than contemporaries, Samuel Butler for example, who said that Oliver Cromwell's style of oratory, plentifully watered with tears and sighs, 'passed with applause among fanatics of his own canting inclination.' Though it has a certain rugged eloquence, it was, like the man, not to everybody's taste.

This is a biography; historically there is a good deal to be said on the other side. Lady Antonia is too sympathetic to the Puritans: in spite of Oliver's love of music and a few performances of opera in London, they did destroy the divine music in cathedrals and collegiate churches, besides all their smashing of stained glass, brasses, monuments, castles, etc.

Nor does she get the Clubmen quite right. The Civil War was a struggle for power between two sections of the governing class; the Clubmen were farmers and peasants who came out against both sides: 'a plague on both your houses' (I sympathise with them, and with the aesthetes).

Nothing of this, surprisingly enough, in either Lady Antonia, or in Dame Veronica Wedgwood, who has largely re-written her earlier book, and now gives us the essence of Cromwell's career in a nutshell, brisk, reliable, brief. *Oliver Cromwell*[2] is excellent in its grasp of the political situation, particularly in the sector of foreign policy, where Oliver achieved glory for his country during his short reign.

What a man! His was a very masculine personality (unlike Charles I), with an appeal for women — to whom he was unfailingly courteous — very potent in all senses, with his long, bulbous red nose. Evidently Lady Antonia has fallen for him — a very good thing in a biographer. Lucky Oliver to be so served by these sympathetic and scholarly ladies!

[2] (Duckworth, 1973).

2

Mr Christopher Hill has progressed a great deal since he wrote his (Stalinist) account of Lenin, for my series of historical biographies, *Men and their Times*. He has not only become Master of Balliol but a leading authority on the Puritan Revolution. I am bound to own that I find this new book[3] on Oliver Cromwell – unlike his old book on Lenin – fascinating and persuasive. It is not a biography, it is argumentative history. I do not much care for argumentative history, usually pushing a thesis round. But this book is candid and honest; Mr Hill has got rid of his (Marxist) King Charles's head, if not quite so drastically as Oliver Cromwell got rid of the King's.

Cromwell is a perenially compelling personality, as everybody found in his own time – the real maker of the English Revolution, victor in the Civil War, which might not have been won without him. Mr Hill gives us a new perspective of Cromwell from quite early on. We used to think of him as an obscure back-bench member of Parliament who rose, rather suddenly by his military genius, to leadership in the Army. He had first-rate military ability all right, but Mr Hill shows that he was always and essentially a politician. He was no obscure country gentleman, but connected with a number of leading Parliamentarian families. Already before the Civil War, he was the trusted colleague of the leaders in the Long Parliament, John Pym and John Hampden, and he had had his apprenticeship in the local politics of the Eastern Counties. He was already a familiar figure there, defending the interests of the people of the Fens against the enclosing landlords, standing up for Puritan preachers against the bishops – though himself living off his leases from the Church.

He was a Radical: what characterised him was his driving spirit, his dynamism, his uncompromising devotion to the cause. He said that, if the Grand Remonstrance against

[3] Christopher Hill, *God's Englishman: Oliver Cromwell and the English Revolution* (Weidenfeld and Nicolson, 1970).

Charles I's government had not been passed in Parliament, he
would have sold all he possessed and gone to America. Mr
Hill does not quote Clarendon's good remark on this — 'So
near was this poor country to its deliverance!' But he does
point out what a prominent part New England Puritans
played in the Civil War. Cromwell made himself the leader of
the Radicals, appealed to and recruited lower-class officers —
the only leader in his class to do so. This naturally caused
scandal among conservatives of social order, not only among
Royalists but Parliamentarians. The plain fact is that they
should never have allowed the Civil War to happen. As
Clarendon said after it all, 'No reformation is worth the
charge of a civil war' — and he had been a reformer, too. On
the other side, Andrew Marvell said, 'the cause was too good
to have been fought for'. It all ended in a military
dictatorship, such as nobody wanted, not even Cromwell.
What he preferred was a moderate constitutional monarchy,
with a representative Parliament as a permanent part of the
constitution.

This should have been possible, if it had not been for
the extremists on both sides. Mr Hill tells us, 'most of the
lasting achievements of the English Revolution came during
the first two hundred days of the Long Parliament's
existence.' Then why was the Civil War, with its long tale of
destruction and thousands of lives lost, ever fought? When
the war, and Commonwealth and Cromwell's Protectorate,
were over the King was restored in 1660, with much the
settlement that had been arrived at in 1640. What had been
the point of it all?

This is the real interest of Mr Hill's book, that it brings
into light these questions that underlie the conflicts of
politics at all times and in all places — but perhaps particularly
with regard to those other civil wars among English-speaking
peoples, the American Revolution and the American Civil
War.

The underlying question is, was in this case the English
Civil War — which set the pattern and influenced the

others — *necessary*? Those penetrating thinkers, the political philosophers Hobbes and Harington, thought not. They considered that the balance of economic and social power in any case was moving on the side of Parliament, and the classes it represented, so that Parliament would have been bound to win. (Much the same argument can be advanced with regard to the American Revolution — the Colonies were bound to achieve independence in another decade or so — and with the War of 1861-5 too.)

Here again, Cromwell was a Radical. The moderate Parliamentarians, once war had broken out, wanted a compromise peace — they feared the destruction of social order. Were they not perfectly right? Cromwell would have none of it: he drove the war on to complete victory over the King. To win it he used the Radicals and Levellers to the utmost, and then cracked down on them and broke them. He was convinced, from his own unbroken victories, that 'God' was on his side. He himself described his elation and assurance of victory before Naseby, which ruined the King's cause: 'I could not (riding alone about my business) but smile out to God in praises in assurance of victory . . . Of which I had great assurance; and God did it.' What did it was a three-to-two superiority of numbers, and complete superiority in artillery and discipline. 'That you have by force I look upon as nothing', he said. Mr Hill adds candidly — 'except when Oliver decided that God wished it to be used: the Civil War, the Army's interference in politics in 1647, the execution of Charles I, the dissolution of the Rump Parliament, the rule of the Major-Generals.' The decisive wielder of force at every juncture here was Cromwell. No wonder people thought he was a consummate hypocrite and dissembler; he was, of course, a consummate politician.

And he made Britain — the kingdoms that he forcibly united — great. The most original part of the book is that which shows how Cromwell and the triumphant Puritans pushed forward British imperialism: not only in Catholic Ireland but as against the Protestant Dutch. Cromwell waged his Dutch war to get the Dutch colonies, his Spanish war to get a dominant position in the Caribbean and the African slave-trade. In everything the Lord was on his side; even Mr Hill, to whom Oliver is a hero, admits that the God of Battles, to whom he was always appealing, in effect was the New Model Army. His compulsive conviction of God's support came from a more powerful ego than anyone else could command.

Actually, Cromwell was a man of heroic stature, an indubitably great man, in his bad deeds as in his good. Except for Catholics – not notably tolerant themselves – he was more widely tolerant than most men of his time. The achievement of power far more absolute than Charles I ever enjoyed made him go back on almost everything he had originally stood for; as Lord Protector he came out for the enclosing landlords against the poor Fens people he had originally championed; he suppressed the egalitarian Levellers, calling them worse than beasts; he suppressed several Parliaments; rising to power through the Radicals, he went over to the 'natural rulers' of the country to whom he belonged. In the last year of his life the great Puritan's daughter was married by the rites of the proscribed Anglican Prayer Book, on its way back. When Oliver died, everything was on its way back; within twenty months, the King was back.

One may well ask, as of other destructive revolutions, to what point had it all been?

# The Rump

Mr Worden has given us what may be regarded as the authoritative account of the proceedings of what was left of Parliament, from Charles I's execution till it was sent packing by Oliver Cromwell in 1653.[1] A younger scholar, he has got fairly away from the thesis-ridden schematism which bedevilled, and befogged, the previous generation. Indeed, he need not apologise for his book taking 'an old-fashioned narrative form': narrative is a far subtler medium of accounting for events than sociological theses are. Nor need he make heavy weather of using the terms 'presbyterians' and 'independents' for polarities rather than parties: as he says himself, 'the usage is justified by contemporary parlance'. Then the gesture to the thesis-mongers is unnecessary.

The story is a complex one, and Mr Worden unravels its complexities with convincing scholarship and commonsense. 'The Long Parliament created an army and a navy that were justly the envy of Europe ... successfully challenged the commercial and maritime supremacy of the Dutch, and reduced Scotland and Ireland to military conquest and political union.' It is to be observed that these very real achievements were those of power; all the rest was largely humbug – the dreams of 'godly reformation', of a broader-based political structure, let alone social reform, came to nothing. Idealists like John Milton may have been disillusioned, but hard-headed realists knew the facts of political life. As to church-government, an able Rump M.P. wrote in 1648, 'there is not a man amongst us that thinks it worth endangering the kingdom for'. But that is what ordinary fools

---

[1] B. Worden, *The Rump Parliament 1648-1653* (Cambridge University Press, 1973).

thought they had been fighting for; in fact, they were, as usual, fighting for power.

The story is full of irony at every stage. The clique that emerged from the war was immeasurably less representative than the Parliament of 1640 that challenged the King and Laud; monarchy and church were far more representative of the whole nation, people and poor. The Rump consisted of only one-fifth of the original M.P.s. What these men fundamentally believed in was just their own hold on power: 'what flourished inside Parliament was less republicanism than a belief in the right of the House of Commons to political supremacy.' Q.E.D. 'It tells us much about the outlooks of M.P.s that many of them – Presbyterians and Rumpers alike – were more deeply angered by Pride's Purge [i.e. of them] than by the execution of the King.' Of course: that is what humans are like, as Samuel Butler saw – and rendered them faithfully as such, to the amusement of Charles II.

As for the Puritan hatred of Laud and his Church, Mr Worden sees that it 'was of course largely political in inspiration, and Puritan laymen were happy to ally with Puritan clergymen to defeat the Anglican establishment.' That is, it was again largely a struggle for power, for preferments, jobs, in the end, cash – for all the offensive humbug they talked. (So far from 'occasions of divisions removed by the sweet and pleasant stream, those rivers of pleasures, the powerful love of God in Christ to the saints begetting in their spirits an overflowing of perfect love towards one another' ... they fell out over their own interests in a very carnal manner.)

As for toleration, the Rumpers were less tolerant than Laud. One of them said, 'where most power of the gospel, most prodigies of heresies and opinions: which will always happen unless you restrain the reading of the Scriptures.' Well, of course: just what poor Laud had thought. Then why describe Laud's rule as 'repressive', when he was struggling in vain, for better order and decency in the churches – let alone beauty? (His philistine opponents were beyond such a consideration.) That excellent Cromwellian soldier, Skippon, thought toleration, with the consequent proliferation of idiot sects, 'more dangerous than the most intestine or foreign enemies. I was always of opinion the more liberty the greater mischief.' Then why execute Laud? His Church was more representative of the nation at large than any brand of Puritanism. Even Cromwell's brother-in-law Wilkins, advised him in the end that the country's religion could not be run without bishops.

The Rump's conflict, having killed King and Archbishop, was with the Army: affairs had been reduced to the naked fact of force. When the Army wanted some useful social reform for all its efforts, the Rump clique dragged its feet and put off the day. The idiotic social radicals outside only consolidated the forces of conservatism within. The two measures of reform achieved – proceedings in Law-courts to be in English, and compulsory church-attendance on Sunday dropped – were chicken-feed to have fought two Civil Wars to obtain.

So there is no point again in making heavy weather of Cromwell sending the Rump packing (Charles I would have been less brutal, and more dignified). The great man was just sick of their palaver – it hardly needs pages of explanation, one has only to look at Parliament today to understand it easily. And, of course, the whole disastrous experience of the Civil War – apart from all the destruction and loss of good men's lives, there was actual famine and people dying of starvation in the North – led to total disillusionment. After all the silly hopes that led men into war, Mr Worden tells us 'the Rump had become intolerably oligarchical, dilatory and corrupt.' As for the great Oliver, 'it never displayed the reforming idealism he demanded of it.' Mr Worden's is the last word: 'the wonder is that he ever imagined that it would.'

# Puritan Administrators

Bureaucrats are hardly the persons to set the heart on fire – except when they become parasitic tax-hounds eating the vitals of the country; and administrative history is a low temperature affair. However, Professor Aylmer is the leading authority on the subject for the seventeenth century, and so is to be taken for the serious scholar he is. Unfortunately he does not know how to write very well. Like most academics, he doesn't know the first rule about building: when the building is up you take down the scaffolding

Indeed, he mixes up the scaffolding with the building. The book[1] is full of comments on historical writing, discussions of points with colleagues, which should have been relegated to footnotes or cut altogether. Who wants to hear any more about the hoary old subject of the Rise of the Gentry, complete with a bibliography for the hundreth time reciting the tedious names of Professor Lawrence Stone, Hexter, Christopher Hill, Uncle Tom Cobleigh and all?

The fact is that these professors write for each other – and then wonder why their books don't appeal to the public, and are envious of those who do (cf. p. 394). The fact is that they do not know how to write and then, being professors – ten a penny nowadays – are too conceited to learn. This book should have been cut by one-third, and then the price could have been. Look at the garrulity of comments like this: 'However, it is a poor historian who spends too long blaming the inadequacy of his sources for what may well be his own shortcomings.' Cut it! I could have gone through this with a blue pencil to some purpose, and saved one hundred or one hundred and fifty pages.

[1] G. E. Aylmer, *The State's Servants. The Civil Service of the English Republic, 1649-1660* (Routledge and Kegan Paul, 1973).

Or take another redundant piece of garrulity: 'Whatever one's views of making moral judgments in history, a historian should always err on the side of charity.' Is this even true? Ought one to fall over backward in order to let off Hitler or Stalin, or Richard III or Nero? These professors haven't thought the matter out; they are subverted by the sentimentalism of their liberal sympathies, which have brought democratic society to the pass it is in today. They have been wrong all along, and are due for a rude awakening: what our society needs is an Oliver Cromwell.

These academics think that I am sentimental about the achievements of the Elizabethan Age, a small society of only five million which produced Shakespeare and Bacon and Marlowe; Elizabeth, Burghley and Byrd; Drake and Ralegh and Ben Jonson. Professor Aylmer has to say it 'was a brutal, coarse, unjust and cruel society': *there* is the sentimentalist — as if all societies are not like that at bottom! You've only got to look around you today to see what the basic elements of human nature are, when released from restraint and discipline. They are far from being what liberal intellectuals suppose them to be. This is the basis of my quarrel with middle-class intellectuals. They have been obtusely wrong: working-class types like Ernest Bevin know better what humans basically are; his last words were, 'The buggers won't work!' Indeed, why should they, unless *made* to, or induced to by incentives or the profit motive? Not much sentimentalism in me — much more, contempt for middle-class and second-rate intellectuals.

That made clear to the meanest intelligence, perhaps I may say that Professor Aylmer's book will be the standard work on the subject. He is reliable in his detailed meticulous way though there is far too much detail, with elaborate statistics to establish something that unaided commonsense would lead one to expect. For example, among Commonwealth civil servants ex-apprentices and Cambridge men are to the fore: nothing surprising in that when you think that London apprentices had supplied the mob howling for Parliament against Charles I in 1641, and that Cambridge was the spiritual home of Puritanism.

Not but what the professor can be caught out in his own special field. He gives us useful biographies of leading civil servants (one does not need to cite the sacred name of Namier to justify so obvious a proceeding). Henry Scobell was an important figure as Clerk of the Parliaments, who published several books of their Acts, Memorials, Proceedings, etc. The professor need not have gone wrong and said that Scobell was 'possibly of Norfolk origin', just because he did well enough out of the Puritan Revolution to buy some property there. *The Dictionary of National Biography* tells us that he was born at Menagwin, in my native parish of St Austell. This is corroborated by all the Cornish authorities, Vivian's *Visitations*, Boase and Courtney's *Bibliotheca*, and Boase's *Collectanea*. Was it too much to expect this painstaking researcher to look up these authorities? It is better not to make a parade of pedantry – and then make such an elementary slip.

Nevertheless, the professor is right enough in his conclusions, platitudinous as they are. We are told that there is 'massive evidence for an element of class division in the struggle', though we are told this is against the views of 'too many historians' struggling to emancipate themselves from the schematic nonsense of Christopher Hill and other Marxists. Why not make the point neat and clean? Of course there was the class-envy of the lesser gentry and town middle-class against the greater gentry and the nobility. Envious enough themselves, these academics lack the imagination to see the importance of sheer human envy in history.

And, of course, it's great fun to watch things breaking up, the landslide to inevitable Restoration after all the Republican illusions, the doctrinaire hopes of liberals like Johnny Milton – just as today, caught out by the folly of their beliefs and convictions. Nothing could have arrested it, for movements in society are generated at a deeper level than men's fatuous hopes: they are quasi-geological, seismological, if not quite inevitable at least unavoidable. Among the professor's comments is one very much to the point, though hamstrung by a qualification: 'the best we can say of these men is that they had learnt only a little and forgotten very little indeed.'

That might serve for humans at any time in history, particularly today.

# Wenceslas Hollar in Perspective [1]

Others have spoken of Hollar as an artist, and we have been given an admirable introduction to his life and work in Mr Pennington's pamphlet. It remains for me only to place the artist in historical perspective: in this case an appropriate task, because Hollar — besides his multifarious work covering all kinds of subjects — might be regarded as an historical artist. He gives us a wonderful portrait of his age, faithful and true, all in perfect proportion so that we can rely on it — in addition to the sensitive delicacy of his art. Indeed, without Hollar's rendering of the age, we should have a much less exact view of it, and our vision would be out of perspective: great figures and grand subjects — like Van Dyck and Inigo Jones, the Court and the Church — would stand out, but many other subjects would have been lost. And they are just as necessary to a full picture.

With his charming catholicity and the universality of his visual response, Hollar portrays for us the social life of his times — particularly what the women looked like, the way they

[1] An address at the unveiling of the monument in St Margaret's, Westminster, given by Dr Sidney T. Fisher, to replace that destroyed by the Germans in the Second World War.

dressed their hair, their costume, the muffs and furs with their fine texture. Then, too, he shows us the public events — sea-battles, the coronation procession of Charles II, the execution of Strafford, the portentous Solemn League and Covenant, which was the price Parliament paid for the Scotch Alliance against the King.

With the penetrating eye of the artist, Hollar looks further into the characters of people than he can have known. There is his speaking likeness of Charles I — as against the romantic idealisation of Van Dyck: one sees the King as he was, isolated in his mistrust, cut off from his people (the Stuarts had hardly a drop of English blood). When Bernini saw that famous rendering of Charles's head from three sides, he said it was a face made for tragedy. There is the etching of the young Charles II, whom Hollar taught drawing: is it fanciful to see in it the embryo debauchee; or in the youthful James the look of obstinate fixation that ruined him as King?

Above all, we are indebted to Hollar for our picture of what London looked like before the Civil War and the Fire — here we should be totally lost without him. There is his rendering of the whole sweep of the river, from Westminster to the Tower, with its many fine buildings standing out in proper relation to the dwellings, that is, in keeping with the human scale (unlike today). Above all, there is the mighty cliff of Old St Paul's dominating the City.

We are so proud of Wren's St Paul's that we are apt to forget that Old St Paul's was one of the greatest churches of Christendom. Without Hollar's illustrations of Dugdale's *St. Paul's* we should have an inadequate idea of its famous monuments; while his etching of the immense nave — one of the finest he ever did — brings home to us the arching splendour, the magnificent vaults of the architectonic forests out of which Gothic building arose.

Those years before the Civil War were a grand period for the arts in England — when Inigo Jones imported the pure classical style with his Banqueting House in Whitehall, the piazza of Covent Garden, the tremendous portico at St

Paul's — the grandest in Northern Europe. Collectors vied with each other in *bringing* works of art to England — and could employ a Rubens in doing so; Hollar owed his introduction into this country to the Earl of Arundel, to whom we owe the Arundel marbles. The foremost patron in Europe was the King himself — only one of whose purchases was the whole Gonzaga collection. After the disaster of the Civil War most of these were dispersed: I go round the Prado and the Louvre noting the Titians, the Tintorettos and Mantegnas that were once at Whitehall. At Aix-en-Provence one finds the tapestries from the choir of Canterbury cathedral, sold by the Commonwealth.

In the blissful decade before the Civil War even a Puritan like John˜ Milton could write masques like 'Comus' and 'Arcades'.

That eloquent Gothic historian, Clarendon, celebrates the happiness and prosperity of that decade, when England was at peace, while the Continent was devastated by the Thirty Years' War. Charles I's

> three kingdoms flourishing in entire peace and universal plenty; his dominions every day enlarged, by sending out colonies upon large and fruitful plantations; his strong fleets commanding all seas; and the numerous shipping of the nation bringing the trade of the world into his ports . . .
>
> O fortunati nimium, bona si sua norint!
> (O too fortunate, if only you had known how well off you were!)

You might say that people had never 'had it so good'; you can certainly say that they never know when they are best off. They proceeded to go in for the Civil War (which drove Hollar abroad); and no one realises the amount of destruction it caused, the artistic losses, apart from men's lives — the most brilliant of composers in William Lawes, poets, artists like William Dobson, at least two brothers of the leading doctor, Sydenham, some of the best men in the world.

Puritan idiots went in for a deliberate campaign of
smashing the stained-glass windows, the monuments, the
woodwork; a Cromwellian officer locked himself with a
helper in Lincoln cathedral for a couple of days and ripped
up a couple of hundred medieval brasses. The cathedral and
college choirs were abolished, the organs smashed, the
wonderful music of the Elizabethan Age dispersed, continuity broken.

And what was it all for? What good did it do?

When it was all over, intelligent people like Samuel Butler
could hardly conceive:

> When civil dudgeon first grew high,
> And men fell out they knew not why . . .

while the Puritans were ready to

> Decide all controversies by
> Infallible artillery;
> And prove their doctrine orthodox
> By apostolic blows and knocks,
> Call fire and sword and desolation
> A godly thorough Reformation . . .

And the result?

We come back to Hollar. I mentioned at the outset that an
artist perceives so much more than ordinary people do. And
John Aubrey tells us what Hollar saw:

> I remember he told me that when he first came into
> England — which was a serene time of peace — the people,
> both poor and rich, did look cheerfully. But at his return,
> he found the countenances of the people all changed;
> melancholy, spiteful, as if bewitched.

How penetrating an observation that is! There is the whole
experience of the Civil War summed up in it. For, of course,
people had been bewitched by the nonsense they supposed
themselves to think. Their happiness, works of art, the works
of men's hands, are more worthy of respect than what they

think – almost always nonsense: their theories, their doctrines, their opinions, their mutually exclusive 'truths' for which they shed each others' blood all through history.

Art is far more worthy of respect, and so above all is the artist. Only art defeats time and survives the ruins of the years; only art remains. – Who now remembers the doctrines, the theories, the quarrelling politicians that led the country into the disaster of the Civil War? Art not only expresses better values, stands for the happier side of experience and nature, and makes us happy; art is saner.

And so we remember Hollar, sanest as well as the most out-giving of men; modest and humble, giving of his best to society. In a world that has gone mad about wages, and is conscienceless in getting as much out of the community as possible (are they any the happier or more contented for it?), Hollar set a more scrupulous example. We are told, 'he did all by the hour, in which he was very exact; for if anybody came in and kept him from his work, he always laid the hourglass on one side, till they were gone.' (Would you see anyone do that today?) 'He always received 12d an hour.'

He was not besotted on wages, did not think in terms of a materialism got out of hand. To an artist – provided that he can live – the work is its own reward. John Aubrey tells us that 'what Hollar did for his delight and recreation when a boy, proved to be his livelihood when a man.'

I suspect that he was essentially a happy man. Aubrey says, 'he has a daughter that was one of the greatest beauties I have seen.' Lucky Hollar! However great our devotion to beauty, we cannot arrange that at will. Though poorly rewarded, he was highly valued by those who knew best, men also touched by genius, John Aubrey, Pepys and Evelyn. We must get our values right.

The world in our time has got out of the human scale, in art and architecture as in everything else. This was not so in Hollar's day; it is one of the unconscious sources of our satisfaction, and even consolation, in contemplating him.

This country owes him a great debt: *he* was the kind of

immigrant that enriches it. It was a happy inspiration on Mr
Fisher's part to renew our commemoration of him; a public
spirited act on the part of a benefactor who is also a scholar.
Mr Fisher knows more about the topography of Elizabethan
London than anyone alive: what could be more appropriate
than such a gift from such a scholarly and generous giver?

# Country Life in Restoration Northamptonshire

How fortunate Northamptonshire is to have this delightful
Restoration Diary![1] – it makes me envious: if only we had
something similar for Cornwall . . . And now rendered doubly
fortunate by this model of meticulous editing. It sets a
standard very difficult for anyone else to achieve, for Sir
Gyles Isham gives us a *Who's Who* to Northamptonshire in
the years after the Civil War and Restoration. He knows not
only the gentry and clergy, who have left more memorials of
themselves, but the yeomen farmers, lawyers, doctors,
schoolmasters, about whom it is far more difficult to obtain
information. He has tracked them all down, with patience
and unassuming learning, to the places, the farms and houses
where they lived, and is able to tell us whether these still
exist, unchanged or no. In the very numerous and full Notes
he succeeds in giving us a portrait of Northamptonshire in
Restoration days.

In the Introduction he places the Diary in the perspective
of the history of those years, and that of the Isham family,

[1] *The Diary of Thomas Isham of Lamport, 1671–3,* trans. N. Marlow, introd. and
notes by Sir Gyles Isham (Gregg International Publishers, 1971).

gives us a biography of the intelligent boy who kept this Latin Diary at his father's behest. We are grateful for this, for we naturally want to know how life turned out for him, lively and charming as he evidently was — rather sadly, for he was a young man when he died, still unmarried.

Some points of interest for the general history of the time emerge. The year 1672 was marked by Charles II's secret treaty with Louis XIV and their joining together to force war upon the Dutch. It is remarkable how unpopular this war was with the nation at large and that both parties were at one in identifying Louis XIV's France as the real threat to England, not the Dutch. Sir Gyles notes that by 1672 neighbours in the country were burying their old Civil War quarrels. The Civil War had of course been an unmitigated disaster, and both sides had learned some sense from its folly; but the quarrels were to some extent continued in the form of party-conflict. Since people must quarrel, this was a less dangerous way of letting off steam.

The Diary also brings home to us how much more informed about events at the centre country-people were than is usually supposed. Of course the Ishams were gentry, on friendly terms with neighbouring grandees to the fore at Court, Sunderlands and Montagus, and received visits from passing notabilities like the Devonshires. But they kept in touch by going up to town or, like the author of the Diary later, living in London; they had their correspondents, and they regularly read their *Gazette*. They soon knew about the battles at sea in this naval war, though there is no possibility of their having heard the gunfire as some folks fancied — a frequent country illusion. It is through the innocent, if intelligent, eyes of a boy that we see events: of the goings-on of the sanctified Charles II we hear of his assiduity in touching for the King's Evil. The boy takes the facts of life in his stride, accepting the King's bastards as he does Dell's puppying, the littering of the ferrets, the breeding going on all round, the quarrels of husband and wife, the illegitimacies. And there are witches; while the outbreaks of violence, the

murders recorded, reveal people as no better (if no worse)
than in our enlightened age.

The abiding charm of the Diary is in the perennial pleasure
of country pursuits: planting out the walks, fruit-trees in the
orchard, bowls on the lawn, horse-racing and cock-fighting
(an old gentleman in Cornwall told me that he could not
restrain the surreptitious delight he still took in it), ferreting
and coursing the hare, like Shakespeare on the Cotswolds.
One disappointment: Sir John Barnard, who married Shakespeare's granddaughter, comes to dinner with news of the
war. The old bore! — if only he had come with some
information about his grandfather-in-law, how grateful we
should be. In a previous generation the Ishams had been
interested enough to purchase a (now unique) copy of the
1599 edition of *Venus and Adonis,* besides quartos of the
plays — all now having left the country for the Huntington
Library in California, where Sir Gyles has piously visited his
ancestors' possessions.

Given such full measure in the editing, there is nothing
that a reviewer can suggest, let alone add. But deer-stealing
*was* a fairly regular pursuit among students at Oxford —
Shotover Forest was much more extensive then — as we can
see from Simon Forman's Autobiography. And one finds in
the Throckmorton Diary that the Isham celebration of
Christmas, entertaining the poor to dinner, calling in the
Daventry musicians for several days, was in keeping with the
custom a couple of generations before, in the Jacobean age,
with Sir Arthur Throckmorton at Paulerspury. No reference
to it — what a pity that Elizabethan house has gone, nothing
but humps under the grass, and a unique monument in the
church.

Anyhow, the book brings Northamptonshire so vividly to
mind that it makes me want to get into the car and go
exploring its villages and by-ways, as in the days when I was
writing *Ralegh and the Throckmortons.*

# Pepys in History

It is always entrancing to read about Pepys — such zest and gaiety, so many interests, such intellectual vivacity, such pure — and impure — enjoyment of life! And it is a double pleasure to anyone who has to read so many history-books, indifferently written, to enjoy so beautifully proportioned and executed a book as this. An artist himself — with the added advantage of a naval background — Mr Ollard[1] appreciates Pepys for the artist he was. Not only in the writing of his Diary but in so many other respects: music, his greatest passion, connoisseurship, book and print collecting, the desire for order in his accounts and files, the Navy Office and the Navy itself. Mr Ollard sums up: 'the artist in Pepys lies at the root of his nature. A passion for perception and a passion for imposing order on everything he perceived runs through and through his life. He was an aesthete' — and Mr Ollard quotes Pater. It is a surprising conjunction, but justified.

In this biography Mr Ollard gets the proportions of Pepys's life right — there is no undue emphasis on the Diary, wonderful as that work is. Indeed a suggestive comparison rises to mind from Stendhal's tribute to Cellini's *Autobiography*: 'c'est le livre qu'il faut lire avant tout si l'on veut deviner le caractère italien.' What more English than Pepys's Diary, in its robustness and naïve directness, its complacency and contentment, its honesty and occasional hypocrisies?

However, the Diary occupied less than a decade of Pepys's early life, and the main theme of this book is, rightly, his place in history, the prodigious work he accomplished for the Navy — though he touched Restoration life (and lives) at so many points besides. He got his leg up through his relationship to the Cromwellian Montagu on the threshold of the

[1] Richard Ollard, *Pepys. A Biography* (Hodder and Stoughton, 1974).

Restoration, in which, along with Monk, Montagu played a significant and secret rôle through his position in the Navy. The Admiral took young Pepys with him to bring Charles II back:

> those happy days aboard the *Naseby* breathe in the Diary the freshness of the season, the sharp tang of the sea air, above all the delight of being alive that makes Pepys, like Falstaff, a favourite in every age. They also introduce us to a number of the principal characters in his life.

The *Naseby* was rebaptised the *Royal Charles* – and what characters bloomed and burgeoned all round Pepys! Restoration people were not afraid to appear somewhat larger than life. There was the Admiral himself, so secret a man that Pepys was rather shocked when he found that he didn't believe anything at all, Pepys himself having a Puritan background – which gave a sharper edge to his amorous proclivities. Then there was the Duke of York, who ruined himself as King by believing far too much. I never knew that Sir Samuel Morland, the ingenious engineer who appealed to Charles II for his mechanical contrivances and raised the water from the Thames for Windsor Castle, had been a double agent in Thurloe's secret service. There is the ambivalence of the age in that – from the shocking streaker, the poet-earl Rochester, the brutal and boorish Colonel Kirke, to the saintly Ken whose company Pepys enjoyed on the journey to Tangier, and the very respectable Evelyn, who seems to have been unaware of the predatory element in his religious feelings for Margaret Godolphin.

The rich contradictoriness of it all is summed up in the strange character of Charles II, so intelligent and so casual, often quite irresponsible. Coventry, an honest and cultivated aristocrat, told Pepys that 'the serving a Prince that minds not his own business is most unhappy for them that serve him well.' Pepys appreciated that Charles knew as much about naval matters as any expert, and yet would allow things to go wrong by making appointments and giving commissions which, 'through a lazy pretence to good nature, favoured the incompetent and the fashionable.' The brilliant Halifax summed him up: 'of a man who was so capable of choosing, he chose as seldom as any man that ever lived.'

Of course Charles was, and had to be, a politician; but the encouragement of personal and party favourites put a premium on factiousness, indiscipline and inefficiency. Apparently 'the Stuart brothers liked it that way.' Mr Ollard puts it down to the shallowness of Charles II's nature. He would have gained something here from Christopher Falkus' understanding of it, in his perceptive biography – the appalling background the boy had had in the Civil War, the killing of his father, the dispersal of the family (only his family spoke to his heart), the shifts and humiliations of exile, the sheer idiocies of politics and politicians. No more *désabusé* man ever lived than Charles II; he reminds me of that other Bourbon, Louis XV, clever as anything, and hopelessly disillusioned.

There followed, as a consequence, the avoidable disasters of the Second Dutch War, with the Dutch in the Medway, etc. 'Why did the First Dutch war, fought a dozen years earlier, result in a resounding victory and the Second, in spite of unparalleled Parliamentary votes of money, in defeat?' The answer was Oliver Cromwell – no one more capable of ruling ever rose to a throne. No wonder an old Royalist's son prompted Pepys to note, 'it is strange how he and everybody do nowadays reflect upon Oliver and commend him, what brave things he did and made all the neighbour princes fear him.' There is no real defence for the divagations and twists of Charles II's foreign policy – not to face up squarely to dangers when they first declare themselves (cf. 1933) always increases them and makes them harder to deal with in the end.

I supposed it is natural that royal persons should be disillusioned, confronted as they perpetually are by sheer human silliness. It was left to solid middle-class types like Pepys to work hard all their lives to staunch the leaks and repair the damage. Both Charles, who knew a good man when he saw one, and James, who rarely could tell, gave Pepys their confidence – and what a good thing he made out of it, for himself as well as the Navy! Mr Ollard sums up that his greatest single achievement was the professionalising of the naval officer. All his life Pepys worked to that end, acquainting himself with everything that could be of use by the way. Before he was half-way through his career 'the plain fact was that there was no doing anything in the Navy without him.'

Gradually the whole field of naval administration came within his grasp. He certainly had genius as an administrator as well as that of diarist, and the two are related. Mr Ollard says of his Secretaryship of the Admiralty:

> tact, mastery of detail, energy, promptitude, all the virtues of a great manager are much in evidence. But beyond and behind this scintillating display of executive talent was a searching, generalising, codifying intelligence: the omnivorous reader, the Fellow of the Royal Society, the historian and the aesthete.

As an administrator Pepys had marvellous opportunities. England was going up in the world then, the oceans were opening before her; and his career lay on those beckoning frontiers between individual enterprise (and indiscipline) and the regularisation of the service which was to achieve such great things up to our own day. It is one of the ironies of history that the navy Pepys created under the aegis of James, Duke of York – which helped to defeat Louis XIV's ascendancy in Europe – also played a part in overthrowing James as King in 1688.

The most touching sentence in this book relates to Pepys's private life, and his wife whom we know so well from the Diary: 'perhaps the bust of Elizabeth, her head turned in laughter towards the Navy Office pew in St Olave's, offers the best comment on his decision not to marry again.' 'Smiling' would be better, and actually truer as one looks up at her there, having survived worse than the Dutch in the Medway, the blitz on London.

# Pepys and his Oxford Friends [1]

Samuel Pepys was one of the best public servants this country has ever had and we all know that he had a streak of genius as a diarist. Then, too, few men have had so full and fruitful a life: not only the devoted administrator of the Navy but scholar and connoisseur, book-collector and musician, the writer and amateur of curiosities, *amateur* – in the best sense – of the fair sex. All these are aspects of his intense vitality and enjoyment of life; the genius consisted in his capacity to express them and communicate them to us, for genius annihilates the years. Mr Pepys is as alive to us today, as when he attended church here.

Various aspects of this many-sided man have been presented from this familiar place: may I offer a side to him that is less familiar? He was a loyal son of Cambridge, and left his nursing mother the magnificent bequest of his Library, so beautifully housed there at Magdalene. But it so happens that in his later years he became acquainted with a number of Oxford men, and much of his correspondence is with them. It was Oxford, not Cambridge, that awarded him a diploma – I suppose an honorary degree – which he much prized: after that, it becomes 'my dear Aunt, the University of Oxford.'

So my subject is Pepys and his Oxford Friends.

The first and greatest friendship, the closest and most

[1] A Pepys Commemoration Address at St Olave, Hart Street.

long-lasting, is, of course, with that Balliol man, John Evelyn.
It is too often overlooked that Evelyn was a projector, and
that the Royal Society was virtually an Oxford foundation.
Evelyn suggested a number of projects of great value to the
country, and one of them was a college to advance
experimental science. He was a foundation-Fellow at the first
meeting at New Year 1661; four years later Evelyn had the
pleasure of welcoming his friend as a Fellow, who became
President in 1684. Evelyn was twice pressed to accept the
office, but declined it.

Both Pepys and Evelyn were devoted to the public service,
the first as a professional, the second — being an independent
country gentleman — appearing as an amateur; in fact, their
interests converged in deep love of their country. Soon they
found that they shared intellectual interests and common
tastes, and then came to have respect and warm affection for
each other. Their friendship is most appealing, and it is
curious to think that it was the publication of Evelyn's Diary
first — he was a much better known man — that suggested
that of Pepys. Pepys's came to overshadow its precursor, by
its sharper vivacity and sparkling sense of life.

Evelyn and Pepys worked together in the Dutch War; the
first, as commissioner for the wounded, conceived the project
for a Seamen's Hospital, which they discussed together in
Lord Sandwich's coach. 'Which I mightily approve of and will
endeavour to promote it', Pepys wrote, 'being a worthy thing
and of use — and will save money.' He was as good as his
word; the Navy Office took it up — the origin of Greenwich
Hospital.

As commissioner of the Mint — and never were there more
beautiful coins engraved than then — Evelyn was in and out
of the Tower, as Pepys was on ordnance for the Navy. Until
the surprising day came when Pepys found himself incarcer-
ated there. Buoyant as a cork, he was not at all downcast —
after all, one was nobody in that age if one wasn't sent to the
Tower; and besides, wasn't it the proper place for peers, not
commoners? The King himself sent him a fat buck from

Enfield Chase to feast his friends, and Evelyn came to sympathise, and dine and wine. 'Mr. Pepys is to be pulled to pieces', someone wrote; not a bit of it: he greatly enjoyed himself as usual, and the added consequence it gave.

Both Pepys and Evelyn were patriots: I gather that one is supposed to apologise for that nowadays – it certainly would not recommend them to the B.B.C., or TV, which perhaps are above such things. After the Dutch War Evelyn gave Pepys a drawing of the Dutch fleet in the Medway, a national humiliation which had so grieved them both. Pepys particu-larly – to the Navy man the reproach gave him as much disquiet, he said, as the man who recognised his portrait in Michelangelo's Hell. He wished that Evelyn's drawing of the disgraceful event of 1667 might take the place in the House of Lords of the famous Armada tapestries of 1588, 'till the depravity of this were reformed to the temper of that age, wherein God Almighty found his blessing more operative than (I fear) he doth in ours.'

So we, in our time, have reason to look back on the wonderful achievements of last century, the Victorian Age, when all went well with us.

Evelyn was writing a salutary History of the Dutch War, from which to draw lessons: which was held up and frustrated by the pro-French minister, Lord Clifford of the Cabal, who carried off Evelyn's papers to Devonshire. I don't know if they are still there at Ugbrooke, along with the unique copy of the Secret Treaty of Dover, the pearls and diamonds that are duplicated in the portrait of Queen Catherine of Braganza and Dryden's white deer in the park.

Meanwhile, Pepys was endeavouring to write his Memoirs of the Navy, and putting a host of queries for Evelyn to answer. Evelyn expressed his readiness to be 'subservient to such a genius as Mr. Pepys.' The latter found the job beyond him: 'it is not imaginable, to such as have not tried, what labour an historian – that would be exact – is condemned to. He must read all, good and bad, and remove a world of rubbish before he can lay the foundation.'

We need not conclude that it is easier to make history than to write it, or that it is less difficult to administer than to be a writer; but evidently these eminent diarists found it a softer option to write a diary than to become historians.

Neither of them finished his history; on the other hand, their diaries became first-hand sources for the historians of their time. Even Pepys's Second Diary is, the Journal of his official Voyage to Tangier, the interest of which people are apt to underestimate — perhaps because there were no ladies present to enliven the diarist's fancy (but he was twenty years older and staider then, in 1683). Evelyn wrote to him with charming courtesy:

> You leave us so naked at home that, till your return from Barbary, we are in danger of becoming barbarians. The heroes are all embarked with my Lord Dartmouth and Mr. Pepys; nay, they seem to carry along with them not a colony only but a college; nay an whole university, all the sciences, all the arts, and all the professors of 'em too.

What a polite way of writing! But that it was not just politeness we know from Evelyn's concern at the wreck of the Duke of York's ship approaching the Scottish coast, when he feared that Pepys was on board: 'which gave me apprehensions and a mixture of passions not really to be expressed, till I was assured of your safety.'

Then as the old friends get older, we find them consoling each other over their ailments, recommending each other possets and medicines. Pepys has left off all malt-drink and is betaking himself wholly to barley-water, 'blanched with a few almonds and sweetened with a little sugar.' Evelyn is down at Wotton gardening and planting, and when it rains too hard, reads and scribbles and builds castles in the air. 'I am sewing [draining] of ponds, looking after my hinds, providing carriage and tackle against reaping time and sowing. *Venio ad voluptates agricolarum,* which Cicero reckons amongst the most becoming diversions of Old Age.' Meanwhile, young John Evelyn is giving up Balliol College; and

Pepys fully agrees 'with your excellent grandson in thinking it no longer worth his while to stay there.'

Pepys having retired from London, Evelyn can never pass York Buildings without a sigh: 'Saturday, which was wont to be a jubilee . . . and the most diverting to me of the weekly circles, is from a real sabbath now become wholly saturnine, lugubrious and solitary.' They had had so much to talk about, shared so many interests — public affairs, books, prints, curios, coins — and now it was over.

In these later years Pepys was making a number of friends at Oxford, though none so close as Evelyn. One of his many good qualities was his faculty for admiration — it shows a want of good nature to be unable to admire, and Pepys was above all good-natured. He had the deepest respect for John Wallis, whom Oliver Cromwell had sent over from Cambridge to teach Oxford mathematics — Wallis was an eminent precursor of Newton in the rebarbative subject.

Pepys formed the project of having Wallis' portrait painted to present to the University. When Kneller learned of this, he jumped the gun — like the boorish German he was — and incontinently went down to Oxford and painted it. Pepys was having a medallion of himself made by Cavalier; but Sir Godfrey writes, in broken English, 'this man having received so much kindness in Germany, has spoiled him, being a Frenchman and should be kept low.' The affair led to a good deal of correspondence, and Pepys's acquaintance, the Master of University College, reported to him: 'It was a very sensible satisfaction to me that the obscurities of Sir G. Kneller's proceedings were unveiled, which to me were all shallow, and natural cause of umbrage.'

However, the upshot was that Oxford got a fine portrait, which Kneller thought one of his best: there is Wallis, in full doctor's robes, in the Bodleian today for us all to see. We owe it Pepys, and Oxford was duly grateful.

The Master of University's young companion, Humphrey Wanley, who shared Pepys's passion for book-collecting, wrote in much better vein than Kneller: ' 'Tis never any

drudgery to wait on Mr. Pepys, whose conversation, I think,
is more nearly akin to what we are taught to hope for in
Heaven, than that of anybody else I know.' This did not go
down at all badly with Mr Pepys.

In fact he became so loyal to his 'dear Aunt, the University
of Oxford' that he took her side against the famous Bentley
in the celebrated controversy over the Letters of Phalaris.
Actually, Bentley though rude, was right: in the end that one
Cambridge man demolished all the young wits and chits of
Christ Church.

Pepys was luckier with his All Souls acquaintance. He
became friendly with the eminent lawyer, Sir Nathaniel
Lloyd, whose portrait hangs in our hall, who went from
Oxford to teach Cambridge law. We find Lloyd, a generous
and philanthropic Welshman, bringing a volume of Oxford
Poems up to Pepys in London.

We know how kind Pepys was in doing good turns to
everybody, how he took on the burdens of his hopeless
brother-in-law, Bartholomew St Michel; and then of his
housekeeper, Mrs Skinner's graceless son, who got into
trouble by getting to know the republican Milton and fixing
up to publish his work in Holland. (I suppose young Skinner
was related to Milton's friend, Cyriac Skinner of the Sonnet;
anyway the young man departed without saying goodbye to
Pepys, but defending himself with the flout, 'as for Milton or
his works or papers I have done withal; and indeed never had
had to do with him, had not ambition to good literature
made me covet his acquaintance.' It seems a sufficient
excuse, but Milton was dangerous ground.)

Pepys had better luck in using his influence with Lloyd to
get the admirable scholar, Thomas Tanner, elected Fellow of
All Souls. Pepys backed a winner in him: not only did Tanner
become a great antiquarian, an authority on manuscripts and
coins, after Pepys's own heart, but he even attained to an
episcopal throne, if the diminutive one of St Asaph.

I do not think that Pepys was a friend of our Warden,
Warden Finch; for, from what the Tory Hearne said about

him, he must have been a Whig. Hearne's principle was that of Dr Johnson, not to let the Whig dog have the best of it – and what Hearne said was, 'Warden Finch is an enthusiastic actor and an outrageous debauch.' I saw that written up on our walls the other day, in the pretty way students have of defacing the premises nowadays. (Very rarely is it so funny as 'Donate your don to Oxfam').

We wonder indeed what Mr Pepys would make of it all – though we may be sure that he, whom neither the Dutch in the Medway or imprisonment in the Tower could daunt, would discover something to amuse him, something to enjoy in it. At the very end we find him relishing a third reading of that great Oxford book, Clarendon's *History,* 'with the same appetite, I assure you, to a fourth that ever I had to a first.' While Evelyn reciprocates with, 'I cannot but let you know the incredible satisfaction I have taken in reading my late Lord Chancellor's *History of the Rebellion,* so well, and so *unexpectedly* well written.' To this day the University profits from its sales.

And so to that last communication from Pepys's nephew, sending Evelyn mourning and mourning rings for remembrance of 'my good uncle Pepys, whose body was last night interred in the parish church of St Olave's, Hart Street, by the Navy Office.'

One word as to Pepys's historic public achievement: it was his energy and efficiency that pushed through the decisive programme of building thirty capital ships from 1677 onwards. Only that saved this country, and helped to save Europe, from the domination of Louis XIV. The sheet-anchor of our security for three centuries – our great days – was to make ourselves the linch-pin of a Grand Alliance of all the smaller powers whose existence was threatened by a greater, whether by Philip of Spain, Louis XIV or Napoleon, or the Kaiser's Germany. We lost sight of that only in the 1930s, to appease Hitler's Germany – and ruined our country.

In Pepys's time the House of Commons, as usual, was slow

to realise the danger. But Pepys not only urged his programme upon the Commons, but carried it through as an administrator. He rightly regarded his Thirty Ships programme as his greatest achievement. A rapid and efficient worker, 'his activities extended over the whole field of naval administration' – he himself saw to everything: the insatiable curiosity we recognise in the Diarist became an asset to the nation.

For his outstanding services he was *twice* put in the Tower. Where do you think we should have put the disastrous makers of the Anglo-German Naval Agreement of the 1930s?

In the long run it was William III and Marlborough who profited from Pepys's ships, and they succeeded, after twenty years, in defeating Louis XIV. Yet, such is the irony of politics, that when William III captured the English throne, Mr Pepys was popped into the Tower again.

But very briefly: he was soon out and about. His comment on this was, 'the worse the world uses me, the better I think I am bound to use myself.'

It seems to me a very good principle to hold on to in bad times.

Pepys's gift for friendship is related to those keynotes of his personality and character: his constant kindness and his enjoyment of life. Though he had a good conceit of himself, he had no spiritual pride. It is sound Catholic doctrine that sins of the flesh are more forgivable than sins of the spirit. He was very human – particularly about the ladies; really innocent and naïf: it is part of his charm, part of his acute sense of life, though his rendering of it back again to us amounts to genius. At bottom he was really a humble man of heart: we might say of him, *anima naturaliter christiana.*

# Langbaine and the English Dramatists

Gerard Langbaine's *An Account of the English Dramatick Poets,*[1] published at Oxford in 1691, is the most important early book on the history of the English drama, the foundation upon which all subsequent writers built for more than a century. It belongs to the small class of key-books, and yet it has for long been hard to come by: it was high time that it was made more available to the public.

The last decade of the seventeenth century was remarkable for the works of literary and biographical scholarship coming out of Oxford. There was the indispensable *Athenae Oxonienses* of Anthony Wood, who knew Langbaine and gives us our best account of him; the *Notitia Monastica* of Tanner, who started at Queen's, Langbaine's college, and became chaplain of All Souls; the Anglo-Saxon scholarship encouraged by Gibson at Queen's, which culminated in Hickes's *Thesaurus*. In a more general way the study of English literature as such became established about this time. Langbaine's book, for all its modesty and the disclaimers of its author, made a no less valuable contribution, more lasting than most, for it was a labour of love – like all the best books.

The simple truth was that Langbaine was in love with his subject: all his life he was stage-struck, in the exact sense of the word he was an *amateur* of the drama. Altogether he collected nearly a thousand dramatic pieces. He loved reading plays, but even more seeing them – the right approach to drama, as against many critics who have preferred the study

---

[1] Reproduction in facsimile (Scolar Press, 1971).

to the stage. He was also an omnivorous reader of novels and
romances in French and Italian as well as the classics; this
gave him a solid basis of comparison, a quite exceptional
knowledge of sources of stage-plots and characters, for all the
light-hearted unpretentiousness of his approach. Then, too,
writing on the threshold of the age of Queen Anne, the time
of Dryden, Sir William Temple and Swift, he wrote an
excellent plain style: no Elizabethan concatenations, nor the
quaintness of the earlier Carolines.

In a way he was recognisably the son of a rather
heavy-weight father, Gerard Langbaine senior, Provost of
Queen's, a massive scholar and antiquarian, who published a
number of polemical and scholarly volumes and still left
twenty-one volumes in manuscript for other scholars to rifle.
Not so the son, however. Anthony Wood tells us that the
young Gerard 'by his mother's fondness became idle, a great
jockey, married, and run out of a good part of the estate that
had descended to him'. Certainly his first published work was
devoted to horsemanship, which appeared at the end of an
anonymous volume of Gentlemanly Recreations.

Then, Wood tells us,

> being a man of parts, he afterwards took up, lived for some
> years a retired life near Oxon [actually up on the hill
> above the beloved city at Headington], improved much his
> natural and gay geny that he had to dramatic poetry, and
> at first wrote little things without his name set to them,
> which he would never own.

It is a charming picture; we see that Langbaine's attitude to
writing was very much that of the gentleman, an amateur
rather than the player — even if his knowledge was more than
professional. With perhaps not quite as straight a face as the
professors have thought he says,

> if I can but be so happy as to obtain a pardon from the
> more solid part of mankind for having mis-spent my time
> in these lighter studies, I promise for the future to employ
> myself on subjects of more weight and importance.

Langbaine did not live to fulfil this promise: he was, to all intents and purposes, the author of this one book, which he was inspired to write. First and last he was an Oxford man, and the book, when written, was printed there.

It had, in fact, a precursor three years before, in 1688, in *A New Catalogue of English Plays,* in regard to which something very odd happened. A hoax seems to have been perpetrated upon him, between sending his manuscript to the press and its publication. A bogus title-page was substituted with the ridiculous title of *Momus Triumphans or the Plagiaries of the English Stage* – Momus being the God of Raillery so frequently and boringly cited by writers against each other, in the name of criticism, for the past century. Whoever perpetrated the joke, some five hundred copies were sold before Langbaine could catch up with it. He could not find out who were the 'obliging gossips' – i.e., godparents – who thus named the brat; but he had to rectify it 'that my friends may not think me lunatick' and revenge himself upon his enemies.

So three years later he brought out this classic book. He had come to think that Dryden and the wits of Will's coffee-house had put this joke upon him, and in this book he certainly gets his own back. Nearly fifty pages – one tenth of the book – besides frequent references are devoted to Dryden: Langbaine cannot get the great man, the Shakespeare of his age, out of his mind. So that the book has a subsidiary dramatic interest of its own, for the attentive reader, besides all the information it has to give us about the dramatists.

This inner tension also plays its part in keeping the book alive, as is the way. And again it was rather a strange thing that happened. Langbaine was not at all an ill-natured man, but his persistency in pointing out Dryden's plagiarisms, his rifling other men's works for plots and characters – just like Shakespeare – had the effect of harming Dryden's reputation. It is all very curious – as if it mattered where Dryden got his sources from! He very often, though not always, turned the lead he plundered into gold. Like Shakespeare, Dryden was a fast and prolific writer, often careless, who rarely blotted a line – and Langbaine obviously admired his genius. But the lesser man got his own back on the great man; as has been said, 'the wits at Will's coffee-house may have laughed loud and long over the Momus joke, but Langbaine's ghost laughed last'. All the same, later admirers of Dryden like Walter Scott took it out on Langbaine, who got less than his deserts in the end. There is irony, as well as drama, in the story.

No one was so much attacked in that age as its greatest writer, Dryden. It is true that his mountain of achievement in every field – prose as well as verse, plays and poems, satires essays, tracts – exposed a wide front for lesser men to attack; but there must have been something in his personality to provoke it. There was an obvious, if superficial, inconsistency in the author of the Heroic Stanzas on the death of the heroic Oliver, who became the laureate of the unheroic Stuarts, the Commonwealth man who became a High Tory, the Anglican who turned Roman Catholic. But this was not it. There was something else. People have wondered 'if there was not about him something provocative even in a negative way, some vulnerable streak of which his enemies were half conscious but which they could not locate'. Dryden was once insulted in public by a Warden of All Souls and, the most devastating of satirists with his pen, was at a loss for a reply. He put the whole of himself into his writing – for the rest he was rather mysterious, impossible to draw. It should be clear that he did not want people to know him: he had no very high opinion of them. A gentleman himself, and really rather magnanimous – considering that he was attacked on all fronts all the time – he assumed that they were inferior, and this maddened them, made them almost incoherent with fury.

This was not Langbaine's attitude: he admired Dryden's superior spirit in spite of everything, and this adds strokes to his book.

For the rest, the book has its own, like its author's, excellent qualities. It is fresh and living, sprightly and gay; it has entire independence of mind. But we must clear out of the way a misconception, very easy to make, that has always dominated discussion of it and has rather distorted Langbaine's claim as a writer. He is so interested in following up the sources of dramatic work, whence the dramatists got suggestions for their plots, situations, scenes and incidents, that people have thought that his chief interest was in detecting plagiaries. This gets him wrong. As he says himself in his Preface, he thought the reader would be interested in comparing the play with the original story. Many were — and still are, as we see from the frequent following up of a film by the issue of the 'book of the film'. Langbaine had a modest pride in his wide knowledge of sources, the range of his reading; but his real interest in this aspect was more like the entomologist's fascinated interest in the origin, environment, and feeding of his creatures.

Langbaine's approach was biographical and human, not bibliographical and critical. 'I am so far from affecting *title-learning'* — as he called it, that he was prepared to leave that to the booksellers. For this he was much criticised by pedants — for whom he had a cheerful indifference, where Dryden described them as 'contemptible' — though a scholar such as Malone always appreciated how much this subject owed to Langbaine. We must remember the absence of reference books for people's biographies; the excruciating delights of bibliography had not yet been discovered: Langbaine was largely dependent on what he could learn from his own collection of plays. Without him a good deal of information would have been lost. Then there were those provoking types — how well we know them! — who promised to send in their material but could never fulfil their promises. 'Should I have stayed for the completion of these promises the Louvre would have sooner been finished than my book.'

We are indebted to him for all kinds of information, drawing our attention, for example, to Dryden's indignation against Chapman's 'Bussy d'Amboise', not only successful in its own time but revived at the Restoration with good

applause. We might not have known as much, but for
Langbaine, about dramatic pieces written under the Protectorate when they could not be performed – some of Davenant's for example, of whom we are given a good account. He
scores a bull's eye against Dryden's absurd condemnation of
*The Winter's Tale, Love's Labour's Lost,* and *Measure for
Measure,* simply on the ground of impossibilities, or 'at least
so meanly written that the comedy neither caused your mirth
nor the serious part of your concernment'. This sprang from
Dryden's modern bias, and the standards he imbibed from
the contemporary French theatre; besides, 'I am sure their
wit was not that of gentlemen; there was ever somewhat that
was ill-bred and clownish in it, and which confessed the
conversation of the authors.'

In the famous dispute of the time between the Ancients
and the Moderns, Dryden was on the side of the moderns.
Langbaine's unfeigned delight in the old Elizabethan and
Jacobean dramatists is an endearing recommendation. Here
he reaps the advantage of being an historian of the drama,
rather than its critic: the result is that he is not dogged by
contemporary critical prejudices, and is therefore not
anachronistic in his attitude to earlier writers. He gets them
right, where critics – their 'views' getting in the way –
are more liable to go wrong. This gives Langbaine, in spite of
occasional errors, a modest trustworthiness.

The posthumous story of Langbaine's book is even more
odd. In 1699 Charles Gildon brought out a much shortened
version of it, *The Lives and Characters of the English
Dramatick Poets,* but bringing it up to date with notices of
Dryden's and Shadwell's later productions along with
younger writers like Congreve and Vanbrugh. Gildon took
leave to differ as much as he could from Langbaine, if only to
hip up the value of his own work – actually it showed that
people were finding Langbaine indispensable. In greatly
shortening the original, Gildon omitted the frequent quotations of verse that are a charming feature of it and are
themselves not always easy to find.

In fact Langbaine became the first and indispensable authority: for the next century there is a distinguished procession of builders upon his work, Oldys, Percy, Steevens, Garrick, Malone. Instead of writing a new and up-to-date history themselves they added marginal notes to Langbaine, quantities of them in their copies. Some of these informative copies provide a story in themselves; those of Oldys and Steevens in the British Museum and of Malone in the Bodleian have constituted authorities for subsequent historians of English drama. But they all go back to Langbaine, the foundation of the coral reef those laborious workers built up. Foundations are apt to be overlaid and not to be visible; it was the fate of Langbaine's book to become 'the most widely consulted on its subject for a whole century, and yet himself to remain hidden and obscure behind the massive annotations of his readers.' It is time that both his book and he were rendered visible once more.

The agreeable young Oxford scholar, the 'fastidious brisk' of Headington, who dedicated this book to the Earl of Abingdon out at lovely Rycote, lived less than a year after its publication. When he died, in 1692, he was only thirty-six or he might have fulfilled his promise to turn to some graver labour or, more likely, have kept his book up to date himself with later editions. The university had been kind to him and provided him with a pleasant little office 'in consideration of his ingenuity and loss of part of his estate'. He was buried in the church of St Peter-in-the-East, next to Queen's College: in the nave where the memorial to his mother, who had spoiled him, looks fondly down upon him. The place has now been turned into a college library: we may suppose that Gerard's agreeable shade has no objection to the books he loved resting upon him.

# Index